Techniques of Successful Practice

For Architects and Engineers

Techniques of Successful Practice
For Architects and Engineers

Edited by William B. Foxhall
Senior Editor, *Architectural Record*

McGRAW-HILL BOOK COMPANY

New York / St. Louis / San Francisco / Düsseldorf / Auckland
Johannesburg / Kuala Lumpur / London / Mexico / Montreal
New Delhi / Panama / Paris / São Paulo / Singapore / Sydney
Tokyo / Toronto

An Architectural Record Book Ⓡ

**Techniques of
Successful
Practice**

1234567890   HD BP   74321098765

The editors for this book were Jeremy Robinson and Hugh S. Donlan.
The designer was J. Paul Kirouac, A Good Thing, Inc.
It was set in Linofilm Helvetica by Black Dot Computer Typesetting Corporation.
It was printed by Halliday Lithograph Corporation
and bound by The Book Press.

Library of Congress Cataloging in Publication Data

Foxhall, William B   comp.
  Techniques of successful practice for architects and
engineers.

  "An Architectural Record book."
  "A re-edited selection of articles . . . [published]
in Architectural Record during the past few years."
  1. Architectural practice—United States.
2. Consulting engineers—United States.   I.   Architectural Record.   II.   Title.
NA1996.F69   720   74-20953
ISBN 0-07-002229-1

Contents

Index

Preface

The business techniques of professional practice have acquired paramount importance for architects and engineers in these times. The internal working methods of practice today have all the accoutrements of program and documentation that now must formalize every business enterprise. Taxation and liability, personnel management and business development, automation and computerization, production and delivery: all these comprise the business climate that is pervasive everywhere. But, for architects and engineers the production and delivery of professional services have a special character—not only unique to the nature of their own business, but uniquely preservative of essential and enduring human values.

The man-made environment is in the keeping of these professionals, who must perform their tasks with art and science and diligence as the professional agents of other men—the owners. In these times of burgeoning invention and stringent economics, both opportunities and perils multiply in the exercise of that guardianship. And the scope of work enlarges even more rapidly than the size of projects.

So, administration and control become a way of life in these professions as in other modes of business—to such an extent, in fact, that one whole segment of professional activities has become structured and identified for these purposes. Project administration and cost control, now acquiring new labels (Construction Management?) and special jargon (Fast-Track? Value Analysis?), comprise one example of one instrumentality preserving the identity of a classic role of architects and engineers—believe it or not!

The fabled master builders had no carte blanche, no limitless resources with which to execute great works regardless of their clients' purses or predilections. Quite the contrary. Clients were patrons or sponsors who bought or hired genius with the total arrogance of princes in a world where princes were themselves creatures of totally manipulative power. The fashion was *sophisticated* power, to be sure. But Esterhazy bought and disciplined his Haydn with no more depth of perception than Morgan exercised with McKim, or Mead, or White.

Today, the architect deals with another kind of prince. He deals with a corporation, a church, a board of directors, a multi-person entity within which the loudest voice is amplified in proportion to the number of dollars behind it. But the voice is not one voice. No member's money is all the money there is. So, although the architect is still the commissioned genius—by now a multi-person himself—he is on his own. He has wrought skillfully to make himself the legally visible and responsible executor of the built environment. Now he must put his artistry where his protestation is. He must deliver a project for which he is responsible to a client who has lost both the identity and the flexibility of individuality.

Well, all of that simply means that the architect and engineer must identify and enlist the elements of management that make large works possible in today's world. Then he must put the elements of ownership and risk where they belong—with the owner, whatever that identity may be—and erect fee structures that accomplish the primordial goals of his profession without jeopardy to his own survival.

These notions are some of the reasons for publication of this book, and indeed were motivation for starting the "Architectural Business" section in **ARCHITECTURAL RECORD** in 1967. The content is a re-edited selection of articles that have dealt with these and other practice matters in *Architectural Record* during the last few years. The articles comprise a statement of current times, current problems and such solutions as can be encompassed in one volume for so broad a context.

Acknowledgments are never complete. The list of contributors appended here omits the names of editorial and publishing colleagues who really made the book possible. Without slighting others, let me cite Hugh Donlan's endless skills and patience as middleman in the publisher's role and Jeanne Davern's editorial support providing incomparable discernment of consistency, quality and balance.

William B. Foxhall

Acknowledgments

This book has been made possible by the generosity of many professionals in sharing with their colleagues their experience on one practice frontier or another. Some of these contributors are quoted or credited in the book; many others have also been, in less explicit ways, contributors to development of the "Architectural Business" section of ARCHITECTURAL RECORD and of this book. To none can an editor be more indebted than to his authors, and their names and contributions are listed below:

Robert Brodsky, EXECUTIVE VICE PRESIDENT, Brodsky, Hopf & Adler, Architects and Engineers, New York City, *Guidelines to European Practice*, pages 57-60

Ernest Burden, ARCHITECT, New York City, *Slide Presentations*, pages 113-117

Earl R. Flansburgh, PRINCIPAL, Earl R. Flansburgh and Associates, Cambridge, Massachusetts, Chapter 4, *Some Thoughts on Starting Your Own Practice*, pages 37-41

William B. Foxhall, SENIOR EDITOR, ARCHITECTURAL RECORD: Chapter 1, *The Changing Patterns of Architectural Practice*, pages 1-6; Chapter 2, *The Response to Change*, pages 7-23; Chapter 3, *The Young Architects: A Profile*, pages 25-35; *Joint-venture Practice*, pages 45-49; *Professional construction management and project administration*, pages 160-163; *Budget control of the phased construction project*, pages 164-167; *Computers: tools for construction management*, pages 106-211; *Interior design practice*, pages 62-75; *Practice problems in remodeling*, pages 75-81; *Survey of architects shows most do some remodeling—and find big jobs and big rewards*, pages 81-85

John Warren Giles, ATTORNEY, Washington, D.C., *Let's clear up laws on copyright of plans*, pages 131-134

Lawrence Jaquith, ECONOMIST, McKee-Berger-Mansueto, Inc., New York City, *The cost index: working tool or trap?*, pages 175-180

Allan Johnson, ARCHITECT, Gruzen and Partners, New York City, *Photo-drafting: time-saving aid to quality*, pages 154-158

Gerre L. Jones, VICE PRESIDENT, Building Industry Design Services, division of Gaio Associates, Washington, D.C., *How design firms should approach government agencies*, pages 109-113

E. R. McCamman, PROJECT DIRECTOR, Giffels & Rossetti, Inc., Detroit, *A critical path example*, pages 201-206

Robert S. McMillan, PRINCIPAL, Robert S. McMillan Associates, New York City, *Practice abroad: a rewarding study in comprehensive frustrations*, pages 60-62

Bradford Perkins, (at time of writing) PRESIDENT, Omnidata, and VICE PRESIDENT, D'Orsey Hurst, divisions of McKee-Berger-Mansueto, Inc., New York City; (now) MANAGING PARTNER, Llewelyn-Davies Associates, USA: *Why and how to plan professional firm management*, pages 88-90; *Financial management of the professional firm*, pages 90-96; *Personnel practices in professional firms*, pages 96-100; *Marketing architectural services*, pages 100-104; *Computers as automated practice aids*, pages 104-109; *Cost knowledge: tool for budget, program and design*, pages 171-175; *Guidelines for early planning estimates*, pages 180-183; *Some common errors in cost control programs*, pages 183-187; *Evaluating hidden cost factors*, pages 187-190; *Computerized cost estimating is ready now—almost*, pages 190-194

Mildred F. Schmertz, SENIOR EDITOR, ARCHITECTURAL RECORD, *Architectural drawing for printing processes*, pages 136-152

Samuel Spencer, ATTORNEY, Spencer and Whalen, Washington, D.C., *Interstate Practice*, pages 53-57

Richard D. Steyert, ARCHITECTURAL ECONOMICS CONSULTANT, New York City, *Architectural economics: the concept of total cost*, pages 167-171

Justin Sweet, PROFESSOR OF LAW, University of California, Berkeley, *New approaches to liability and legal service costs*, pages 127-131

Roland D. Thompson, PARTNER, Gruzen and Partners, New York City, *Photodrafting: time-saving aid to quality*, pages 154-158

E. Van Krugel, DIRECTOR OF TRAINING COURSES, U.S. Army Corps of Engineers, *Introduction to CPM*, pages 196-201

Nathan Walker, ATTORNEY, and **T. K. Rohdenburg,** ARCHITECT, New York City, *Legal pitfalls flagged in book for architects and engineers*, pages 120-127

The
Changing
Patterns
of
Architectural
Practice

Architects face new and larger tasks in the midst of the huge works now shap-
ing every aspect of the environment of man—his resources, transport, recrea-
tion, whole cities, forests and the crucial marshes where life begins. It is to the
architectural profession that those who feel the need for these great works
are turning, not just for the complex specifics of design, but for skilled and
thoughtful help in setting new goals. And the profession is taking up such new
tools as it needs to execute these great commissions.

This is an evolved profession, called forth to deal with the crowded plight of
mankind in a time of technical and social revolution. It is the logical extension
of an ancient concern of architects with the commodity, firmness and delight
of buildings. But now it must embrace the whole environment of man in an
ever more demanding complex.

As man has multiplied and his structures and devices saturate the earth, his
every exposure becomes man-made. He makes waste and generates friction.
His natural resources are depleted or polluted. The very air he breathes is
charged with the noxious exhalations of his own machines.

But somehow the last great strangulation is averted. Man has survived and
will continue. He reaches out for new devices, new resources, new lubricants
for the order of his ways. A profession evolves that plans the controlled resources of a state; that devises transport for a nation; that shapes the features
and the future of cities, new and old. It is a profession that pulls together a
stupendous multiplicity of hardware and the skills for its deployment. It makes
of all that multiplicity a cohesive and intuitive whole. It is an art. And its name is
architecture. But the future depends on the capacities of practitioners to grasp
it. "The question confronting us," says AIA past-president Morris Ketchum Jr.,
"is whether or not we, as individuals and as a profession, can rise to the demands of our new destiny." What are these demands? By whom are they imposed? What capacities must architects develop or enhance to meet them?

The surge to bigness   The individual architect, as artist, remains and shall remain the dominant conceptual force in the design of man-made environment. The architect as pro-
fessional, however, is operating in an era when the surge to bigness has
brought business and government to ever more complex corporate and bureaucratic structures. Architects are facing fundamental changes in both the
nature of their clients and the milieu in which their work is done. They have
themselves been caught up in an economy in which a large office no longer
reflects a simple and happy multiplication of commissions. Today, size is very
often fundamental to staying in business at all in certain kinds of practices now
developing.

This is *not* to say that the big architectural office is the only office of the
future. By the very nature of the professional relationship, the classic dialogue
between architect and client remains at all levels; and the very multiplicity of
jobs of all sizes assures continuance of and opportunities in individual relationships.

But even the solitary practitioner must now approach the smallest commission with a bigness of mind that is prepared to encompass a whole new spectrum of consulting services.

One aspect of change was aptly illustrated in an interview with William H.
Scheick, then executive director of the AIA. Consider, he suggested, the
relationship of J. P. Morgan and Charles Follen McKim. Morgan owned a site
on which he wanted to build. He simply called McKim and instructed him to

design a bank. The job was done and bills were paid. It was an interchange between individuals, complicated only by the possible clash of strong opinions. Nowadays, the client for a large project is generally a corporation, a syndicate, a foundation, or a government agency. The dialogue becomes diffuse and complex, subject to new disciplines of organization and new lines of authority.

The demand for comprehensive services

In any business today, consultation has become a way of life in dealing with any situation that is out of the normal stream of operation. For example, new construction for expansion—while an outgrowth of normal operation—involves expertise in feasibility, construction, location and programing that is beyond the in-house scope of most business organizations. They seek guidance in these matters from a consulting profession. They find one that is uniquely endowed to provide or to coordinate that guidance. They turn to architects, because those pre-construction problems are the familiar prelude to the daily work of architecture.

But the traditional practice of architecture, while it generated familiarity with many of these pre-project problems, had not set up fee structures or habits of operation geared to participation on the developing large scale. When the challenge of increased demand presented itself, the profession took up arms to deal with it. "Comprehensive services" became the rallying cry. And the means of providing and charging for those services are being worked into the professional structure. Demand and fulfillment have generated more demand and higher capabilities for meeting it. Corporate clients, governments and institutions now enlist architects on a widening front of attack on problems related to planning—larger-scale complexes of buildings, whole new campuses, vacation and recreation complexes, bigger and more carefully thought out residential communities—new cities, in fact.

The demand for urban planning

In communities all over the nation, there is a great and growing awareness of the impact even a single building may have on the appearance and viability of its surroundings. Recent Federal administrations have actively fostered that awareness in a climate of cultural and esthetic emphasis. The establishment at cabinet level of the Department of Housing and Urban Development, and more especially the assignment of architects to key roles in administration, are significant and far-reaching in relating the public mind to architecture as an instrument of urban planning. While the planning of cities is no new role for architects, the crisis of rapid growth in this field, brought on by vast appropriations for urban renewal, has opened the door to personal involvement by hundreds of architects on a scale never before realized.

It is perhaps this character of personal involvement that puts the architect, as citizen, in a key role in the implementation of urban renewal. Architects are tending to participate more in community affairs—not just because their voices are more needed, but because this involvement is increasingly related to their professional roles. As problems in urban renewal come up, fellow citizens are calling upon architects for leadership in planning their own home towns. Center-city merchants, especially, who have felt centrifugal losses to outlying suburbs, are asking architects to redesign the centers of cities in more inviting aspect. City officials are meeting the pleas of citizens with ready funds and enabling acts. And so the battle with our staggering urban problems is effectively joined.

The demand for regional planning

Success succeeds, as the saying goes, and the step from successful urban planning to commissions on a regional or statewide basis would seem a logical one. It is; but there is an exponential factor of complexity as it relates to size. Further, the product of this kind of practice is not always one to delight the eye of the artist by its line and form. It does have, however, an architectural quality of organization, and it is calling forth every talent of a considerable body of skilled practitioners. It is truly architecture; specialized, perhaps, and practiced on a grand new scale.

Those who are responsible for vast enterprise in transport, conservation of resources, statewide health or education systems, recreation areas, or any of the complex regional facilities that transcend local boundaries, are turning more and more to architects who have demonstrated capability in planning on a large scale. A regional system of airports and ground transport to serve them in a huge metropolis; a statewide program in mental health facilities; a control system for a whole coastal watershed—all these have been real commissions for architectural offices.

The key factor of agency

Thousands of architects, especially those in smaller offices, do not now consider themselves geared to offer many of the so-called "comprehensive services" including urban and regional planning on a broad scale. And in strict fact, there is work enough to suit the proclivities of any architect at whatever scale he may elect. But many small and medium firms are offering these services successfully. The practice modes by which consultants are assembled *by the architect as agent for the owner* are opening up opportunities in comprehensive services for even the smallest offices.

This factor of agency has not only legal and fiscal implications (with their attendant and familiar pitfalls); it is the key device by which a whole battery of inter-reacting disciplines can speak with one voice to the owner. As ownership becomes more complex, it must, of course, seek similarly complex channels of response to a professional identity, so that the classic dialogue between architect and owner continues unobscured in a changing world.

Changes bring new problems and solutions

All of these forces for growth and change have exacerbated the problems of architects by the very nature of growth and change in themselves. Technological advance imposes a staggering body of data on the background of design. The individual technical mind is forced to specialize and the designer is forced to call on specialist consultants in new techniques for the exercise of his practice. Unfortunately, complexity breeds error; and in the world of architecture and its attendant professions, errors can be costly and of long-term consequence. The instinct of all concerned is to relieve the financial and professional consequences of error by finding someone who can be proved legally and perhaps morally responsible. Who better than one——the architect——who comes naturally to the role of agency and accepts the rewards of that role as well as its responsibilities?

Architects have been through a period of horrendous and inhibiting liability suits. Often these grow out of the "let's sue somebody" attitude nurtured by the climate of insurance and judgment practices. If architects are to retain the stature implicit in their role as owners' agent, they must do something to bring reason into the contemplation of liability. As individual citizens and as a profession, they are urging and slowly achieving revisions in statutes of limitations. Contract documents are getting intense scrutiny and revision. Clauses pertaining to construction site work are being clarified to specify "field administration" rather than to leave interpretation by the courts open to the implication of liability for "supervision" of construction down to the safety of the last scaffold.

Even the time-honored prohibition against "free sketches" is coming under review and clarification. As architects are called upon for judgments and ideas earlier before commissions for design can be formalized, there is an increasing urgency that some means be available whereby they can express those ideas on a provisional basis without jeopardizing their standing in the profession. The notion of a "contingency fee" is finding favor in some cases where a firm time-charge is not feasible. Under its terms, an architect may elect to participate in early work provided he has an understanding that he is to be architect for the job if and when it goes forward.

The magic word of "guarantee"

Today almost every new facility must be rigorously budgeted and fitted into a firm time-slot. Frequently, corporate or bureaucratic clients insist that the designers give an early guarantee as to completion date and cost. In this hard school, many architects have learned to guarantee bid prices within a small per cent of estimates at early phases of design. For those who have not so learned, here is a new breed of cost consultant and construction manager that can help in this regard.

The need is for estimating skills in the very early design development stage, and for strong discipline in design changes once preliminaries have been approved. The consequence of these disciplines is a new look at the design process itself, so that costly excursions in trial and error are not condoned in the name of art. Means are devised to bring diverse disciplines of technique and management to bear on conceptual phases of a project.

The fee structure must keep pace with complexity

Almost no one believes that the long-established mode of setting architectural fees as a per cent of construction cost is ideal, reasonable, workable, or even moral in the more complex situations of today's market. Alternative methods now in vogue such as "cost plus a fixed fee" or "direct technical expense plus" depend for their validity upon firm knowledge of what the cost of the design processes really is.

It is generally acknowledged that the current level of fees is not high enough to assure across-the-board excellence and inventiveness on the part of all disciplines. Further, it is felt, even by some contractors, that higher architectural and engineering fees, shared in proportion with consultants, permitting more careful work on specifications and detailing, eliminating conflicts and errors, could be more than offset by savings in overall cost to the owner.

The architectural profession is finding that in order to demonstrate the need for higher fees and to arrive at truly equitable ratios of distribution among the consulting professions, it must learn more about the cost of doing professional business.

Emerging techniques in the management of work

Nine techniques adapted from the advanced processes of business have found their way into the modes of architectural practice, according to publications of AIA. A 92-page paperback, under the title, *Emerging Techniques of Architectural Practice,* reports on a study prepared by members of the Department of Architectural Engineering of the Pennsylvania State University and based on interviews with architectural firms from coast to coast and management experts outside the profession. The nine techniques found to be of growing importance in modern practice are:

■ *Network planning.* Finding increasing application in architectural offices are graphical devices of the critical path method (CPM) and the program evaluation and review technique (PERT).

■ *Management science.* In the new interplay between people and machines, decisions by intuition and calculated risk are being replaced by techniques of management science. These techniques include statistical decision theories, managerial forecasting and controls, effective communications, probability theories and value theories.

■ *Systems development.* Recurring problems in the architectural process are problem definition, goal setting, systems synthesis, systems analysis and selection of alternate systems. New techniques for space analysis and human engineering offer designers new methods of approach.

■ *Construction cost management.* Evolving into a vital aspect of architectural services are cost management systems which permit the control and prediction of construction costs. Some firms are applying such systems, and the term **construction management** is gaining definition.

■ *Quality control.* Architects are adopting relatively new techniques which grew out of aerospace and automotive fields by establishing standards of design quality to be used as yardsticks to measure actual performance under tests. Post-construction data are analyzed and applied in determining degrees of reliability for various design techniques.

■ *Communications technology.* In addition to the well-established technology of business communications, architects are using advanced methods of indexing, abstracting and systematizing source material, sometimes enlisting the aid of computers in efforts to solve complex problems in information retrieval.

■ *Reproduction systems.* Standard reproduction systems for graphic and written material are being supplemented by photographic film techniques not only for the review of information pertaining to current work, but also for microfilming of drawings and records. The SCAN system, whereby subscribing contractors and supplies are provided with microfilmed sets of architectural drawings and specifications and a viewing device, is in this category.

■ *Automated graphical systems.* In addition to the emerging graphical capabilities of computers, the study points to the potential use of automatic data plotters, "digitizers," and magnetic display units that will permit architects to maintain communication with previously computerized information for design and analysis.

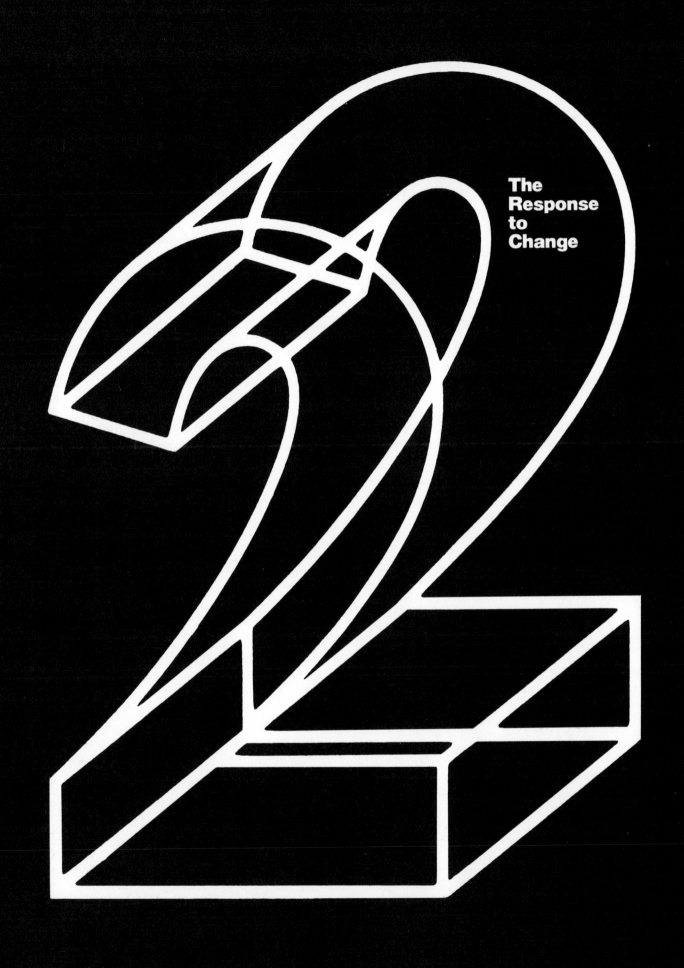

The
Response
to
Change

Increasing attention to management and the new supporting tools that help get bidding documents produced and construction put in place sustain architects in a role that is primary, exclusive and undiminished.

Management is a broad-gage word; and some would tell us that it is a more or less exact science. Perhaps, for now, we can agree it is an umbrella word for many sturdy talents in this field. Then we can separate some nodes of emphasis in what is, in fact, a single unifying array of talents and tools for one purpose— the practice of architecture. In this and following chapters, we have arranged to look at: organization for management, tooling up for management, architectural job management, and that catch-all phrase, project and construction management—and we are not deceived into belief that these are truly separable subjects.

The organization chart: framework or limit?

For a generation, the pages of the architectural press have repeatedly shown ingenious charts of firm organization. Reproduced here, for example, are two charts from an early article ("CPM: What factors determine its success?" by Francis A. Sando of Day & Zimmerman, Inc., *Architectural Record,* April 1964) illustrating how CPM fit at that time in a design firm.

The purpose here is to show graphically the difference between vertical and horizontal organization. Two actual and reasonably current (1970) charts for the firms of Golemon & Rolfe and RTKL Inc. show how these forms can evolve in response to the logic of good management so long as the lines and boxes are not considered to express inviolable, "scientific" rules. (Charts, pages 10 & 11.)

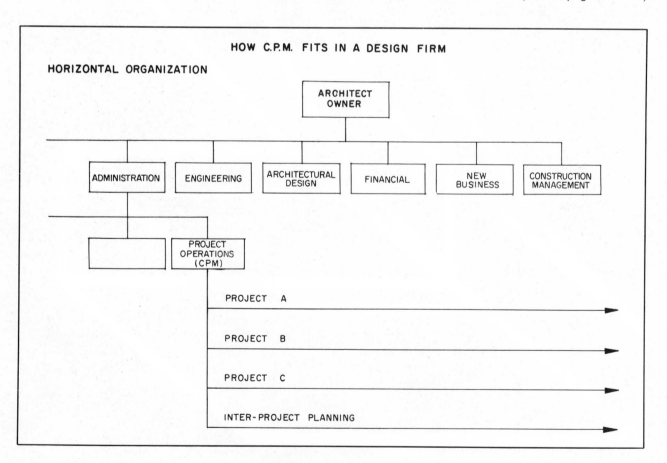

HOW C.P.M. FITS IN A DESIGN FIRM

HORIZONTAL ORGANIZATION

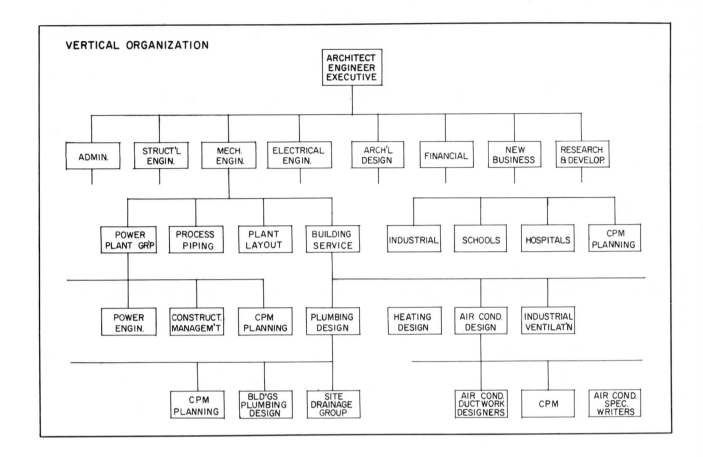

VERTICAL ORGANIZATION

"At Golemon & Rolfe, we consider the practice of architecture to be the creation of art through . . . creative management, scientific method and talented persons."

Thus, Harry Golemon, second-generation president of this long-established Houston firm, states the philosophy by which he hopes the firm will evolve from its well-established image of skilled, engineering-oriented projects toward what he calls a fourth dimension, the spirit of the design.

The responsibility flow-chart shown reflects a conviction that certain persons of specific experience and talent should be provided with both opportunity and responsibility for exercising their talents throughout the project development process. Thus, projects proceed, not through departments, but through a succession of special inputs to the design process.

This is the applied logic and the firm's stated position: *that the architect must become involved in the decision-making process wherever it occurs and with ever deeper penetration into those decisions that shape the environment*— even before a building design is considered. This means penetration into social, political and economic arenas.

The board of directors, then, is made of the president and executive vice president, an attorney and a real estate economist who is also a certified property manager. This composition reflects broadening services in the special interests of a growing clientele among developer-builders—about half their practice in 1970. In this kind of work, says Golemon, a team approach is essential, and the architect needs a new arsenal of coordinating knowledge in real estate, finance and rental management.

The directors of facilities are all partners in the firm and are directly responsible to the client for all matters pertaining to a commission in any of the three special categories shown. Matters of contract are coordinated by the executive vice president, and the directors themselves report to the president. Not shown on the chart is a development committee made up of the president as chairman and the directors of facilities as advocates for their fields of interest.

The executive vice president has reporting to him an operations committee made up of the two vice presidents in charge of construction systems and business and construction administration. These two vice presidents, although they have no personnel assigned to them as such, are involved in decisions affecting the entire project development process, as indicated by the dashed lines on the chart below.

Project development for each job is set up in a network scheduling process similar to CPM. Network task assignments and the man-hours estimated for each are related to computerized schedule and cost control.

Management for growth in size and scope

The emergence of urban planning on a big scale as real commissions for architects has introduced a management requirement for those firms who intend to offer that service. Further, the giant scale of work for some other clients

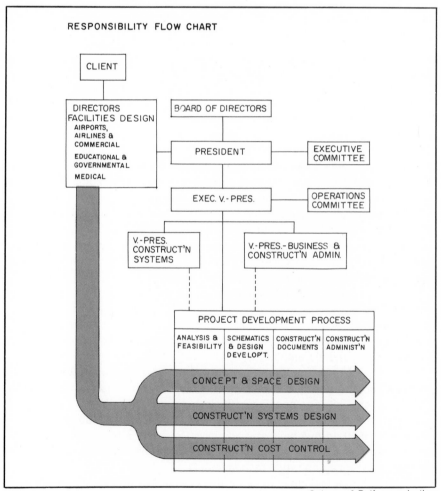

Golemon & Rolfe organization

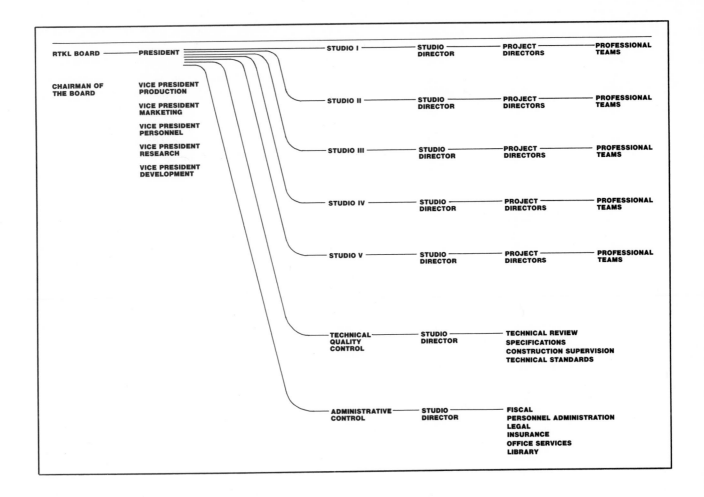

—corporate, government, and investment developer—is such that large, diversified firms are the most visible first call for those clients. Good architectural firms of moderate size are faced now with a decision either to begin choosing clients to fit their capacities or to embark on rigorously planned programs of growth to handle the larger work. That decision will be based on the personal proclivities of the firms involved, as well as on the fact that there will continue to be a substantial market in moderate commissions.

These were some of the background ideas preamble to a description of growth plans for the firm of RTKL Associates Inc. (the name adopted in January 1969 by the Baltimore firm of Rogers, Taliaferro, Kostritsky, Lamb). The firm began in 1946 as a small architectural office in Annapolis, Md. Since then, the scope of practice has expanded to include downtown development plans, new town plans, campus master plans, and special studies, as well as a full panoply of more conventional building design work. At about the time of its incorporation, the firm had grown to 100 employees, of whom more than half were either registered or had master's degrees in architecture, planning, or urban design.

The RTKL organizational flow diagram illustrates two important aspects of the firm's approach to management. First, the president, Harold Adams, is a young architect whose interests center on management. (This kind of bent, many practitioners say, is one that should have better opportunities to flourish in the curricula of architectural schools.) The decision to appoint an exclusively management head becomes important as firms reach 50 to 60 employes and is clear-cut as the 100-mark is reached.

The second point seen in the diagram is that the firm is structured in a series of more or less parallel studios for which management activities are shared by several principals. Each studio has a principal-in-charge, a studio manager and directors for each of the assigned projects for which the studio is responsible from beginning to final documents. An additional studio handles all working drawings, specifications, estimates and construction supevision. There is a cross-feed of management and technical experience at key points for all projects.

Joint ventures offer relief of growing pains

The joint venture as a means of mustering diverse talents for accomplishing single large jobs is a familiar form of organization. RTKL brought a new on-going interpretation to the joint venture concept as a means, not only for marshaling talent, but also for gaining geographically widespread points of outlet for their own considerable resources.

As the first step in a two-phase organization plan to reinforce the firm's resources in urban problems, RTKL looked into the possibility of a series of joint ventures in growth areas across the nation. Instead of setting up branch offices, they sought out compatible moderate-size firms in such widespread locations as Puerto Rico, Hartford, Minneapolis and California. The idea was to set up standing joint ventures in advance of any specific job.

The objective was to add expert people to the total scope of their firm and gain widespread geographic representation without the capital expenditure usually associated with setting up branch offices. Further, they would acquire the background knowledge of local conditions and other specific areas of expertise by the simple expedient of carefully selecting those firms with which they associate. RTKL, in return, would offer the local firm the advantages of their own resources.

In response to the question as to whether spreading work across the whole of the nation is a sound procedure in this field, RTKL points out that this is the way many large corporate clients work, and as clients they may find some advantage in working with a firm similarly distributed. The joint venture mode of geographical distribution may indeed be a response to some of the lessons of the past in over-extension of branch offices in the profession. The course of development of the network has, of course, provided other lessons in diffusion, agreement format, marketing and management that call for particular study in each case.

How one post-war firm is organized for service

A chart of organization for professional services is shown as a segment of the overall logic by which the firm of Lyles, Bissett, Carlisle & Wolff has grown from its founding in 1948 to its present 200-plus complement in four office locations. A comprehensive chart of the whole organization might show a management nucleus of the home office at Columbia, S.C., surrounded by and connected to satellite representations of offices in Washington, Alexandria and Raleigh and all neatly framed on one side by administrative departments channeled to the executive director and on the other side by operating departments (planning, industrial, hospital, interior, etc.) channeled through the director of professional services who is directly in charge of a central core of architectural design, engineering and technical services. Supporting this core would be a construction division in charge of all field work.

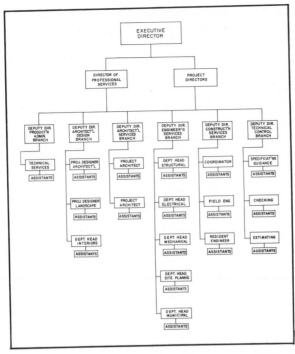

The fragment shown marks a significant adjustment in 1968 of some aspects of professional services. Especially fore-arming for practice in the 1970s is the addition of a coordinating department in the construction services branch. This change was "to facilitate the processing and record keeping of shop drawings, samples and comparable submissions during the construction phase."

Another significant adjustment in organization, perhaps reflecting foresight in emerging "systems" applications, was a linkage of structural and electrical/mechanical engineering operations under a deputy director of engineering services and establishment of a new position called "electrical consultant, special projects" reporting to the deputy director.

However deeply this firm may elect to penetrate into the role now popularly called "construction management," it is—like many others—setting itself up with competence to do so. And it is a competence backed up by computerized job-watching whereby the director of professional services gets a status print-out of every project in work at every significant interval and in all details of estimates, allocations and actual performance.

How another young firm gears up for developer clients

Well, organization isn't everything. Some firms, young firms, have problems of growth, not size; problems of getting started, not turning around an aging name-firm against its own momentum. William D. Peckham says he and his partner Fred F. Guyton had started in 1962 "with not much more than a conviction" which was that if they as individuals and architecture as a profession were to prosper—or even survive—in today's scene, they would have to design better mousetraps as well as better monuments. So they started with warehouses.

They did homework on investment-development in such matters as true total costs and rent returns and they welcomed developers as clients. They rejected those in-and-out developers who have only short-term commitments and chose only developer clients who retained at least 65 per cent of long-term ownership in their projects. Notable among these was the Linclay Corporation for whom in 1970 they did all the architectural work in planning, design, interiors and landscape; but further, they begin very early in the search for real estate, analysis of economic feasibility and determination of the mix of industrial, commercial and residential buildings. Linclay is developer of large projects in the St. Louis area. Current at press time was a giant development of over 800 acres planned for virtually "new-city" balance.

The mode of operation of the Peckham-Guyton 30-man organization is to assemble a task force for each project headed by a project architect who is responsible for all phases of services. If the project is in another city, the whole task force may move there for the duration. The firm principals also take an active part in all phases, and the virtually unpartitioned aspect of the home office in St. Louis makes for unlimited—not to say uncontrolled—cross-feed.

Organization chart? Peckham says it could only be a straight line. "It's esprit de corps that holds the whole thing together"—plus the fact that a project manager, after about five years, may be taking home as much pay as a principal. We're really in it for architecture, says Peckham, and all these real-world services aim at that goal.

Two other trends in architectural organization may gain momentum in the 1970s: First, there seems to be an increasing role for the self-client architect in developer affiliations a step further than Peckham's. Second, is the architect coordinator of other architects as were Rogers/Nagel/Langhart for Denver schools, Ferendino/Grafton/Spillis/Candela for Miami and others.

New tools foster new methods

Computer hardware, data plotters, microfilm retrieval and display systems, photo reproduction devices, automated typewriters and other adjuncts to the business and processes of architecture have had profound effect in implementing and actually fostering changes in practice in the 1970s. Purveyors' and users' inventiveness has been directed toward three important areas of practice routine: information retrieval, specification writing and the graphical output of coordinated information. It is to the last of these that exotic adjuncts to computerization will increasingly address themselves in the 1970s. Photo processes, too, are taking an increasing amount of the repetitive drudgery out.

Graphical computer output is scarcely new. *Architectural Record* reported on the potential of the oscilloscope and light-pencil as early as March 1963—and has recorded "sketch-pad" and other developments periodically since then. But "exotic" and "development" are the operative words that have meant high cost and limited application. Now, there are converging streams of development that may bring cost and application into better focus in the 1970s: 1) computer programs in A/E fields are more abundant; 2) architects are more familiar with them and more sophisticated in their instincts about the limits of design application; 3) hardware in smaller, more flexible sets is available; 4) dataplotter output is more useful and the machinery less formidable (although still costly); 5) an increasing number of computer service centers has made expensive hardware available on line or shared time so that the investment picture is changing; 6) many architects are beginning to realize that a close-held proprietary attitude toward programs they have developed may be self-defeating—if not unprofessional. It forces them as well as others to keep reinventing the wheel in building their own libraries. AIA's continuing support of Masterspec may be an avenue toward broader professional attitudes and input.

Several architectural offices have, in fact, made their in-house programs available to the profession, with or without fee. Some such offices are Reynolds

Smith & Hills of Jacksonville, Dalton, Dalton & Little of Cleveland, Perry, Dean & Stewart of Boston, CRS, Houston, and others.

Computer equipment was set up by RSH at a separate location for developing a set of programs called Architectural Design Systems. ADS has been used on large airport, military, and school commissions to quickly assess cost and other implications of design alternatives. Stored geometric models are related to materials and cost subsystems. The designer talks to these programs through simple English-language coding sheets, and the machine responds with estimate printouts. RSH has since withdrawn from the business of serving other architects while ADS programs are further and independently developed.

Skidmore Owings & Merrill, whose pioneering installation of computer hardware has been a display center in their Chicago office, is another firm whose building optimization programs have been a more or less public spin-off.

William R. Orr of the Ft. Worth firm, Construction Service Company, developed computerized construction cost, graphics and schedule programs which are available on a time-sharing basis through the McDonnell Automation Company of St. Louis.

The former computer applications department of Caudill Rowlett Scott, having developed an array of programs in information retrieval, cost estimating, campus planning and feasibility studies, decided to make these programs available to other architects. CRS set up a separate corporation, CRS 2, to continue further development and release; but that service, too, has been discontinued.

The A/E firm of Dalton, Dalton & Little in Cleveland and its highway engineering-oriented branch in Akron have invested heavily in both hardware and personnel to set up a computer service division of 16 specialists (including an architect) under the leadership of Irving I. Budish, a principal of the firm. The division has been under development for more than eight years and serves both the firm itself and outside clients. Its computer library contains over 60 programs including several that extend the capabilities of graphic plotter outputs beyond most conventional limits. Other engineering programs coordinate geometry problems (COGO), surveying systems (SASSY) drainage, roadway, bridge construction and various building programs in structural, electrical and mechanical.

A Cleveland A/E firm offers computer services

Dalton, Dalton & Little has about 14 programs of special interest to architects. These have to do with spatial allocations in multi-story plan layouts, estimating, lighting, perspective, drawing, working drawings and schedules, mapping, urban land use and campus planning systems.

Cal Dalton, DDL principal, would be the first to caution those who would go forth and do likewise that computer hardware is expensive and its load factor is critical to any economies it can produce. As Robert F. Hastings, the late chairman of Smith, Hinchman and Grylls, has observed: the decision to invest in computerization will depend on the short-term ability of computers to save on conventional business services while firm professionals are developing their programs.

Prudently, Golemon & Rolfe called in an outside consultant (Lockheed Electronics) to study feasibility of computerization of that highly organized firm. The conclusion was that even their internal network scheduling and highly developed statistical and estimating procedures could best be handled by outside services.

So the tools are marshaling, and modes evolve for their employment.

The management response to change

It is not always clear whether such techniques as phased construction and construction management are changes to which architects must increasingly respond or are in themselves a response to deeper changes in the economics of construction. The difference is more semantic than real. In the context of this chapter, the following is adapted from an article in the *Architectural Record* for October 1970 on the response of practice to changes in the 1970s. It is more reportorial than definitive, and later chapters will deal in more detail with the content of these techniques.

Under pressures of increasing construction costs and urgent needs for space—especially in educational and socio-medical facilities—some of the techniques of industry have been refined and applied to the design-and-construct sequence. The techniques have been evolutionary rather than revolutionary. But their application to these human-oriented types of facilities (rather than to warehouses and heavy industry) has introduced new complexities of program and new priorities for quality to what has heretofore been a rigorous demand for time and cost control.

Further, a spin-off from diverse attempts to probe and identify the developing concept of "systems building" has been effectively applied so that new meanings are implicit in phrases that, to some, may already have a familiar ring:

- Fast-track scheduling
- Pre-selected systems
- Continual delivery process
- Surge building
- Simplexes and subsets

The last item in the above list of jargon phrases may be a misfit in present company. It comes from the computer world glimpsed in previous pages and is illustrated in the diagrams that deal with a management technique to handle sheer complexity of program.

Hand finishing the perspective output of DDL's data plotter takes care of "lost lines" and provides what they call "instant renderings" at any selected point of view. Plotter's area/juxtaposition output can be hand-converted to a floor plan retaining essentials.

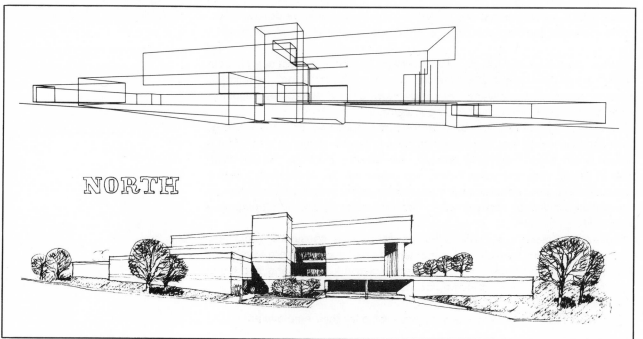

Well, not much is really new in this new world of management, except perhaps our willingness to really organize and use the experience and knowledge we already have.

New York sets a fast-track pace

The State University of New York, faced with horrendous problems of over $3-billion-a-year worth of construction on multiple campuses, calls on the State University Construction Fund for money and construction know-how. SUCF, in turn, calls in private professionals—architects and others—to work with their own in-house professionals on design, construction and method. For example:

A 1969 SUCF commission in the study of method went to architects Caudill Rowlett Scott. A 40-page report dated November of that year is entitled "Fast-track and other procedures; a general study of design and construction management." The first three items in our phrase list are in its table of contents. Here we can only quote the conclusion:

"Substantial reductions in project delivery time (25 per cent) can be achieved with fast-track scheduling.

"Remarkable savings (45 per cent) accrue if a pre-selected systems approach is integrated into the process.

"If the continual delivery process were fully operative, the whole notion of project time would need to be rethought since, as classically defined, the project delivery time could be reduced to less than a year. Construction could operate in cycle with the university's annual incremental growth."

In October 1969, CRS put their money where their method was. They had been commissioned for additions to three elementary schools on Long Island: a total of 25,600 square feet. Here is the schedule they met:

30 October	1969	Board of Education engaged CRS
3 November	1969	CRS selected project team
19 December	1969	Four sub-systems released for bid
11 February	1970	Out-of-system work released for bid
11 March	1970	Construction begins
1 September	1970	Schools completed

     Budget: $1,415,000
     Estimate: 1,028,756
     Bid: 953,931

Every architect will recognize the implications of such a schedule in matters of detailed handling of procedures and people. The quality of the product? A quality that only architects preserve and that need not be compromised by any schedule.

SUNY musters forces for the battle of Stonybrook

Design forces, management forces and construction forces, armed with the know-how of fast-track and all its implications, were the primary need when SUNY faced an awesome crash program for its campus at Stonybrook on Long Island. Starting with a bare site in the fall of 1969, they had to provide 190,000 square feet of facilities (2/3 laboratory space) for a student population of 4500 ready for September 1, 1970.

Smith, Hinchman & Grylls Associates, Inc., long in the vanguard of management and resources for getting things done with sustained quality in the demanding arenas of Detroit, got the commission. James P. Gallagher, SH&G's director of public affairs, describes ensuing events as follows:

"Here is a blow-by-blow account of what happened between our commissioning in December, 1969, and delivery of the buildings on September 1, 1970. I

Simplexes and subsets

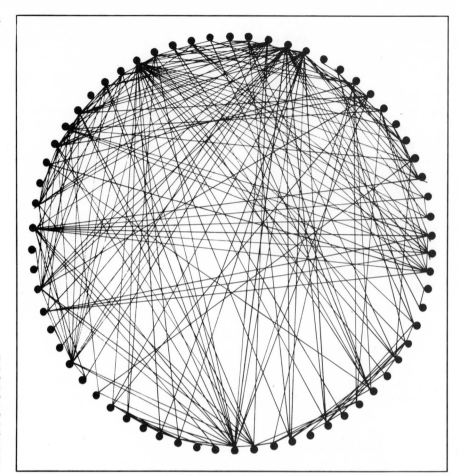

These sketches illustrate a computerized approach to sorting out complexities in the master plan for Brooklyn State Hospital for which Max O. Urbahn Associates were the architects. Some 65 requirements for commerce and communication among departments were input to the CLUSTR computer program described by Murray Milne (MIT Press 1969). Relationships are diagrammed in the circle. Simplexes and subsets are assembled in nodes, opposite page, and built into the plan superstructure, below.

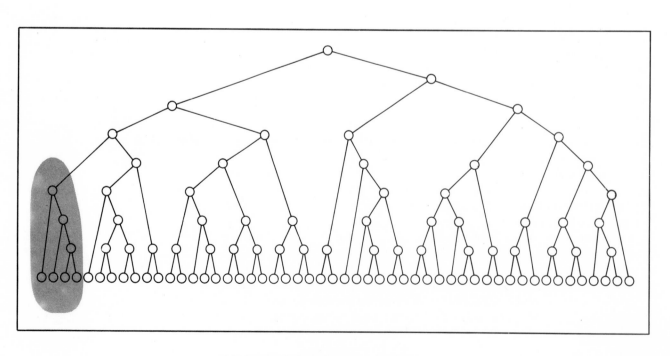

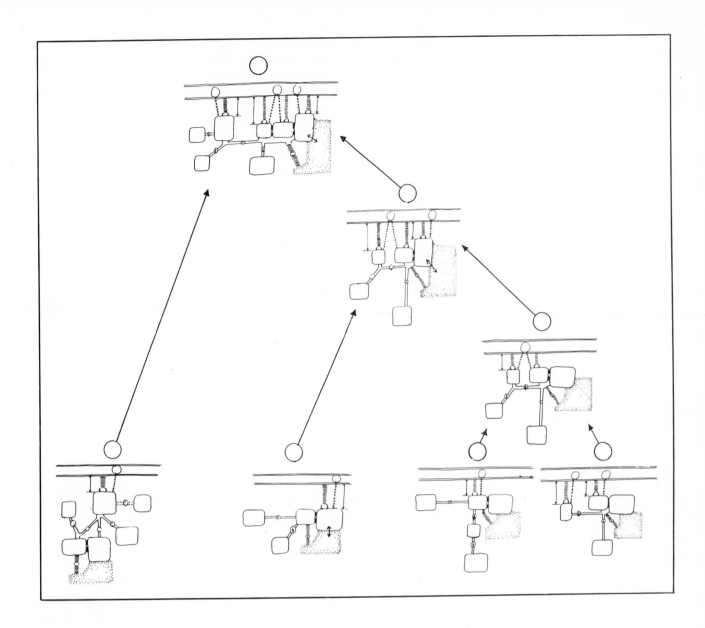

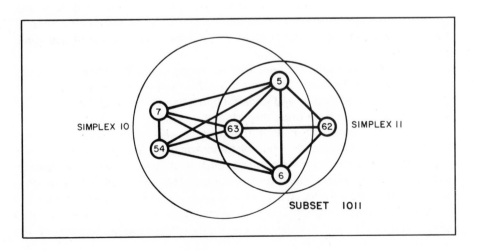

have included the major reasons we were able to meet such a schedule, but there is no way of putting into words the determination by all hands that these buildings were damned well going to be ready when the students turned up in September. They were really built on faith: faith that everyone was working toward the same end.

"On December 18, 1969, SH&G sat down with SUCF and SUNY while they set their program requirements. The next day we told them of certain building shape requirements they should accept if we were to get the buildings finished by the September 1 deadline. Among them: a number of buildings rather than one or two larger ones (we wound up with 11); one story, with flat roofs. And bay sizes and ceiling heights were limited. SUCF accepted these limitations, and we said we could deliver.

"Within days, we had settled on a 5- by 5-ft planning module, and 30- by 40-ft structural bays. On January 5, we started grubbing out the land, and shortly thereafter poured foundations (since bay size had been established in the initial decision) and started erecting columns.

"By breaking up the general contract into subcontracts, and by giving potential bidders an exact schedule for putting their products into place, we were able to get a number of bidders on each contract, and they could bid closely because they knew what their costs would be. If they had had to bid on an installation 18 months or two years away, they would have had to allow for all kinds of contingencies.

"Then we set up weekly meetings of architect, client, and contractors to iron out any difficulties that had come up. Everything on the agenda had to be decided at that meeting. Nothing could be put off for the later discussion. If there was disagreement on any problem, it was to be referred to Phil Meathe, our executive vice president, for his final and binding decision. Throughout the entire schedule, only one item was referred to him (something about a slight change in siting of one building). Everything else was hammered out at these weekly meetings, where the representatives of all three organizations had the authority to make decisions without checking with the front office before they acted.

"The contractors' agreements called for them to go on overtime whenever they fell even a day behind schedule, and our computer readouts gave us immediate warning if this was happening.

"Very early in the game, we knew that the manufacturer of a certain piece of electrical equipment was not going to be able to make his schedule. We had been in his factory and knew that no crash effort could make up the time. So we found another supplier on the West Coast who could meet the date, and gave the order to him, and canceled out the first supplier. We didn't wait until the date came up and he didn't meet it. We were not interested in penalties, only performance.

"At Stonybrook, we did the construction management as well as the design, which meant that we were enforcing the CPM, and we could get immediate decisions whenever design and construction clashed. If something had to be changed, we did not have to go through a third party.

"Another key reason for meeting the timetable was the willingness of prime manufacturers to bid on component systems. Again, this was due to the fact that they had a definite date for start and completion of their installation. A number of firms bid component systems on an installed basis. This applied, for example, to all the steel and roof trusses, the HVAC units, interior wall systems, etc.

"Every effort was made to approve payments immediately for work put into place, without the normal 10 per cent holdback of the general and subcontract system. This meant that subs could count on getting their money fast if they got the job done.

"In the spring, an appropriation that didn't come through caused SUCF to pull five of the 11 buildings out of the schedule, but later, the appropriation was made, and the five buildings went back in. They will be ready about Christmas, as we just couldn't make up the time lost waiting for the appropriation. But it would have been just as easy to finish the 11 on time.

"The criteria on which we base our estimate of $3.4 million in savings reside in the last 25 buildings built by the Fund in New York. They took an average of 43 months from commissioning to delivery.

"This dollar saving does not take into account the money that SUNY would have had to spend to provide classroom space for the students for the 43 months of normal construction time. While the figure is a guess, we estimate that it might have cost the university another $3 million.

"Smith, Hinchman & Grylls did all the design, engineering and construction management at Stonybrook, and Johnson, Johnson & Roy (which is now a division of SH&G) did the planning, siting, and landscape architecture. Project manager was John Solo Rio, out of our Detroit office, and field superintendent was Mark Wilson. The buildings were under the overall direction of our General Building Division headed by William Jarratt."

Further detail on this SH&G project will be found in the chapter on construction management and cost control, under the section on budget control of phased construction (pages 164–167).

When the Canadian Imperial Bank of Commerce had at last assembled all the parcels of land for a "super-block" development in downtown Toronto, management wanted to move very fast. They wanted to start construction way in advance of having a complete set of construction documents.

A knowledgeable client fosters project construction management

Five years earlier they had finished a large development in Montreal, and still had retained a skeleton "construction management" staff.

Consulting architect I. M. Pei and Toronto architects Page & Steele had worked out a large number of schemes that would have permitted developing the super-block in land-purchase stages; but all at once the few property holdouts sold their land. With zoning restrictions putting a ceiling on the maximum number of square feet of building, the final project—Commerce Court—evolved as a 56-story office building, two low-rise office buildings, and the bank's existing high-rise neo-classic office buildings.

The bank first thought it would manage the project with its own staff, but very soon decided to have it done on the outside, because they would in any case need a general contractor to handle coordination of general construction and the usual specialty subcontractors. The bank, however, does maintain a very active supervisory role with its own staff of construction specialists. Thus there developed an overall management role called project management, provided by the client, and a construction management role filled by the contractors in concert with consultants.

What is different about this project is that the client became convinced, at the urging of its mechanical and electrical consultants—G. Granek & Associates and Jack Chisvin & Associates—that it should divide the construction management into three parts: general construction (including structure), mechanical systems and electrical systems. Straight fees were negotiated with Mason-Kiewit, a joint venture, for general construction; with Sayers & Associates for mechanical systems, and with Standard Electric for electrical systems.

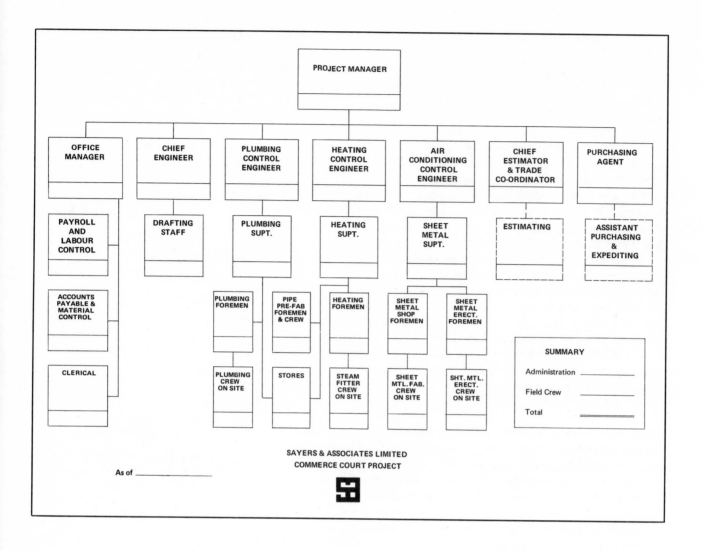

PROJECT MANAGER

| OFFICE MANAGER | CHIEF ENGINEER | PLUMBING CONTROL ENGINEER | HEATING CONTROL ENGINEER | AIR CONDITIONING CONTROL ENGINEER | CHIEF ESTIMATOR & TRADE CO-ORDINATOR | PURCHASING AGENT |

PAYROLL AND LABOUR CONTROL

DRAFTING STAFF

PLUMBING SUPT.

HEATING SUPT.

SHEET METAL SUPT.

ESTIMATING

ASSISTANT PURCHASING & EXPEDITING

ACCOUNTS PAYABLE & MATERIAL CONTROL

PLUMBING FOREMEN

PIPE PRE-FAB FOREMEN & CREW

HEATING FOREMEN

SHEET METAL SHOP FOREMEN

SHEET METAL ERECT. FOREMEN

CLERICAL

PLUMBING CREW ON SITE

STORES

STEAM FITTER CREW ON SITE

SHEET MTL. FAB. CREW ON SITE

SHT. MTL. ERECT. CREW ON SITE

SUMMARY

Administration _____

Field Crew _____

Total _____

SAYERS & ASSOCIATES LIMITED
COMMERCE COURT PROJECT

As of _____

With the specialty contractors involved as management contractors, there was a much freer working relationship between them and the consulting engineers. This paid off in terms of improving the functional quality and performance of certain components. Example: a new type of trench duct for under-floor distribution was developed that has more rigidity and better access than conventional types.

The mechanical management contractor was to be responsible for expediting, coordination, project programing, checking, and also for such items as balancing, interference drawings and field engineering. The project was then split up into the following categories: 1) pre-ordered equipment; 2) pre-ordered materials, such as repetitive typical-floor ductwork and diffusers; 3) the sub-trades, such as insulation and thermostatic controls; 4) field contracting for piping and ductwork.

The advantage of splitting the mechanical contract into many separate direct contracts was to gain lead time and to permit the owner, through the construction management consultants, to control costs. The total number of separate contracts in the mechanical area was in the fifties.

Bid openings were held weekly, with representatives of the owner, architect, consulting engineers, and management contractors all present. Thus all fifty-plus bids in the mechanical area were out in the open for all those involved to evaluate. Of course the engineers look at the bid-alternates from a technical point of view, the management contractors from an installation and delivery point of view. Much of the equipment could all be pre-ordered. Repetitive elements such as typical-floor ducting and piping could be fabricated off site.

To encourage the more accurate bidding of off-site fabricated items, the owner authorized the construction of mock-ups of various sorts, including an entire 50-ft bay of induction units.

The consulting engineers report that they have spent a lot more time in management than they had ever expected: reviewing multiple bids, revising drawings many times, etc. But on the basis of records kept on costs, the client will come out way ahead in terms of his costs and the quality of the building. Moreover, he will have his building two years ahead of normal schedule.

Project/construction management, whatever the refinements of its definition and whatever its lines of protocol; whether it is performed by the architect, the client, or a specialist consultant; has one overriding characteristic: it brings order and unity to an historically fragmented procession from program through design to construction. The efficiencies and accelerations that redound to the economy are services to a prevailing goal of architecture.

The
Young
Architects:
A
Profile

If you analyze the 1972 surveys of young architects reported in the next few pages, you'll find that . . .

■ Young architects are not much different from their older colleagues in terms of general goals.

■ They expect large firms to become larger and more numerous to cope with large commissions.

■ They do not expect the demise of the small- or medium-sized firm; and most would prefer to work in that size range.

■ They want their own firms to offer a full range of architectural, engineering and construction management services—although individual preferences for their own occupations run strongly to architectural design and planning.

And a general conclusion emerges—more from the cumulative sense of essay response than from any tabulated data. Insofar as you can make any generalization about so heterogeneous a mix of individualists as is implicit in the two words, young architects, it seems that they are neither dismayed nor entranced by computerized technical and economic changes that have given some of their elders pause.

To gain perspective for reports about and from young architects, it seems appropriate to review some of the trends and changes that are affecting the professional and economic milieu in which they must operate. Changes in the format of client-architect relationships, for example, have been reviewed in the previous two chapters. Those changes have been brought about by the need for multi-service architects to meet multi-headed corporate and governmental clients on their own multi-level planes.

Huge and complex projects with stringent budgets in the midst of inflationary costs have set more inexorable values upon time and money to the point where the management of projects, formerly normal within the fees of architects and the profit margins of contractors, now spins off as that separate professional expertise called construction management.

Another shift toward size and complexity in practice has been the increasing participation by architectural firms in the actual processes of project development and construction. While this participation, thus far, is usually structured through organizational channels separate from the work of architectural design, its presence is nonetheless felt and reflected in a whole new set of attitudes toward its ethical acceptability. Young architects, having grown up among these concepts—and without prior commitments of reserve against them—bring unencumbered élan to their views of practice in these fields.

Youthful views of practice also now encompass an expanded social consciousness of architects' responsibilities in urban planning and ecological controls. The increase in public monies available for real commissions in these areas has multiplied opportunities for career specialization in them. Here again, the required backup of interdisciplinary expertise carries with it implications of increasing firm size.

How, then, do young architects propose to reconcile their acknowledgment of broad-gage professional needs with their explicit yearning for the personal identity and that "close touch with the job" they see as best available in the smaller firms? How, too, are big, established firms adjusting their own organizations to accommodate these valid yearnings for professional and personal identity so that young architects will gladly work for them?

Here are just two examples of this reconciliation:

The first is the shift toward the "studio" format of organization by the large and growing firm of Heery & Heery. The other is the firm of Gaio Associates, established in 1970 by a "young architect" for the sole purpose of pooling the resources of a nationwide network of small- and medium-size firms in proposals for large jobs. Neither the studio format nor the joint venture is a new concept, but these two examples come to view as specific to the confrontation of young architects with today's world.

Long before construction management and fast-track became the catchwords of the day, Heery & Heery of Atlanta had gained a reputation for delivery of substantial works (especially industrial plants) on time and within stringent budgets. The firm grew, and the variety of work increased. Commissions for stadiums, public facilities and, more recently, the Cincinnati Airport broadened the scope and extended the organizational talents of the firm. They became forerunners in the economics of systems and modular construction. Now, with about 150 architects and engineers, more than double the size of three years ago, they are responding to a sense of unease about losing the rounded, personal participation essential to full effectiveness of professional staff.

A large and growing firm reorganizes for staff identity

George Heery, who heads the firm, became increasingly aware that his own contact with the work of architecture was being obscured by the problems and business of management. He recognized the stifling effects of losing contact, and that these would be aggravated among staff who needed career growth along with firm growth.

The Heery solution was to create six or more complete integral practices within the framework of his firm. These practices are organized in groups of six to eight key people. Each group organizes its own practice along whatever lines it chooses, and each is responsible for its own work from beginning to end. They are called project-control groups, and each has access to corporate support capabilities in engineering, interior design, etc. Each of the 16 principals is a member of one group or another. Only two executives, George Heery and Louis Maloof, have overall responsibility outside the groups.

This form of organization has done away with overall management and supervision along classic lines. There is, of course, surveillance of the design quality and profitability of the groups, much as might be the case in any consortium of firms. The surveillance is not so much over-the-shoulder interference as it is a continuously stated policy of design quality and time/cost control.

The youngest group is headed by Larry Lord, Ennis Parker and Mack Scogin, each 30 years of age or less. This group has in work about $60 million worth of buildings, including a condominium, high school, office building, industrial building and the Cincinnati Airport.

The point of it all, says George Heery, is that these young people—and the older ones as well—conduct their business and their practice with a full-scope approach to each project. There is no middle management. There are conferences with top principals during pre-design analysis and regularly scheduled meetings and reports to George Heery, but the usual prevailing welter of paperwork and inter-office communication no longer submerges either individual architects or the principals. The principals themselves feel better related to the design purpose and the central motivations of architectural practice.

This idea of the studio format has been tried by other firms and will be tried again in many variations. Its emergence in the Heery organization is notable because of the realism that has been characteristic of this firm. One of the newer young firms (Designbank) that is committed to this studio idea is quoted at some length in following pages dealing with survey results.

A young architect sets up to bridge the red-tape gap

One firm, established in 1970 and headed by architect Raymond L. Gaio, now 34, is a clear demonstration of the diversity of opportunity in architecture and related fields today. Gaio Associates, Ltd. is an inter-firm collaborative idea serving a clientele of ten small-to-medium sized architectural firms located in widely scattered regions throughout the nation. None of these firms is formally or permanently related to the others except through application of the Gaio services. Those services include skilled representation and pooling of affiliates' resources in various combinations for making proposals for all manner and size of Federal and other governmental construction programs. Other activities of the Gaio firm are: a constant search for upcoming jobs, business development in both public and private sectors, business management advice and personnel search.

Raymond Gaio acquired his knowledge of Washington affairs during about a decade of intimate professional activity on the Washington scene. About five of these years were spent on the staff at AIA national headquarters where he directed the departments of State Chapters and Student Affairs. The first Grassroots programs were under his direction. He had also worked as an architect for several architectural firms. Other members of his firm, Robert S. Carter and Julian Singman, provide an aggregate of about 50 years of Washington experience in governmental, architectural, and legal practices. Jerre Jones, formerly in business development roles with Ed Stone, Vincent Kling and Ellerbe Architects, joined Gaio in October of 1972.

In addition to its permanent roster of ten firms (which may increase to a dozen or so distributed roughly as one each among the regional divisions of AIA) the Gaio firm has a first-call relationship with some of the large engineering and other professional firms for the purpose of presenting a rounded capability of various combinations of his member firms, tailored to the scope of specifics of prospective work. Expansion of the membership is not contemplated as a

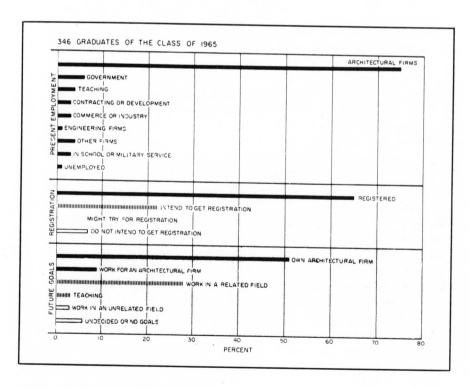

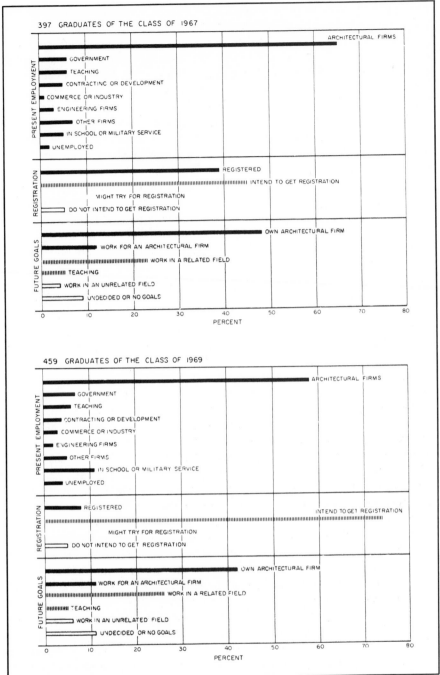

397 GRADUATES OF THE CLASS OF 1967

PRESENT EMPLOYMENT
ARCHITECTURAL FIRMS
GOVERNMENT
TEACHING
CONTRACTING OR DEVELOPMENT
COMMERCE OR INDUSTRY
ENGINEERING FIRMS
OTHER FIRMS
IN SCHOOL OR MILITARY SERVICE
UNEMPLOYED

REGISTRATION
REGISTERED
INTEND TO GET REGISTRATION
MIGHT TRY FOR REGISTRATION
DO NOT INTEND TO GET REGISTRATION

FUTURE GOALS
OWN ARCHITECTURAL FIRM
WORK FOR AN ARCHITECTURAL FIRM
WORK IN A RELATED FIELD
TEACHING
WORK IN AN UNRELATED FIELD
UNDECIDED OR NO GOALS

0   10   20   30   40   50   60   70   80
PERCENT

459 GRADUATES OF THE CLASS OF 1969

PRESENT EMPLOYMENT
ARCHITECTURAL FIRMS
GOVERNMENT
TEACHING
CONTRACTING OR DEVELOPMENT
COMMERCE OR INDUSTRY
ENGINEERING FIRMS
OTHER FIRMS
IN SCHOOL OR MILITARY SERVICE
UNEMPLOYED

REGISTRATION
REGISTERED
INTEND TO GET REGISTRATION
MIGHT TRY FOR REGISTRATION
DO NOT INTEND TO GET REGISTRATION

FUTURE GOALS
OWN ARCHITECTURAL FIRM
WORK FOR AN ARCHITECTURAL FIRM
WORK IN A RELATED FIELD
TEACHING
WORK IN AN UNRELATED FIELD
UNDECIDED OR NO GOALS

0   10   20   30   40   50   60   70   80
PERCENT

Charts of survey reported next page.

primary goal. Mr. Gaio insists that there be no regional conflict of interest on the part of any two of his firms and further that the resources of his own firm be made available on a clear-cut professional basis guarding against dilution of the personal relationship between his staff and his subscribing clients.

Young architects? Small firms? The permutations of opportunity and enterprise are endless.

What has happened to recent architectural graduates

(See charts, previous spread)

The research department of *Architectural Record* conducted a study in 1972 about recent graduates of architectural schools—specifically the graduating classes of 1965, 1967 and 1969—to find out what the graduates were doing and what their future aspirations are. The deans of 34 of the 70 accredited schools of architecture in the United States provided the names and addresses of graduates with professional degrees (B.Arch. or M.Arch.) in those classes. Of the 2,858 graduates surveyed, 43 per cent replied. There was no significant difference in profile between the graduates of one university and another.

The following questions were asked: 1) Are you currently employed by an architectural firm? If not, in what type of firm do you work? 2) Are you registered? If not, do you aim to be? 3) How many different full-time jobs have you had since graduation? 4) As a graduate architect what are your long-term goals (start your own architectural firm, work in a large architectural firm, go into a related field, etc.)? Charts (pages 28–29) present a general order of results in each class. The question about number of jobs does not emerge in detail on the charts. Tabulated results for that question showed that 85 per cent had changed jobs three times or less, but about 25 per cent of the class of 1965 had changed four or five times—not surprising in the light of recent economic conditions.

The manager of the research department, Elizabeth Hayman, draws two general conclusions from this study. 1) The graduated classes do not differ from each other in any significant way (other than the normal accretions of experience, of course). 2) These graduates do not differ from older architects in any statistically significant way.

For example, a quick look at the per cent of graduates employed by architectural firms seems to reveal a decline from 75 per cent of the class of 1965 to 58 per cent of the class of 1969. However, 15.7 per cent of the class of 1969 is either unemployed, attending school or in military service. Only 4.5 per cent of the class of 1965 was so removed from active employment. The tight employment situation of 1970–1971 and the military draft operate on these figures. They do not reflect any difference in aspirations of the graduates.

It is also noted that the per cent of graduates employed by firms other than architectural is much the same as that reported by the AIA study of the profession in 1950.

The number of graduates who are registered or intend to be remains fairly constant at about 65 per cent. Also the future goals of graduates present a consistent pattern across the three classes.

However, analysis of written comment with replies shows there is some difference between these young graduates and their older colleagues. Although the evidence is not statistical, it is nonetheless apparent that there is greater interest among these younger people than among their older colleagues in development, planning, construction and building. "A number mentioned wanting to be builders as well as architects," Miss Hayman observes, "and this is a fairly new, though already known, attitude. On the other hand, evidence is beginning to come in that more and more established architectural firms are getting involved in development and construction, so maybe these young architects aren't different after all."

A second survey of young architects probed ideas, ideals and goals

About 200 young architects were asked to summarize their experience and views regarding their education and their goals. The candidates receiving the questionnaire were selected entirely at random, and the number of questionnaires was determined largely by the practical capability of handling the response. There were about 175 replies ranging in scope from simple checkmarks and phrases on the questionnaire itself, to several pages of essay.

The questionnaire itself was presented as eleven questions. Three of those questions had to do with the architects' evaluation of their own educational experience and their suggestions as to changes they might recommend in academic programs or professional training for architects. The review of responses to these questions, and other matters dealing with architectural education, are outside the scope of this text.

Other questions dealt with the young architects' views of the future of the profession and their own preferences about size of firm, building types, scope of services, and the general sphere of desired employment.

The thoughtful quality of replies precluded much tabulation by numbers, as might be inferred from the following recap of questions other than educational:

Question 4: From where you now stand, what do you see as likely and/or desirable for the future of architectural practice in terms of firm size, organization, services, pre- and post-design responsibilities, inter-discipline relationships, etc. and why?

Question 5: For your own professional fulfillment, what size of architectural firm would you like to head or be an associate of . . . and why?

Question 6: What building types do you want your firm to handle—and why?

Question 7: What general services do you want your firm to perform: architectural design only, planning, A/E, A/E-contractor-developer-construction manager, other . . . and why?

Question 8: What kind of work do you personally prefer: design, management, planning, promotion, research, or . . . ?

Question 9: How do you regard computers and other technical developments in the professional scene: as good tools, as bad tools, indifferent; what are you using and why?

Question 10: Would you consider or even prefer working as an employee of a firm other than architectural: developer, manufacturer, package builder, government, other; and why?

Question 11: Would you comment on other aspects of the profession today: the AIA, the team approach to design, licensing, ethical standards, fee structures, Federal (or other) selection procedures. What bugs you, what inspires you, why practice?

**A sampling
of thoughtful response**

The process of review of replies was a conscientious outline of the points of emphasis, agreement and disagreement of each return, whether brief or copious. The sampling of replies that follows is an attempt to reflect the frequency and weight of each opinion.

The very first sample is perhaps typical of the quandary of emphasis we face. It is a letter that acknowledges and states our problem about as adroitly as any. It reads in part as follows:

■ "Louis Kahn, if he were under 35, might be answering that 'a good question is greater than the most brilliant answer.'

"With all due respect to the listed eleven questions and their good intentions, there hastens to my mind a sensing that by their very form you will be submerged with more quasi-erudite, scholarly type answers than you may have bargained for.

"To add to your burden, let me preface some very general comments on the whole quandary of education and practice by offering to you a reminder that I have carried about with me through school and from office to office, invariably finding its way over my drawing board, tacked somewhere between a very fashionable 'Knoll' Bertoia poster, perhaps a MOMA postcard, plenty of yellow tracing paper and the New York Giants' football schedule. It's Thoreau and it reads simply: 'The youth gets together his materials to build a bridge to the moon, or perchance, a palace or temple on the earth; and at length the middle-aged man concludes to build a woodshed with them.'

"In essence, this reflects my outlook on both *learn* and *do*. It seems that we architects, whether we are championing systems design, advocacy planning, POP solutions or whether our Utopian dreams are couched in Mies or Corbu, have all been ill equipped in some measure to cope with (much less change) the restrictive and limiting forces that prevail in our society.

"Therefore, no matter what numbers game you play, whether you advocate a five-year or six-year masters program (which I prefer), it behooves the institutions to deliver something more than a perfunctory exposure to the world of finance, law and government so that the practitioner is able to put into being that place of wonder rather than playing it safe in favor of that woodshed.

"Playing it safe is the curse of the large office, despite the absolute necessity of inter-disciplinary team approach to complex problems and corporate clients. Since, all too often, the emphasis is just to please the client, there is little time for excitement, inspiration and discovery in the mind of the architect; compromise and expediency rule, and efficiency and motivation diminish to that point where two or three middle-aged men are doing the work of one.

"At the other end of the scale, you have the private practitioner working in a vacuum, dealing with limited problems and few variables, offering somewhat less than the optimum effectiveness of a professional problem solver and client server.

"Presently, I'm building my practice (which will sustain itself for five years) on a single inter-disciplinary team basis; one architect, one planner, one engineer and one finance consultant." —*Don Alvaro Leon, North Wales, Pennsylvania.*

Well, we are not dismayed—nor are we building woodsheds with your dreams. We cherish them. You are not alone. Nor are you typical. Praise be that in this world of architects no one is.

Before we continue with quotations in support of that thesis, here are a few numbers that help show the drift of response:

■ Probable future firm size: large, 50 per cent; medium, 25 per cent; both large and small, 25 per cent.

■ Preferred firm size: small to medium, 70 per cent.

■ Preferred building types: variety, 77 per cent; residential, 8 per cent.

■ Firm services intended: full, including construction management, 60 per cent; architecture and planning, 25 per cent; architecture only, 10 per cent.

■ Work personally preferred: design, 44 per cent; variety, 35 per cent.

■ Work for non-architect firms: no, 60 per cent; developer, 18 per cent (but with design control).

We hold no brief for the deep significance of these numbers as such, but some general conclusions were stated at the beginning of this report. The following excerpts from replies are the real essence, unhappily curtailed by the limits of space.

Young architects deal with the modern world

■ I feel that the profession now is in a state of schizophrenia: one part denying the central ego and promoting the disenfranchised ego or the watered down team and producing a corporation machinery encased in organization, bureaucracy, hierarchy, money and power games with extensive involvement with technology and growth and large-scale thinking. On the other hand, there is centralized ego clinging to the sanity of a coherent unified creative effort, seasoned with a personal touch and nowhere near the capabilities of handling large or complex programs.

Each denies the other; each destroying the other. For myself, right now I favor the smaller, more personal approach, as I look at it from the standpoint of the building. I would rather be a smaller piece of the pie that still stands after a large political riot; the piece that can really touch the lives of the individual.

I think architecture should inspire, charge, move, stimulate, function, arouse, soothe, foil, supplement, reinforce, amplify, respond, communicate, suggest, grow, live, contain, combine, collide, and spring from the roots of social needs, aspirations, and capabilities of the constantly changing civilization of the present. —*Philip J. Tabb, RNL, Inc. Denver, Colorado.*

■ I see the architectural profession entering more of a full service field from site selection to building construction. Architectural firms will enter the building construction field and furnish contracting services. As computers begin to play a major role in providing the architect with services, separate computer corporations will be established inside large architectural firms. Because of economy of scale, computer services will be sold to smaller architectural practices. Thus a three-man office will be able to do the work of a thirty-man office. Architectural firms may then function similar to the doctors' clinic, which uses the back-up support of a large hospital. Small- to medium-sized firms will become a more viable size again.

—*Robert W. Dvorak, University of Arizona, Tucson, Arizona.*

■ Personally, I have had it up to here with these voguish public images of architects as businessmen—smoothies who "coordinate" and provide "services." That sort of thing hardly results in anything more than zippy technological découpage. After all the ballyhooing and promise, we should expect no less than wonderful work from this kind of approach everytime. But more often than not, we get the equivalent of a Jeanette MacDonald/Nelson Eddy style of extravaganza, very expensive, often well manicured, but heavy-handed and just a little too dumb for my taste. The paradox is: currently, there seems to be some sort of showy, pragmatic, Southern California style of right-wing thinking in the profession that looks down its nose at the conventional problems and their solutions, which I personally think are often very wonderful. Yet after all the talk, the right-wingers still seek out the middle of the road solutions to architectural problems. So that what often happens is that a building that is too wonderful or too conventional is self-righteously put down as irrevelant or unimportant. And we get a chancy "good design" that hopefully satisfies as high a percentage as possible of the public and private agencies that have a grasp on our very vitals. —*Dario Santi, Hickory, N.C.*

■ Architectural practice should be centered around small teams of professionals that are directly responsible for the environmental solution: understanding the problem of the program, providing the solutions and implementing the building process. Any organization that does not provide the structure of the team of responsible professionals, interdisciplines, and consultants to respond to the client and social needs does not contribute. The organization can be of any size, shape, offer any services, as long as this responsibility is maintained by the creative team.

—*Laurence O. Booth, Booth & Nagle, Chicago, Illinois.*

■ The range of architectural services and involvement will and must expand into political and community-oriented problem solving. This will not mean the proportionate expansion of office personnel. The desirable trend for myself would be the employment of sophisticated office equipment and methods to limit physical office size and employment. I believe we are seeing the return of the individual, with new technical resources of graphic and communication techniques available for him and to provide expertise in the largest context of problem solving. —*Edward R. Niles, Malibu, California.*

■ A/E-contractor-developer-construction manager. I personally find this very challenging because you have control over the entire project. Many of my clients are asking for comprehensive services. For a small office, this is financially rewarding and allows the architect to spend more time with the client. The architect receives an architectural fee plus a construction management fee.

—*Joseph J. Railla, Hollywood, California.*

Size and studio approaches to organization

■ Our approach to firm size and organization is essentially based upon a studio concept. As we grow we plan to expand based upon a 4- or 5-man studio concept which we hope will prevent the development of huge anonymous departments. Each studio will theoretically be able to handle any job which the office produces. We will attempt to balance each studio in terms of talents, experience and interests so that each one is to the maximum degree possible, self-sufficient. For large jobs, two or more studios might be combined during the duration of a particular project. Certain individuals in the firm will move horizontally through the firm where these individuals are particularly strong in a given aspect such as urban design or architectural programming.

If we can make this type of concept work, we have no real limits to ultimate size. It theoretically should not make that much difference provided our management system is properly designed and maintained.

—*James C. Morgan and Paul J. Foster, Denver, Colorado.*

■ I think there is a great excitement today in all of the environmental arts, something which was not present in the early sixties. At least a partial understanding of what the environment is all about has permeated all areas of life, all economic levels . . .

The future of the profession-art-business of architecture is optimistic. Major problems are going to be attacked in major ways, by major firms who have a professed expertise in the solution to complex environmental problems . . . We can no longer afford the luxury of building something we think will work; we have to know it will work. We can no longer exist in a vacuum without the lending institutions, real estate brokers, marketing analysts, management and legal professions, and the computer . . .

We hope to create with Designbank an organization with the vast resources of a large firm, with all necessary disciplines housed together to help each other but with each remaining autonomous. Designbank, the name, becomes a corporate umbrella under which singular staffs of architects, interior designers, graphics and industrial designers, planners, and eventually developers do their own thing, each with their own principals and profit incentives . . . We want to keep the organization as loose as possible, and perform in all areas of environmental design.   —*Nathan S. Leblang, Designbank, Baltimore.*

Kicks and kudos for the AIA

■ We strongly support AIA as it currently exists. Its position of advocacy for the profession is long overdue, particularly in the area of advertising, technical services, lobbying and continuing education. Our desire for a day of quiet for research and personal renewal has led us to give serious consideration to a four-day week, although maintaining 40-50 working hours per week.

—*David E. Nordfors; Joyce, Copeland, Vaughan, Seattle, Washington.*

■ The AIA should take a far stronger stand on the quality of architecture, rather than on just the quality of architecture produced by their members.

Obviously, there is a need for licensing various levels of architectural practice.

One license for all people, regardless of their interest is absurd.

—*Clark H. Neuringer, Frost Associates, New York, New York.*

■ The AIA is by and large the organization which protects the employers. There is a need to have similar protection for employees.

—*Jacqueline Stavi, Kamnitzer/Marks & Partners, Beverly Hills, California.*

■ While the AIA provides certain services at relatively low cost, it should confine itself to those activities and any other non-coercive and needed services. The AIA's political activities should be discontinued. While I suppose these activities are well meant, they do more harm than good for both design professionals and everyone else. The recent AIA task force recommendations on land-use policy are immoral as well as impractical. To forcibly take from one to give to another solves no problems—it only creates the problem of another established injustice. The task force architects are dabbling in a dangerous game of power politics with men who are far and away much more adept at the use of political power than they are.

I am disturbed by the willingness of many design professionals to endorse a policy of government-initiated force to solve social and environmental problems. As mentioned before, force doesn't solve problems, it creates them. This willingness to endorse force bespeaks a miserable lack of imagination—possibly understandable in bureaucrats, but unthinkable in designers.

—*John B. James, Denver, Colorado.*

Thoughtful, articulate, enthusiastic, angry, optimistic, conventional, radical, inventive, artistic, undaunted; these are the young architects.

One respondent, Phillip J. Tabb, provided the following diagram of his preference for a medium to small organization and concluded with the melting figure at the bottom—which seems an appropriate terminus for this profile.

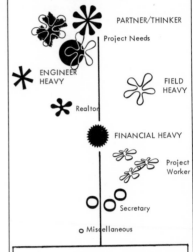

Office Personnel:

PARTNER/THINKER

Project Needs

ENGINEER HEAVY

FIELD HEAVY

Realtor

FINANCIAL HEAVY

Project Worker

Secretary

Miscellaneous

"You can say about art—meaning the inner psychological side of the creative process—that it is the process of solving problems that cannot be stated clearly before they are solved. The process of orientation to a new problem is practically one hundred per cent of the solution."
—PIET HEIN

Thank you for the opportunity to express my views.

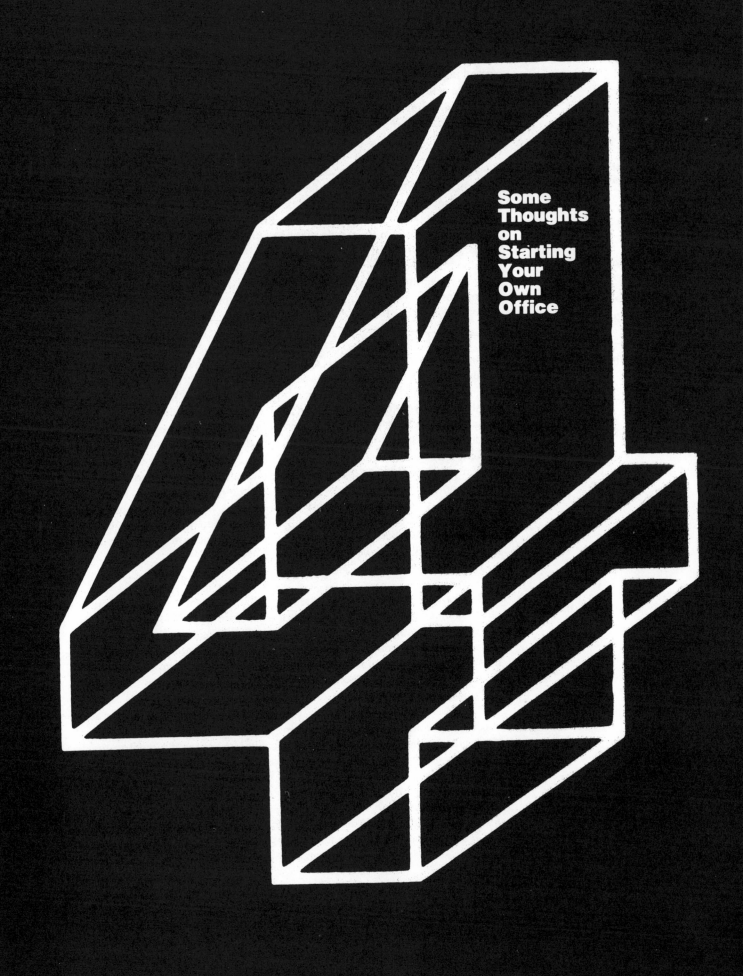

Some
Thoughts
on
Starting
Your
Own
Office

For the individual who starts out by himself or with partners, there are some questions that are of utmost importance to consider. 1) Who will be your partner or associate? 2) When will you launch the venture? 3) Where should you locate? 4) What do you want to do in terms of design goals, building types, or firm size? 5) Why do you want to do it? Earl Flansburgh writes as follows:

Partnership, like marriage, is a contracted commitment

Who will be your partner is extremely critical. It is normal for designers to choose designers as partners. This does not always produce successful results. The best partnership, in a way, is a partnership involving complementary disciplines, experience and interests rather than similar interests. It is important in selecting a partner to be certain that he or she is as dedicated to the ideas that make you want to start a firm as you are. Nothing causes more strain in a partnership than a disparity between the amount of work one partner is willing to do compared with the amount of work the other is willing to do. Starting an architectural office requires a substantial personal commitment. A part-time partner can strain even the best of personal friendships.

Strike while the iron is hot

When is the best time? Obviously, the architect must be licensed. To attempt to establish an office prior to this is simply foolhardy. But more important than age, and, actually, even more important than the license itself, is experience. Establishing an office is an experience that has a special charm and a special opportunity. At the time of establishing your own office you are a new commodity. Your skill as an entrepreneur is untried. If you do have a depth of experience, it may be fairly easy to start your own office. But if your skill is untried and you have had little experience, you may indeed be limited to work in the form of porch remodelings and an occasional house for friends.

This kind of work can be as self-destructive as no work at all, because it consumes great amounts of time and does not really give you substantial opportunities. Very few commissions for larger works are awarded because someone's back porch was skillfully remodeled.

Location can be the key to the future

Where you should start your architectural office is an important question, because architectural opportunities do not exist uniformly throughout the world. If a student wishes to start his own office, it may be valuable first to get a couple of years of experience in a prestigious architectural firm in a large city. Then he should move to the location where he hopes ultimately to have his office, so that he becomes familiar with the environment, the problems and the people he hopes to have as clients.

It is also important here for the young architect to look impartially at his chosen community from the standpoint of growth during the next 20 years, for a practice built on personal friendship may very rapidly outstrip the resources of one's friends. Many small towns grow slowly, and a community that is not growing is a very difficult place to practice architecture. It is important to choose a dynamic place with some real and demonstrated growth opportunities.

Having decided upon the city or the town, the logical place to put an office is in a neighborhood that is easily accessible for clients and engineers, but which also has some appeal in terms of its surroundings. You may occasionally want to take a client to lunch. Another important consideration is accessibility for employes.

What, the next question, is probably the most difficult. For those of you who wish to begin on your own there is a burning desire, after receiving your license and with enough experience, to immediately take the first porch remodeling, hang out your shingle and say, "World, I'm ready." There is a tremendous tendency to take almost any job that becomes available. The best investment of your time in your early years is not to do as much work as you can in the field of porch remodeling and additions to small commercial buildings, but to do very well a limited number of projects that are broader in scope. The unfortunate problem is that porch remodelings, and even houses, although they may be wonderful cocktail party conversation, are hardly projects from which a strong, dynamic office can grow. It is possible to do a series of houses well and gain a reputation quickly. This, in itself, is a very valuable thing. But it should not be the utlimate goal. Therefore, if you are working in a responsible position for another firm, and suddenly you have a house to do, do it on your kitchen table while continuing to work for your present employer until such time as you have access to a project of slightly greater magnitude.

It is important here, however, to indicate that there is no good time or best time to go into business for yourself. There are only a series of better times. As soon as you have a reasonably big job, a job that is really going to happen, then is a good time to hang out your shingle.

One thing here is extremely important. When you leave your present employer, do not leave him in the lurch, because if he is like most architects, he will not begrudge your going into business because you may someday offer competition. Rather, he may be helpful in sending to you commissions that he considers too small for his office to handle.

The most important rule about setting up your own office with that first job is to go after the second job before you finish the first, because it is really not the first job that is the source of problems in most architectural offices. It is the failure to get the second.

Try for jobs that help you grow

Why start your own office? There is no why, really. There is a certain excitement, a certain challenge in having an office of your own. It is the same kind of mysterious euphoria that infects mountain climbers and glider pilots. If you have it, it is almost impossible to describe. And it is certainly impossible to communicate to someone who does not have it.

When you start out in business as an architect, you should have a goal as to what it is you are trying to achieve. One goal of course, is self-expression in terms of design. But architecture today is not limited to design. It is not simply the merging of forms in pleasant proportions producing interior and exterior spaces. And for the architect who seeks to establish his own practice only to interpret his particular stylistic form of architecture, great problems may be in store. For architecture today deals not only with the molding of space and the creating of an environment, but with problems of complexity in both the specific, technical sense and in the general sense. Architecture today does not acknowledge a simple monument, but rather evaluates a building in the human sense, in the way it embraces the people that create the environment that it shares. In this regard, architecture has passed from visual problem-solving to the world of social and economic problem-solving, a world that architects must approach with care.

In many architectural schools today, there is a great concern about the relevancy of the architecture that we have been practicing for the past twenty or

Why start? Because you must!

twenty-five years. This is a legitimate concern, for in far too many cases we have been awarding prizes for pleasant visual non-solutions of problems.

If we bear in mind the role of the program in today's architecture, and the role of the need to incorporate many complex ideas, which are often pulling in contradictory directions, then we can see how an architectural office can be established. For the practice of architecture today is as much decision-making and problem-solving as it is the abstract world of esthetics.

But to return to the central question—How do you find the client who will invite you to function on this level? How do you obtain a project other than a house that is given to you by a friend? The field of educational buildings is a good place to start. This is an area of continually recurring needs, with great attraction for the architect whose professional skill is his main attribute, and whose contacts with the business world are somewhat limited. Often a group of young architects, combined in joint venture, have a good chance of getting that first school.

Being interviewed for a school immediately forces the architect to contemplate the basic philosophy of the contemporary practice of architecture. He is being interviewed for a specific school and he is being asked to solve a specific problem. There has always been a concern on the part of the AIA that an architect should not work for nothing—that is, do free drawing or sketches—in order to obtain a job. We are not suggesting for a moment that the architect offer free advice. However, there is a very basic need for the architect to put the level of advice he will offer clearly in perspective. That means that when you are being interviewed for a school, it is important to know what the town's educational problem is. Is it the replacement of an existing elementary school too venerable to be renovated? Is it the need to build a new elementary school for a growing population? Is it the need to build a secondary school? What is the educational philosophy of the community? It is important for the architect to come to his interview with the ability to deal with such specific questions. For in selecting an architect, although the community will to some extent weigh your previous experience, it is in essence saying "How would you handle our problem?" And it is concerning *their* problem that they want their answers.

You may receive half an hour or an hour's exposure to the committee. In that period of time, it is important that you communicate how you would approach the solution of *their* problem. The needs of the school committee are frequently quite specific, but also they are frequently quite diffuse: It is important to know which in each case. The work that you show should be directed toward their particular problem with enough other examples to give some depth to your presentation. It is always helpful to leave a brochure of your work with the committee to give them a longer time to absorb it. Most important, bear in mind the needs of the committeeman. He is not interested in carrying outsized working drawings or 2 x 2 inch slides. What he is interested in seeing is something he can look at in the light of day and can easily carry under his arm.

It is also important to consider "what the client should do until the architect comes." Once you have gotten the job, it is very important that your client participate in the process and that your method of operation be clear to him. In other words, what you are doing should be stated to him at the outset. Organize your presentations to him so he sees what his role is. Your client, by and large, will be interested in exactly what it is you are doing. The world of mystical architecture is no longer with us. Most clients are relatively educated and will understand when you talk about esthetics, and you in turn must understand what they are talking about when they talk about economics. Today the world of professional responsibility is important. This means that when a client says he wishes to spend $750,000, he will not overwhelm you with praise if the project comes in at $1,200,000. It has nothing to do with whether he has the money or not, but rather with how much he proposes to spend on the particular project. This means that there is a requirement, a role which you as architect must play, in which at particular stages of the game no matter how painful it is you must say to your client, "This is how much it is going to cost, and it is going to cost you 'x' number of dollars more than you anticipated." You must be prepared for the client to say, "Well, that's too much," and then redesign it so it can be accommodated within the budget, or to say to the client, "It is not possible to build what you want for the amount of money that you wish to spend, so therefore, we propose that you either cut your requirements or increase the budget." Now, this may sound like a harsh or difficult thing to say. It is, for the first two or three times. After that time, it becomes part of your professional stance. And it is important. Most clients are reasonable, and they will accept the fact that they cannot buy the moon, provided that they are told about it in time.

The next step has to do with design. There is a real need, in designing public buildings today, to deal with what you might call economy of form. That means that it is not possible in most public projects to have a vast, unlimited amount of money or a vast, unlimited amount of architectural expression. Therefore, you must select, with considerable care, those areas where you wish to invest the client's money in special effects, because there are only a few places where you can do this. The design should enhance these particular places of accent. The industrialized building becomes important and details become important, for the simplest project frequently is disastrously dealt with when the details are done in a complex fashion inappropriate to the over-all design.

When the building is finally done, if you have conducted realistic estimates at various stages, you will discover when you bid the project and it comes in at the price that it is supposed to, that suddenly your client is much more impressed with you than you ever thought would be possible. This makes relations in the future much more pleasant. If you do nothing else in your first buildings, work very hard towards the objective of having the cost of the building and its budget bear some relationship to each other. It is possible to build a firm on the strong base of professional responsibility. Building on a prima donna, esthetic approach is no longer really a relevant approach. Most clients, as I mentioned before, are sophisticated. Most clients are interested in knowing what you are doing and most clients are particularly valuable during the program phase if you spend enough time trying to get to know what the program is. The client will appreciate the time spent. Further, he will allow you to do what he has hired you to do if you spend time trying to know what it is he wants you to do in a rather precise form. Knowledge of the program is really a double-edged sword. If you have it, you can use it to your own advantage in terms of generating the kinds of architecture you would like to generate. But secondly, you understand what it is you are being asked to accomplish.

I use the words professional responsibility. This is important because we are no longer in the world of clients who wish us to reproduce Greek temples or Gothic cathedrals. Contemporary architecture, which has been very readily accepted, is indeed the vocabulary of the land. Therefore, the excuse that the "client wouldn't allow me to do it" is by and large not as valid an excuse today as it once was. It also may mean that the architect didn't try hard enough. It also may mean the architect did not try to explain to the client what he was trying to do or that he was not willing to deal with the problem intensively enough to convince the client.

In architecture there is a continual question about what to do about failure—a project that does not advance, a client who does not pay, etc. There is very little you can do about a project that does not advance. For a client who does not pay, the solution to the problem is to sign a contract for every project, no matter how large or small. If the client is unwilling to accept a contract the chances are also good that he may be unwilling to pay when a bill is presented. But there is also a problem about what to do about success, because you may very well discover that not only have you done all the things that you set out to do in your initial buildings, but that you have done them well enough that you are suddenly faced with the problem of several conditions.

Success has ruined the architecture of more than one office. It is important to control the growth as much as it is important to control the quality of your architecture. A number of years ago, when exposed to a brief encounter with military science, I read a military book that indicated that one man can effectively control seven other people. I don't know what the current thinking in management is, but I think this system may very well be a good guide—that as the office grows it is also very important to make sure that its ability to manage itself grows with it.

Whether your office structure is a partnership, a collaborative, or a sole proprietorship, as it grows it will still need people in responsible positions. The choice of these is as critical to your success as your ability to solve that first problem. Suddenly you have grown. Suddenly you are at a point where you are faced with the delirious possibility of having more work than you can possibly do. This is a very serious problem, for it is very difficult to make a reputation but it is possible to undo a good portion of it with a single bad building. Therefore, it may very well be better to do one less project and do all the ones that you are doing well, than to take on more work than it is possible for you to handle.

Oh yes, one final thought. You may have worked for an architectural firm on an eight-hour-a-day basis. When you have a firm of your own, the eight-hour day will look as obsolete as a steam motor car. Because having a firm of your own is a 12-, 14- sometimes 16-hour-a-day mistress, it is extremely demanding, always requiring your attention. And if you are unwilling to work long hours to establish your own office, chances are very good that you won't succeed.

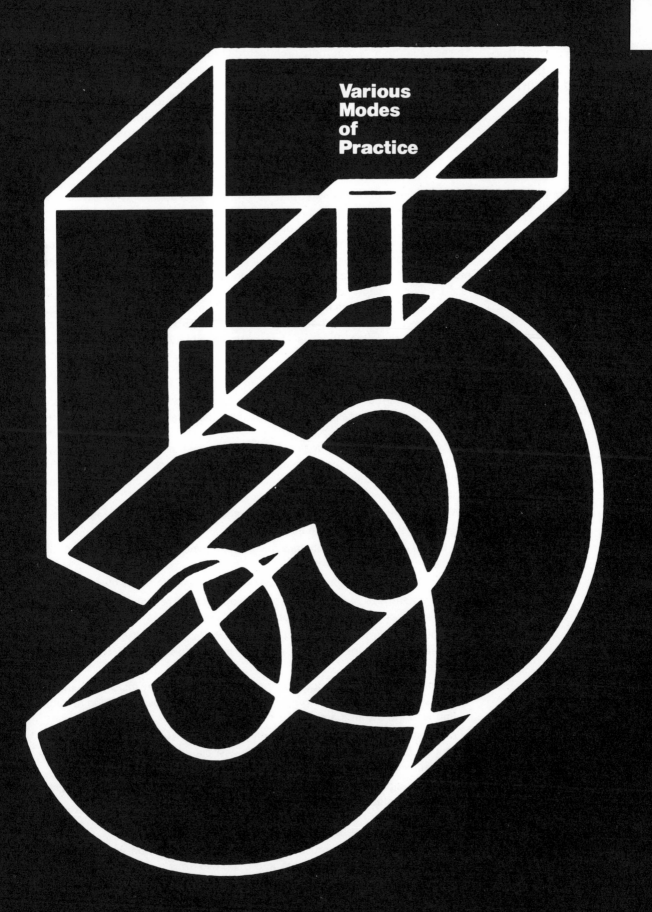

Various
Modes
of
Practice

Associated practice: Ground rules and variations

The association of two or more architectural firms in a formal agreement for the execution of a commission offers many advantages in the complex, frequently long-distance operations required of today's expanding architectural profession. But it can also introduce complications and frictions. The ground rules listed below were developed in an interview with Richard Roth Sr., a partner in Emery Roth & Sons, a firm with long experience and notable successes in associated practice.

The most important condition: complete mutual respect

Although one firm or the other may have primary responsibility in, say, design or production phases of the job, each firm must feel that the other is qualified to criticize or make suggestions on any phase of the work. Actually, association between two firms is not very different from the kind of association that occurs internally in any large architectural office staff, and the criteria for success are much the same. If one office is assigned only the design work, it must nonetheless be vitally concerned with the execution, if the finished building is to be attractive and also within the client's budget. It is important, too, that the association between two firms should be voluntary—where the client insists upon a particular association, there is always the possibility of resultant friction or misunderstanding.

Different kinds of associations: effective teamwork vs. shotgun marriage

Mr. Roth describes nine variations of the associated arrangement, some of which reflect differences in motivation, while others describe differences in the actual working relationship itself:

Where a large job introduces building types which are unfamiliar to a firm—for example, a large shopping center with one or more theaters—a firm may suggest to the client that an association with a firm specializing in theater design might be an advantage.

A public agency may insist upon association for various policy reasons, and a kind of shotgun marriage may result.

A firm of moderate capacity may have a client who suggests association with a larger firm.

The prime architect may elect to associate for reasons of his own.

The type and size of job may warrant association for reasons of workload and diversification of talent to be applied.

On out-of-town jobs, the client may want a local man associated with his project, even though the local architect may not be equipped to handle the whole job.

The major tenant of a proposed commercial building may insist upon involving its own architect in the project. This makes for a loosely defined relationship with the owner's architect.

Where an associated architect merely inspects construction, the association may also be a loose one in which the associated architect has a separate contract with the client.

An association may be formed to demonstrate combined capability to a client at the presentation stage of the project.

The mechanics of association: fees and arrangements

Fees for associated work must be slightly higher than for non-associated jobs, since there is an inevitable loss of time when two firms are involved. The client must understand this and be willing to accept the premium fee in exchange for the inherent advantages of the associated firms' resources.

Every association should have a formal agreement, which spells out in detail the scope of each firm's work and responsibilities and the division of the fee. If one of the firms is responsible for engineering consultation, the fee is adjusted accordingly. In the case of the association for the building of the World Trade Center, for example, the basic agreements were with the Port of New York Authority (the client) but associated architects and consultants all signed an agreement to work together.

An associated architect may have engineering or local talent available to deal with specific problems, but in every case communication—particularly between architect and engineer—is of vital importance to the work.

About one in every five jobs going through the Roth office is done in association with other firms. The circumstances of each new association have proved to some extent unique, and have added something to the experience of the office as a whole, Roth reports.

A notable association in which the Roth organization was deeply involved was the Pan Am building in New York. There was reason to believe that any building of such a size and in such a location would inevitably be controversial in character, and further, Roth felt that many minds should be brought to bear on so prominent a building. The Roths decided to invite the participation of the best minds in the country. Pietro Belluschi and Walter Gropius both accepted the challenge of this controversial commission, and their work with the Roth organization is now history.

The Roth organization has also been engaged on another exciting and no less controversial association with Yamasaki for the development of the new World Trade Center for the Port of New York Authority. In this case, the Authority approached both Roth and Yamasaki independently with the suggestion of association, and each firm selected the other. One of the chief reasons for association was the vast size of the job, which could have tied up the complete resources of any one office. Association in this case permits each firm to handle its load efficiently without risking the economic dangers of total commitment of its entire staff to one huge project.

Unlike many architectural offices, the Roth organization does not assign particular jobs to an exclusive job captain. Instead it operates on the principle of guidance and supervision of each job by the top people in the firm. The associated arrangement therefore works out very well for this type of internal office organization, since each firm can supervise its own phase of the work without the serious dislocation and problem of excessive supervision which would result if the firm had to add several hundred extra personnel to handle a given assignment on its own.

Mr. Roth has found from his extensive experience in associated practice that each office learns something as a result of working closely with another firm. The exchange of knowledge and experience, if handled sympathetically, ultimately makes for a stronger profession. Ideally, all architects should practice to the utmost depth of their capability, but it takes time to acquire knowledge. Mr. Roth felt that association is one means of accelerating the learning process, and of deepening the experience of architectural practice.

Experience in the Roth office

How one architectural office has developed the joint-venture technique for handling sophisticated problems in extraordinary commissions—whether the project is large or small.

Joint-venture practice: Problems and procedures

A joint venture in architectural and engineering practice is a close contractual union, a "civil marriage" so to speak, between two or more professional firms for the purpose of bringing their combined resources to bear on the acquisition and/or execution of a commission. Usually, the commission is a complex one, and the union terminates on completion of the single job for which it was created. As with most marriages, civil or otherwise, there is a great iceberg of problem-solving savvy under the bright surface of compatibility.

These are some of the characteristics summarized by Max O. Urbahn in a review of some 20 years of experience with the joint-venture technique. Continuing participation in various joint ventures, although by no means an exclusive preoccupation of The Office of Max O. Urbahn, provides a broad view of the adaptability of this mode of operation to sophisticated problems. These ventures include: the world's largest enclosed volume (the Vehicle Assembly Building at Merritt Island, Kennedy Space Center), the National Accelerator Laboratory, Batavia, Illinois, to house the world's most powerful nuclear particle accelerator (a mile-diameter, 200-bev cyclotron) and a relatively modest lecture hall and cafeteria for an international clientele (at AEC's Brookhaven facilities).

The joint venture operates somewhat like a partnership

The joint venture, Mr. Urbahn points out, has some of the operating characteristics of both a partnership and an association but differs from each at key points. The joint venture is more tightly drawn than the association in its joint commitments to the client and in the formal definition of member responsibilities. As in a partnership, all participating members of the joint venture are individually and jointly responsible to the client for completion of the whole job. Unlike the partnership, however, the joint venture has no continuing existence beyond its one-job purpose. As an entity, it retains no profits and is therefore not taxable. That is, all profits are disbursed to participating firms on an agreed basis and are taxable as income to those firms.

Joint ventures in which the Urbahn firm participates generally work under two agreements: first, the joint-venture agreement itself, which stipulates the purpose, composition and operating principles; second, the operating agreement, which details the day-to-day work assignments and contributions, financial and otherwise, of member organizations. Similarly, there are two checking accounts; one into which all monies received by the venture are deposited and from which withdrawals require signatures of two or more participating principals; the other is an operating account which receives its funds from the first and is disbursed by the single signature of a managing director designated by agreement of the joint venturers.

A policy board makes all the rules

Such agreements, and all other matters of policy and joint commitment, are the province of a policy board or executive committee established specifically by terms of the joint-venture agreement. This board consists of a designated principal and alternate from each participating firm.

Regarding the operation of the board, Mr. Urbahn holds two strong opinions: first, that each of the member principals should be of equal status in his authority and responsibility to the client; second, that the board should operate on a basis of unanimous agreement in matters of management policy. It is possible, says Mr. Urbahn, to operate on a basis of majority rule. Or the joint venture can also operate under decisions of an executive elected by participating members. Either of those two methods, however, undercuts the principle of joint and individual responsibility and can result in both legal and personal complications.

The form of the joint-venture agreement can vary in depth and detail with complexity of the project and preferences of the members and their legal advisers. As a legal document of contract, however, it must be as explicit and comprehensive as possible. An agreement typical of the Urbahn operation has 17 items of consideration, each of which is detailed in unequivocal legal language.

At risk of losing something of the firmness of the document in translation from the legalese, it may be helpful to summarize. The purpose is not to present a pattern to be followed in detail, but to underscore the many facets of attention that must be given to this kind of contract.

An introduction dates the document, lists the participating offices to be known as the "joint venturers" and states the nature, location and ownership of the work contemplated. Specifics of the agreement are:

1. *Right of the parties.* Commits the parties to the terms of the agreement and to the conduct of all work of the undertaking contracted for by the joint venturers.

2. *The name.* States the name under which all activities of the venture are to be conducted.

3. *Interest of the joint venturers.* Specifies the percentage division among parties to the venture to be applied to profits, losses, working funds, liabilities and obligations.

4. *Representatives and policy board.* Designates membership of a policy board as a partner or associate from each firm to serve as principal representative and another partner or associate to serve as alternate to represent the firm in transactions of the joint venture and in dealings with other parties to the venture. Further stipulated are provisions for absences or changes in membership of the board, meetings, compensation (usually none for board membership *per se*) and liability of members to the other joint venturers (none except for gross negligence or fraud).

5. *Supervision of the joint venture.* Gives the policy board full responsibility and authority for performance of the undertaking and for appointment of a project manager who will be responsible for management of the work and contacts with the client.

6. *Financing of services.* Sets up a joint bank account with initial deposit determined by the policy board and contributed *pro rata* by joint venturers each of whom designates an authorized signer of checks and endorsements. All receipts and payments in connection with the undertaking are made through this joint account. In a multi-member venture, the board may designate fewer signatories and/or limit check amounts as it sees fit. The board may also require additional contributions from the venturers as they are required and assess penalties for delinquent contributions. When the board decides funds are in excess of needs, pro-rated distributions can be made. When the undertaking is completed and all bills paid, a terminal distribution is made.

7. *Performance of services.* Locates one or more places for doing business of the joint venture and gives the policy board power to determine which activities are to be performed in any offices maintained by the joint venturers. Arranges for reimbursement of members for an audited account of the cost of doing work on the undertaking and for payment of expenses incurred by the joint venture itself.

8. *Preliminary expenses.* Allows out-of-pocket expenses incurred by members prior to an award of contract by the client to be reimbursed out of joint-venture funds.

9. *Technical assistance of each joint venturer.* Makes personnel and resources of each venturer available for the undertaking to the extent that is "reasonable, necessary, or desirable to the end that the undertaking may be promptly and successfully carried out."

10. *Disputes and arbitration.* Provides that unresolved claims or disputes among venturers in connection with either the agreement or the undertaking shall, upon written request, be settled in accordance with rules of the American Arbitration Association and entered as judgment in an appropriate court having jurisdiction in such matters.

11. *Assignment of interest.* Prohibits any venturer or his firm from disposing of or encumbering his interest in the venture except as, with prior written agreement of other venturers, that interest may be assigned to a successor to the business of the venturer if the succession is voluntary and not from bankruptcy or for benefit of creditors. The right of any assignee, in any event, is limited to the stipulated share of the assigning venturer and may not be claimed until after completion of the undertaking and closing of the joint-venture account.

12. *Relationship of the parties.* Limits the engagement of each venturer toward all others as being confined to performance of the undertaking and specifically exempts the agreement from any implication of partnership or agency for any other work and from placing any limit on the freedom of the venturers to conduct their respective businesses. Nor does the agreement impose or imply any liability among venturers or their firms except in performance of its specific terms.

13. *Continuity and performance of the agreement.* Assures full performance of the undertaking by committing the parties, whether individual or corporate, and their executors, legal representatives, sucessors and assigns to full completion of the undertaking should any individual member die or corporate member be dissolved for whatever reason. Should any party withdraw from the joint venture for any reason, the others may, with the consent of the client, complete the work. If, upon completion, there is a profit, the withdrawing party will receive his pro-rated share as of the date of his withdawal. If there is a loss, he must bear his share without regard to his withdrawal.

14. *Interpretation of the agreement.* Refers all questions relative to the execution, validity and interpretation of the agreement to be governed by the laws of the state in which it is executed.

15. *Term of the agreement.* Terminates the agreement as of completion of the undertaking and satisfaction of terms of the agreement.

16. *Persons on whom agreement is binding.* Excludes all but the joint venturers and their legal assigns from provisions of the agreement.

17. *Notices.* Asserts that any written notices required under provision of the agreement shall be mailed to the principal offices of the venturers for whom they are intended.

The operating agreement is made up as you go

As a practical means of getting things done and retaining the necessary flexibility for change or emergency action, the operating agreement can take the form of a series of numbered Executive Committee Memoranda. These are drawn up as the censensus of meetings and are headed by a statement such as: "The following agreements were reached by the Executive Committee and are hereby made a part of their contractual agreement dated____." The memoranda are then signed by all members of the committee.

The kinds of items of agreement covered in these memoranda are infinitely various. Following are a few examples: 1) Qualifications of executive committee members (as, for example, architects or engineers registered in a given state); 2) frequency of meetings and disposition of minutes; 3) compensation of members for administrative and technical time spent on the joint venture; 4) compensation of all others including employees of the joint venture and ground rules covering overtime, benefits, etc.; 5) basis of overhead computation; 6) bank accounts; 7) insurance; 8) accounting; 9) travel and entertainment; 10) reimbursement to joint venturers from control account; 11) reserve funds, etc.

Basic elements of success in any joint venture, says Mr. Urbahn, are mutual trust and respect of the venturers and the clear delineation in writing of all elements, scope and limits of the working arrangement.

Pros and cons of corporate professional practice

The professional service corporation has been a legal entity in all states except Wyoming ever since New York's Governor Rockefeller signed the enabling law for that state in May, 1970. The New York law is similar to others that require all officers of the corporation to be licensed professionals. While there are state-to-state differences, in that and other requirements, there are also many common questions regarding taxes, liability and other matters that warrant the following review in anticipation of legal counsel for architectural and engineering firms contemplating incorporation. Indeed, it will be seen that the case for incorporation per se in these fields is not always a clear positive.

Frank Smith and Louis DeBiase, principals of the Poughkeepsie, New York, consulting firm, Probus Pension Programs, Inc., have prepared a seminar outline on the professional corporation from which the following summary of precautions and advantages is extracted.

Complications of incorporation for professional practice

Practical problems arise in the processes of formation and operation of a professional corporation. Many of these problems are general and solvable through conventional business decisions. Some are particular for the profession involved; and some arise out of the unique set of people and goals of the firm itself. Hence the following points are regarded as guidelines to alternatives rather than clear disadvantages.

1. The cost of establishing a corporation is substantially more than that of a proprietorship or partnership. But incorporating costs are tax deductible over a five-year period.
2. The professional stockholder-employe will have to pay unemployment and workman's compensation costs, and his social security taxes will be slightly higher than the self-employment tax. But the employer's portion of the social security tax is a deductible expense of the corporation.
3. Benefits such as pension, profit-sharing, group life insurance, medical plans, etc. will create additional costs—also deductible by a corporation.
4. Since 1963, self-employed individuals have been permitted by IRS to establish retirement plans—so-called Keogh plans—which enjoy some of the tax advantages of corporate plans. Under Keogh (HR-10) plans, tax-free annual contributions cannot exceed 10 per cent of earned income or $2,500, whichever is lower.

    If you already have a Keogh plan and you incorporate, you have two basic choices. You can withdraw the money in the plan and pay 110 per cent of the tax that would have been applied over five years or the number of years the plan has been in effect if less than five. Or you can simply leave the money in the Keogh plan and add it, plus accumulated interest, to your income when you retire. Under certain circumstances, it is possible to have both Keogh and a corporate pension at the same time.

5. Fixing compensation income of principals who are, in fact, employes of the corporation will probably be one of the most important problems the corporation will face. A corporation can deduct only "reasonable" compensation paid to employes. A major pitfall is the possible disallowance by IRS of part of the corporation's deduction for compensation to shareholding principals. That would result in the disallowed portion being taxed at both corporate and individual levels. The trick is to fix the compensation at a "reasonable" amount for which there is no clear-cut formula. Factors in the computation include the nature of services performed, qualifications of the employe, comparable amounts paid by others in the same profession and in the same region, etc. Even where there is no conflict of interest, and all shareholders participate in setting compensation for all (as in a father-son practice, for example), IRS may rule that some profit be left in and taxed to the corporation.

6. While the professional is considering how to split income between himself and the corporation to result in the lowest possible tax (especially where there are only one or two shareholders), he should remember that IRS might also determine that compensation is "unreasonably low" and that too much income has been left in the corporation, which then faces a shifting of the excessive amount to the shareholder-employe as personal income. IRS will require reallocation only where individual rates exceed corporate rates and where there is a legal requirement that shareholders have effective control over the corporation—as they must in most professional service corporations.

Advantages of incorporation: less tax, limited liability, fringe benefits

The greatest advantage of incorporating is to give the professional the tax status and fringe benefits enjoyed by other corporate employes. By incorporating your practice, you become an "employe." Among some of the specific advantages are:

1. A corporate characteristic of real significance is permanent existence. The death of one of the members of the corporation will not, in itself, result in dissolution of the corporation or demise of the practice.

2. Closely related to continuity of existence is the matter of evidence of ownership. Each stockholder of the professional corporation would have stock certificates evidencing his ownership interest. When you sell your interest in a professional corporation, any profit on the transaction will ordinarily be treated as a long-term capital gain. If the practice is not incorporated, a portion of the purchase price may represent your share of accounts receivable, and as such be taxed as ordinary income. Such transfers could be made pursuant to a purchase and sale agreement entered into between the members of the corporation, with the transfer of stock back to the corporation to take place either at death or retirement. Similarly, when a member wishes to leave a professional corporation, the integrity of the practicing group can best be preserved by such a buy-sell agreement. It would seem that this agreement should run between each shareholder and the corporation rather than between the shareholders individually. In this

way, the estate of a deceased shareholder could be equitably paid and the corporation would continue without interruption or harassment by heirs.

3. As employes, the professionals could participate in a wage continuation plan established by the organization. Such a plan would provide for continuing wages to an employe in the event of his disability. There is a very attractive tax climate for establishing these plans. If an individual purchased a disability income policy, he would not be entitled to deduct the cost of the premiums. The corporation may purchase disability insurance for an employe and fully deduct the premiums, which will not be taxed to the employe. At the same time, the disability income payments which the employe receives are tax-free up to a maximum of $100 a week. The tax-free status of these payments requires that certain conditions be met as to the length of the waiting period and the amount of the payments. In any event, significant amounts of tax-free income can be received under this type of arrangement.

4. Another attractive benefit available to corporation employes is the medical expense plan. Again, premiums paid by the corporation for medical insurance are deductible by it, but they are not included in the employe's income.

5. Group life insurance is another important benefit available to employes of professional corporations. The professional corporation could purchase group term life insurance for all its full-time employes and take a tax deduction for the premiums paid. Such premiums are not considered income to the employes, and the death proceeds received by the employe's beneficiaries are income-tax free.

   In addition to group life insurance, individual life insurance protection can be provided by the corporation on a selective basis through split-dollar plans. The personal life insurance needs of a professional may be met by the corporation with only a small portion of the premiums taxable to him as income.

6. Professionals, as employes of the corporation, could participate in a qualified pension or profit-sharing plan. Contributions made to the plan by the organization would be fully deductible.

   Contributions to a profit-sharing plan for an employe can go up to 15 per cent of his compensation, to 25 per cent if combined with a pension plan, and pension plan contributions can exceed 25 per cent if actuarial computations show the necessity for such funding. Contributions within these limits are deductible by the corporation, and the employe-shareholder owes no tax until payout. This compares with the limits of Keogh plans.

7. As employes, the professionals could consider a deferred compensation agreement with the corporation. Such arrangement would defer current highly-taxed compensation until the low tax years after retirement. This could be in addition to any formal pension or profit-sharing plan. However, some professionals within the same corporation may want more cash income and others want more deferred income. Employment contracts are drawn with each employe. They can specify type and amount of compensation, as long as total compensation is reasonable.

8. In a partnership, each partner is personally liable for both his own negligent acts and for the acts of all other partners and employes when acting on behalf of the partnership. By contrast, the stockholders of a professional corporation are not personally liable for the acts of fellow stockholders. Instead, the doctrine of limited liability requires an injured party to seek

redress from personal assets of only that professional who has committed a negligent act, or from the corporation.

Liability for negligence of corporation employes other than professional principals is limited to all corporate assets plus the personal assets of the practitioners, if any, who were in direct control of the employe.

This limited liability concept also has significance in the case of dealings between the corporation and its contractors and creditors. These would be limited to recovery through the assets of the corporation and could not reach the personal assets of the individual members.

Calculating the financial incentive to incorporate

A professional firm can make a fairly simple calculation of the financial consequences of incorporation. If you are an unincorporated individual practitioner or partnership, assume your net income before taxes is about $60,000, your net income after taxes is about $37,700. Of this amount, if you set aside $7,500 (20 per cent of net income after taxes) for savings and investment, and $2,400 (4 per cent of net income before taxes) for disability, health and term life insurance protection, you have spendable income of $27,800.

Under the same general conditions of scope and gross income, assume you incorporate. After deducting the same business expenses as you did when unincorporated, your corporation will have $60,000 of taxable income remaining.

Of this amount, the corporation can save and invest for you $9,600 in a qualified corporate retirement plan and contribute the same $2,400 for disability, health, and life insurance. These sums will be deductible to the corporation and thus reduce its taxable income to $48,000. If you draw a salary of $48,000, the corporation will have no taxable income. You will have, after taxes, spendable income of about $31,900.

Similar calculation of the financial incentive to incorporate at various income levels using the same assumptions as in the above example show similar gains in total benefit on the order of 10 per cent.

The fine print on tax law is worth the labor of reading

Generally, an incorporation has no immediate tax consequences. When a taxpayer transfers assets to a corporation and takes all of its stock in exchange, no tax is due on the transfer (IRC Sec. 351). The transferor's *basis* (i.e., total value, whether book or market) for the stock and the corporation's *basis* for the assets after the transfer is the same as the transferor's *basis* for the assets before the transfer (Secs. 358, 362). Basis is important because it will fix the shareholder's gain or loss on the disposition of the stock and the corporation's gain or loss on the deposition of the assets as well as the corporation's depreciation deduction. But many incorporations involve more than a straightforward swap of assets for stock, and so there are qualifications to this general rule.

In one-man corporations, the classically simple situation—a straightforward swap—is most likely to occur. For example, an architect who is a sole practitioner transfers the lease on his office, office furniture, drawings, tools and library to a corporation in exchange for all its stock. No tax is due from the architect or his new corporation. The corporation's basis for these assets is the same as the basis the architect had immediately before the transfer, and the architect's basis for his stock is the total of the basis of the assets before the transfer.

Let's change one fact. Instead of a lease on an office, the architect owns the building in which the office is located, and he transfers the building subject to a mortgage. A corporation can receive property subject to a liability or assume the transferor's liability, and the transfer will still be tax-free. But the architect's basis for his stock must be reduced by the amount of the mortgage—(Sec. 358 (a) (1) (a) and (d).

There is, of course, more than these pages can encompass. A few words of caution: Don't get too smart with your "pre-incorporation bailout of earnings." For example, if you mortgage your building to let the corporation pay off the debt, there is an excellent chance that a borrowing immediately before incorporation, when the incorporator uses the proceeds for his own purposes, will be considered tax avoidance.

For professional corporations with more than one shareholder, all of the rules discussed in relation to the one-man corporation will apply. But note this. In determining whether liabilities exceed basis, each incorporator will be considered separately. This is also true in determining whether the transfer of a liability is so tax-motivated that it will result in gain.

It will be an unusual situation where one shareholder owns more than an 80 per cent interest so that Sec. 1239 will apply. But Sec. 1239 applies if all the transferors, as a group, receive 80 per cent or more of the stock.

One possible way of circumventing the problems that arise when one shareholder contributes most of the assets would be to create two classes of stock. For example, a preferred stock with redemption price equal to the value of the fixed assets might be given to the contributor of those assets. The common stock would then be received for minimal cash contributions.

The potentials of corporate practice are substantial, but there appears to be a minimum firm income below which the costs of incorporation may exceed its benefits. The New York State Association of Architects has circulated a suggested minimum of $30,000 a year.

Interstate practice: Legal and accounting problems

When an architectural office contemplates extending its practice to another state, it is important to remember that the various territories and states have enacted over 50 different statutes regarding qualifications and registration for the practice of architecture. There are wide variations in the provisions of these statutes—and particularly in their application to practice by architects from other states. There is much variety in detail and little reason for some of the differences. Thus it is difficult to generalize—and easy to trip up.

This was the caution urged by Samuel Spencer of Spencer & Whalen, legal counsel to the AIA, in a talk before an AIA convention.

"If there is one thought I would like to leave with you," Spencer said, "it is that when you or your firm are considering undertaking a commission or opening a branch office in a state or territory where you have not practiced previously, you should consult your attorney to be sure that you take the necessary steps so that you will not be practicing illegally in the new jurisdiction." What follows is extracted from Mr. Spencer's remarks.

When architects are contemplating opening a branch office, there are—in addition to legal problems—a number of accounting and tax matters on which they will probably need the advice of an accountant working in conjunction with their attorney. The lack of uniformity of the law frequently makes what should be a fairly simple matter into a complicated and cumbersome one. The practicing architect must comply with these laws and regulations, or he may find that he is guilty of a crime or cannot collect his fee.

Here are some examples of the kind of problems which you may run into in extending your practice to other jurisdictions. There are two basic situations: (1) where you or your firm want to handle a single commission in another jurisdiction; and (2) where you want to open a branch office and practice in the new jurisdiction on a continuing basis. Further, it makes a difference whether a single architect, a partnership, or a corporation is involved.

Proprietorships   If you are a single architect practicing as an individual proprietorship and wish to undertake a commission outside the state where you have your office, there are ordinarily two ways that you can do it: (1) you can become registered in the jurisdiction where the building will be constructed; or (2) you can associate a local architect or firm with you in the project. It may be that you will want to do both. It should also be remembered that in some jurisdictions, such as the District of Columbia, some public work is exempted from the registration requirement.

Most states now recognize an NCARB certificate and will register an architect who holds one without his having to take extensive examinations. Thus it is clearly to your advantage to have an NCARB registration. However, even with such a certificate there may be considerable delay in registration being issued.

Because of this time lag and for other reasons, it may be necessary for you to associate a local architect or firm with you. This practice has been widely used throughout the country and has been broadly accepted for a great many years, even though in many cases the local architect has almost nothing to do with the design and even during the construction phase may have little responsibility for the work.

In spite of the widespread nature of this practice, a word of caution is in order: Many architectural registration acts provide that no one who is not registered in the State shall engage in the practice of architecture. The practice of architecture is often defined substantially as rendering or offering to render services by consultation, preliminary studies, drawings, specifications or any other service in connection with the design of a building or alteration or addition thereto. Where an architect with his office in state A enters into a contract with an owner in state B to design a building to be constructed in state B, has various conferences in state B with the owner, draws the plans and administers the construction contract in state B, it is entirely possible that a court would hold that he was practicing architecture in state B even though he had gone through the form of associating a local architect with him and adding his name to the plans submitted to the building permit office.

Fortunately, such matters are not very frequently litigated, and there has been a reluctance by prosecuting authorities to bring criminal charges against professional men for failure to comply with registration acts—except in very flagrant cases. However, there is always the possibility of a criminal prosecution, and this issue may easily arise if the architect gets into a dispute with his client over his fee. It is a well established rule of law that if an architect is practicing illegally, he cannot collect his fee. Thus, you should be quite careful in the manner in which you associate a local architect with you and how much you have him do, in order to be sure that you are complying with the registration act of the particular state involved. In a few states, such as Kentucky, you can only be a consultant to the local architect, who must make the contract with the client.

If you, as an individual proprietor of your own firm, wish to open a branch office in another state, it would ordinarily be essential for you to be registered in the state before you do so. Further, some states have an annual professional license fee which must be paid by anyone engaging in certain professions. In Alabama, for example, there is a rule of the State Board for the Registration of Architects that no firm or individual may establish an office or branch office to engage in the practice of architecture unless it is under the "immediate day-to-day control and direction" of an architect duly registered in the state "who is a bona fide resident of the immediate area in which such office or branch office is located and whose sole place of business shall be such office and whose sole responsibility shall be the management of such office or branch office".

Partnerships

If a partnership is extending its practice to another jurisdiction for a single commission, there is a question of whether one or more of the partners should obtain registration in the new jurisdiction and whether and to what extent it should associate a local architect with it. With regard to the association of a local architect or firm, the same questions arise regarding the extent to which the registration law of the state requires the local firm to participate and assume responsibility. This necessitates a careful examination of the state registration law and a division of work and responsibility between your firm and the local firm to meet the requirements of the law. There are not many decided cases on these matters, and frequently your attorney will be somewhat in the dark when endeavoring to advise you about what is permissible and what is not.

Frequently, architects are under the impression that if they associate a local architect with them for a small fee so that his name can go on the drawings there is little else the local architect need do. The originating, out-of-state firm does all the work and takes all the responsibility. No doubt this has been done many times by reputable architects and no trouble has resulted. There is, however, always the possibility that if a controversy arises over the architect's fee and he is forced to litigate, the owner may claim that he is practicing illegally and is therefore not entitled to his fee.

There are some states, such as Ohio, where a partnership may not practice in the state unless all the partners are registered. This may not be practical where only a single commission is involved. In such cases it may be necessary for the partner who does become registered to make the contract with the client individually rather than in the name of the firm.

When a partnership is opening a branch office in another jurisdiction, one of the first things to check is whether the state requires all partners of a partnership practicing within its borders to be registered. If it does and if it is practical for all the partners to be registered in the state, that is one solution. In some cases, however, this may not be practical. It may then be necessary to set up another partnership to operate in the new jurisdiction, having as its partners only those who are registered in the new jurisdiction. In such cases the new partnership should maintain a distinct identity.

Contracts with clients in the new state should be executed in the name of the new partnership and carried out by its personnel. Partners should be careful not to hold the main partnership out in the new state as practicing architecture there. This involves not placing its name on the door, in telephone directories, on signs and on stationery used in the state, or doing anything which would indicate that the main partnership is practicing architecture in the state.

You should also be careful regarding the name which the new partnership uses in the state. Some states, such as New York, prohibit the use of assumed or fictitious names. Others, like the District of Columbia, permit only the names of persons who are registered in the District to be used in the name; it has been ruled that it is a violation for an architect registered in the District, who is associated with others who are not registered, to use the words "and associates" after his name. Some states prohibit the use of a deceased person's name.

It may be that where the intention is to have one resident architect who is locally registered run the branch office, he will have to do so in his own name, signing contracts, etc., in his own name and indicating, if local regulations permit, that he is associated with the firm in the other state. These legal requirements are necessarily reflected in the arrangements of the local man with the main partnership regarding the handling of his compensation and his responsibility for actions of the firm in the other jurisdiction. Sometimes, rather than being a full partner, it may be preferable for him to be considered as a consultant of the main partnership and compensated as such.

Again it should be emphasized that in all these situations a firm is wise to consult legal and accounting counsel who can tailor the organizational and contractual arrangements to comply with the applicable statutes and to meet the desires of the professional men involved in the venture.

Corporations

The problems arising with respect to an architectural corporation extending its practice to other jurisdictions are more complicated and troublesome than for either a proprietorship or a partnership.

The problems arise primarily from the varying treatment of architectural corporations by the different jurisdictions. Some jurisdictions prohibit registration of corporations but permit architects to organize into corporations as long as a responsible official of the corporation is registered and is responsible for the work. A number of jurisdictions prohibit registration of corporations but authorize corporate practice subject to various limitations regarding who may be stockholders, directors, officers, etc.

This widely varying approach toward the corporate form of organization for architectural practice has been caused by a number of factors. One is the concept that professional service is essentially a personal service which must be rendered by an individual and which must have individual liability and responsibility behind it. For example, in the great majority of states, lawyers are not permitted to organize in corporate form for the practice of law. Working in the opposite direction is a line of thought that professional people should have the same advantages regarding pensions, profit-sharing plans, and the like, as business people, and that therefore they should be able to organize into corporations or associations treated for tax purposes as corporations. These conflicting lines of thought, and considerations, have had varying impact on state legislatures producing the present diversity of law.

The most acute problems occur when a corporation, organized in a state like Massachusetts, which permits corporate practice, wishes to extend its practice to a jurisdiction in another state that prohibits corporate practice. In that state, the corporation as such cannot contract with the client to provide architectural services. The contract must be executed by one or more individual architects who are officers or directors of the Massachusetts corporation. It may be necessary to set up a separate proprietorship or a partnership of certain of the corporate officers and directors to practice out of state. This proprietorship may have to assign its fees to the corporation. It may not be possible for it to practice in the corporate name because of a limiting law which prohibits anyone from practicing under an assumed or fictitious name.

There are many complications with respect to accounting, allocation of costs, and federal and state tax liabilities. Questions also arise regarding who is the employer of employes in the New York branch office. Can such employes participate in the pension and profit sharing plans of the Massachusetts corporation, or must they be considered in all respects employes of the out-of-state proprietorship or partnership?

You can readily see that this situation raises many practical problems of how to set up and run the branch office which can only be solved in each case with the help of an attorney and an accountant and after a careful examination of the applicable laws.

Guidelines to European architectural practice

The following outline of what American developers and architects should know about European practice was delivered as a talk by Robert Brodsky, executive vice president of the New York firm of Brodsky, Hopf & Adler Architects and Engineers, to a mid-1973 seminar in Marbella, Spain, sponsored by the Real Estate Review and Real Estate Institute of New York University.

Although the subject of this discussion has to do with the development of a general understanding of the architect's problems and responsibilities in European practice, my remarks will be primarily predicated on project development in France, where my experience, and that of my firm, have been most recently concentrated.

In this experience, although we have learned that there are many similarities to problems and ground rules in the United States, there are vital differences. Although I am not quite inclined to say, "vive la différence," the American developer and his architect had best get to know these differences well if they are to realize the very attractive potentials that await them on the European continent.

These differences have to do with zoning laws and ordinances, ecology, esthetics, costs; they deal with local customs, and with materials. As they relate to these considerations, European policies are, you will soon find, considerably more restrictive than those of the United States. And these restrictions, although certainly not insurmountable, must be included in your initial planning of real estate development in Europe.

All of us are, of course, quite familiar with the problem of conforming with zoning and ordinances. Most of the countries of Western Europe have adopted zoning laws very similar to our own. These pertain to requirements of land area per dwelling unit, road frontage, yard requirements and parking, among others. But today European zoning codes are becoming more stringent. They now include provisions for such matters as architectural review, engineering requirements for sewers and water, road specifications, and other factors.

In France, the zoning and building codes are tied together. To file plans in France, one is required also to engage the services of a consulting French architect. The plans are then filed at the Prefecture General level and, on their approval, you are provided with a *Permit de Construire,* the paper that says you may begin construction.

Before obtaining this permit, however, one must go through a number of formalities.

First you are required to prepare a site plan, in which you will indicate the scheme: the type and number of buildings, number of units, density, parking, and so on. A meeting with the local equivalent of a zoning board is then arranged for. There, you will be confronted by the *Architecte de Conseil,* the consulting architect, who will ask most of the questions and whose opinion will carry considerable weight. Most often, a second meeting will be required before you are permitted to make your formal submission to the board.

This formal submission consists of a set of preliminary plans for roads, water, sewers, ducts, buildings and of the other facilities to be provided. If public facilities buildings, such as restaurants or hotels, are to be included, preliminary plans for ventilation, heating and plumbing facilities must also be shown. And cost estimates must be provided. Then, it will take from two to three months before you will receive a response. Once approval is given, no additional plans need be filed.

No additional plans—but—one more interesting surprise does await you. You will be invited to participate in a discussion related to Z. A. C. I'm not quite certain of the words constituting this acronym, or whether it may not be more appropriately designated "Z.A.P.," but I can tell you with some authority what, in plain English, it does mean. Literally translated, it stands for, "How much will you pay for schools, hospitals, water, garbage disposal, etc. . . . . *If we give you an approval?*" It is, in effect, a tax levied on the developer for putting his facilities in that area. The developer's contribution could take the form of a donation to a new school, adding a wing to the hospital, building a sewer plant, or whatever, the size of this contribution being directly related to the scope of your project.

It goes without saying that you will be well advised to take into consideration such supplementary costs when developing your initial project cost estimates.

As we've seen, European zoning problems are quite similar to those we know in the United States. Building codes contain the same fire and health protection requirements we know at home, but, added to these, are social requirements that are much more stringent than those with which we are familiar in the States.

In Europe, esthetics are a particularly important consideration and your compliance with the regulations pertaining to them is vital to the acceptance of any real estate development plan.

The use of the land area and how it is developed is a matter of real concern in Europe today. Wooded lands are fast disappearing and, in France, special areas have been designated for the express purpose of protecting the woods. The design of villas and apartments must take into consideration the desires of the prospective client for such amenities as gardens, pools, tennis and horseback riding at the time site development is started. As a means for providing green space as well as for preserving wooded areas, the concept of cluster housing is a preferred alternative in Europe to the more prevalent American practice of providing for one house per acre or half-acre. All plans must be submitted to a Review Board.

Other matters related to esthetics which are of vital public concern have to do with the design of the buildings and with the materials to be used. In preparing your proposal, the design concept is usually covered adequately by a simple statement to the effect that the buildings will blend with the surroundings, but the material selection can be a problem unless agreement regarding their choice is reached early. Color of tile for roofs, exterior walls, etc. can be dictated by the zoning board if the problem had not been discussed and agreed on beforehand. The architectural façades of old buildings will be carefully scrutinized before approval is given.

There is one area of special public concern that has now taken the spotlight in Europe with an intensity at least equal to that in the United States. The protection and rejuvenation of the ecology now has top priority in Europe—and with good reason. Since pollution has already affected the Mediterranean, the Atlantic Coast, parts of the English Channel, and most of the rivers in Europe, stringent rules and regulations planned to implement effective controls are being adopted and enforced. Strong measures are now being taken to regenerate that which has been ruined and despoiled, and to save that which remains in reasonably healthy condition.

In France, strict regulations have been instituted for the control of sewage treatment plants. B.O.D. requirements on the order of 95 per cent removal mandate the utilization of complete treatment plants. It is, however, possible to deposit this effluent in a river, but always with careful monitoring.

All matters affecting the protection and maintenance of green areas and beaches, as well as the habitats of fish and wildlife, have become the concern not only of the press and the general public, but of national and local governments as well. There is an all-encompassing interest that constitutes a hurdle that would be quite difficult to overcome. It is, therefore, an area of development activity that must be carefully considered—one which should be discussed with authorities in order to determine specific requirements before plans are developed too far—and along forbidden directions.

In Europe, as elsewhere today, special consideration must be given to control costs. But, particularly in Europe, in view of the situation we have just outlined, special thought must be given to the factors affecting costs that can be controlled by the architect. This includes planning for engineering economy, and I stress engineering, since it represents almost 40 per cent of the total project cost. Layouts of roads and utilities, including sewage plants and water systems, reflect importantly on the cost per unit of building and in order to establish and maintain an effective control of cash flow, proper phasing of site work is a vital consideration.

Costs are affected, too, by the availability of materials. With changes now taking place as a result of the Common Market, and these include the removal of tariffs on many products, the architect has more freedom of choice in the selection of materials.

Labor, then, becomes the next factor affecting costs. This varies with the type of labor required, whether skilled or unskilled, its level of productivity and with its ability to adapt to the use of new materials. Shortages of skilled labor in most of Western Europe have had the expected effect of escalating costs.

No differently than in the United States, the European architect is totally and personally responsible for all of his work. In France, the architect *must* carry "Errors and Omissions" insurance to the full value of his projects. But in Europe, the architect seldom does a complete set of plans. He develops the design concept and will then allow the contractor to prepare the engineering drawings. Occasionally, an architect will hire a *Bureau d'Etudes* for a large project. This is the equivalent of a large architectural drafting company to which design drawings are furnished, from which they prepare working drawings.

In Europe, the architects are usually small practitioners. An office of 20 men is considered quite large. Their approach to architecture is usually the "Beaux-Arts" approach, quite different from that of the business-oriented American architect. The concept of time being money does not seem to exist there. You can also readily sense the fear of governmental authority which obviously colors their thinking and approach. Our American attitude of "let's try it this way, if it doesn't work we'll change it" is a frightening one to the French architect. Yet, surprisingly, our experience has been that the local authorities view this in the light of being something new and novel—and we have found that they do not resent it.

Working in Europe is a challenge. Some things are different, many are the same. Special care and good management are the key, and these must be paired up with competent professional architectural and engineering help.

Practice abroad: A rewarding study in comprehensive frustrations

Robert S. McMillan returned to New York to set up his own U.S. practice after many years of practice abroad. As he concludes in this report: Diversity is interesting but it can be wearing over the long pull.

There is excellent opportunity for architects with American know-how and technique in the field of international practice, especially as it pertains to the emerging nations of Africa and the Middle East. Despite the abundance of work, however—and fewer building restraints—the American architect practicing abroad can expect to meet with a battery of peculiar and often amusing problems arising out of differences in custom, religion, climate and geography. The new nations are expanding rapidly, and nationalistic pride demands that conditions be improved and facilities created to enhance each country's "new image." They want change and want it fast. There is money to be spent, but there are few local planners, architects and builders.

I became involved with the special problems of international practice in 1957 when, as a partner in The Architects Collaborative, I went to Baghdad with Walter Gropius to negotiate a contract to design a new university. In 1960, I moved to Rome to conduct other TAC projects in the Middle East. But it was in 1963, when I set up my own Rome-based practice and tackled projects in Africa and Europe as well, that the full scope of diversification, excitement—and often enough frustration—became a way of life. I found myself filling the role of diplomat, public relations expert, artist and politician. I sat out revolutions in both Iraq and Nigeria, and had to begin the same negotiations many times over, since the people I had been negotiating with had suddenly been jailed (or worse). Often, I had to establish a completely new set of contacts with new ideas —not necessarily better, but necessarily different.

I located my office in Rome where, aside from the obvious advantages of physical beauty and ease of life, there are many Italian architectural assistants who have had years of experience with successive waves of Rome-based American architectural firms. Rome's airport is almost completely "weather-free" and offers a mutliplicity of flights to all points from Aden to Zanzibar. This is an important consideration since travel is a necessity. Foreign dignitaries consider the ability to travel a status symbol, and promoting a project often involves a great deal of travel and entertaining. For weeks on end I would only touch base in Rome between trips to Lagos, Nigeria (five hours by jet), where we had an office and were building the University of Lagos as well as three military installations for the Government of Nigeria; to Nairobi (eight hours by jet), where we were constructing an office building for the East African Moslem Welfare Society (the Aga Khan's group); to Iran (five hours by jet), where we were designing Pahlavi University in Shiraz; and to Libya (only two hours by jet—when the planes were flying), where we had been commissioned to build two hospitals, two office buildings and 18 clinics. I encountered different languages, different religions and customs, and different monetary systems. My passport became a dog-eared tome of visas—so full and fat that occasionally I had trouble finding the pertinent visa for inspection at customs.

Negotiations call for endless patience

Appointments hardly exist except on the highest level. One just drops by the Ministry in the morning, and waits with all the others, drinking endless cups of tea. This may well occur in the Minister's own office, where everyone's problems are given public hearing. Secretaries are almost nonexistent, and if you want your "hard-bargained-for" agreement typed up and translated into Arabic, you had better do it yourself. Government offices, in general, only work until lunch time, and one has to be aware of the different national and religious holidays in setting up a schedule.

Negotiations that are started at a lower level and apparently successfully concluded are often just the beginning. Usually, you have to start all over again higher up. In one memorable deal with an "emerging nation," I spent weeks negotiating with a special committee set up specifically for dealing with my particular problem, only to repeat my efforts when the prime minister decided he wished to conduct the negotiations personally for political effect. He then called his whole cabinet together with a dozen assorted generals and bodyguards, and we negotiated for two hours in front of television cameras with many official references to the love of our two great countries for each other declared against an obligato of constant clicking of the guards' nervous Sten guns in the background. Having reached a well-publicized agreement, another three to five months went by while the agreement was moved through ministry offices. This is not just bureaucratic slowness. Often there are pro-American and anti-American factions in the government, and one has to be very nimble to keep the agreement from being "lost" in some "anti's" office.

Money and politics color exotic practice conditions

The major sources of work in Africa and the Middle East are governments, oil companies, U.S. Government agencies such as AID and the Corps of Engineers, and occasionally a private client. Generally, U.S. agencies will be smaller in the countries where the governments and/or the oil companies have the money to give out work.

Competitors run the gamut from the British (who have been working overseas for generations and have the full backing of their commercial attachés), to other nationalities whose concepts of architectural practice may be considerably different from ours. One well-known practitioner in the Middle East was rumored to have accepted his fees in camels when hard currency was scarce. Often governments reflect their "middle line" foreign policy by trying to select a mixture of architects—one from one of the Iron Curtain countries, one from Scandinavia, and one from the U.S., for instance. This is to "bring more ideas to a project."

The American practice of complete working drawings and specifications as a basis for contract documents is seldom adhered to abroad. The form of contract documents perfected by the British, with the addition of a quantity surveyor and bills of quantity, is the more normal method used for tendering. Drawings may be dimensioned in feet or meters, and serve mainly as a guide to the building process. The bids are usually based on the bills of quantity, which accurately describe the amounts of all the diverse pieces which go into making up the building. Architectural details follow normally during the construction phase.

Construction techniques may be ancient and immutable

Generally, one or more resident engineers hired and supervised by the architect will be stationed on the site throughout the job to handle the daily problems that come up for their distant offices. Construction problems can keep one's sense of humor alive in the 104°F tropical heat. Most countries use massive untrained labor forces and relatively few mechanical devices. Concrete is placed by laborers carrying about three shovelfuls of concrete in headpans.

At one point, we suggested to our contractor that he would have a better chance of meeting his daily pouring schedule if he used wheelbarrows or dollies instead of headpans. He agreed, and the next week there were eight or ten wheelbarrows at the site. But by the next day, all the wheels were missing. The fellows had substituted the barrow for the headpans, and the work progressed apace. Clearing a site for one of the jobs also turned up some unexpected difficulties when we learned that there was a religious shrine in the area. The native priests kept darting in and out of the bush to put a hex on the machine.

Programing abroad can be a most demanding art

The client usually does not have the experience to develop a program and expects the architect to be the expert. This means that the architect must correctly judge the client's wishes and present these completely and expertly or not get another chance. While working on Pahlavi University in Shiraz, Iran, the effective client was the Chancellor of the University and former Prime Minister. Since the Shah was the sponsor of the University, however, it was to him that the project had to be presented for approval. This took place in the garden of the Shah's palace. Both he and the Shahrina (who had studied architecture at the Beaux Arts in Paris) reviewed the project, quietly asking questions for about an hour and a half and only relieved the suspense at the end by saying how pleased they were. During our long wait to see the Shah, the Chancellor had seemed especially nervous. It was only after the presentation that I realized his concern had been because he had recommended us, and he was anxious for approval of his choice.

All in all, practice abroad can be rewarding and—to say the least—interesting. Diversity, however, can be wearing over the long pull, and one may yearn (as this practitioner has done) for the regenerating challenges of more purely architectural pursuits in the U.S.A.

Interior design practice

There has been a resurgence of professionalism in interior design. This has been substantially a return to the ''mother art'' of architecture and has run parallel to the expanding scope of other architectural services.

This is not to suggest that professional levels of skills required for interior design are inherent in the training or talent of every architect. Further, many successful and gifted practitioners, who have never registered, or practiced, or even trained as architects, qualify as interior designers of the very highest caliber.

The point here is an important one: The practice of interior design today calls upon an array of talent and detailed competence that is unique to its own success and must be learned by anyone through basic design education honed by exacting practice in the field. It has a generic bent of effective sensitivity to form and function in human environment that is essentially architectural. Therefore, it recruits heavily among those who have pursued that bent through architectural schools with adequate design emphasis. Further, it has a special immediacy for many practicing architects in that it completes and integrates the overall design of many types of buildings.

The field of interior design is complicated by a number of demanding and limiting factors—artistic and economic—some of which are carried over from the business and professional doldrums of the thirties. During that depression, interiors commissions were scarce and mostly residential. Many of them were handled by a coterie of variously talented amateurs, among whom were furniture sales departments, housewives with rich friends, dealers and contractors of various sorts, and—let's face it—unemployed architects. Formation in 1931 of the American Institute of Decorators put a name on the profession of the time and at the same time it raised the first concerted voice of recognition of the fact that qualifying standards were essential, even—or perhaps especially—for so mixed a group.

How did we get here? Where are we now?

The war years generated new demands and provided opportunities for what is now called the contract furnishing industry. Postwar potential greatly multiplied demand on all fronts of interior design and furnishing. Sharp and preferential trade practices developed, however, which were harmful to almost everyone involved.

Although the reviving business economy supported an increasing number of commercial "space planners" for both offices and retail stores, the custom of providing layouts and specifications for minimal or no fees and relying for income on the mark-up of furnishings carried over from depression practices. The custom was further entrenched by certain furniture outlets, which maintained planning service departments as part of their sales operation.

But the demand for truly professional services in both programing and design of business and institutional spaces gained more and more support from prospering and sophisticated clients. Some architectural offices were already providing such services. Others prepared to do so.

Strong evidence of the drive toward professional status for interior design was the formation in 1957 of the National Society of Interior Designers followed, in 1961, by a change in name of A. I. D. to the American Institute of Interior Designers. The substitution of the term *designers* for *decorators* was a clear statement of intent. Both organizations set up membership-qualifying standards of education (four-year college degree with a design component) and training (three or four years of work in a "recognized establishment"). Thus the term *decorator* was relegated to those who could not qualify, and the term *designer* was used to designate a category of practice advancing toward professional standing.

While these moves have worked no sudden magic in the marts of trade, they have had at least two marked effects on how architects and other acknowledged professionals can set up to do business as interior designers. First, they have gained the mixed blessing of increasing surveillance by the Federal Trade Commission over pricing practices of the furniture industry. Possible consequences of a ruling by FTC early in 1969 that only one price prevail for furniture sold to either retailers or professional designers were viewed with alarm by A.I.D. when it appeared that certain manufacturers would thereupon require professionals to purchase from designated distributors, many of whom themselves maintain competitive "design" services. An A.I.D. resolution sought the support of N.S.I.D., AIA and the Industrial Designers Society of America to keep the FTC informed of such ramifications, and some of those problems are now resolved.

A second and perhaps more profound effect of emerging professionalism in interior design has been to free architects—already secure in their professional status—from any compulsion to set up separate departments or corporations in order to obtain "resale numbers" for the discount purchase of furnishings. This has not been an insurmountable problem for many years, and those relatively few architectural firms which now separately incorporate their interior design services do so for other business reasons. The point is that full options of organization now exist.

Interior design work affects architects' office organization

The best organization for interior design services in a fully integrated architectural office could be none at all; or a cell of enthusiasts; or a tasteful young girl in a sunny corner; or a separate corporation; or a filer of samples in a closet; or an outside consultant; or . . . As is so often the case in practice, it all depends.

The serious fact is that unless the architect approaches interior design with the same respect for its special character that he might bring to, say, urban planning or any other of the "expanded services" proliferating these days, he is in for a rude awakening—if not disaster.

Organization for interior design can be—indeed must be—as flexible and varied as the building types involved. Further, it will be affected by the point in the overall building design development at which the interior design is introduced. The annual volume of work will, of course, determine some of the limits of organization, as will the consistency or fluctuation of the work load.

Architects in practice are already familiar with the basic modes of organization for doing business as professionals in their states. Proprietorships and partnerships are the predominating if not the only form of organization permitted by the laws of many states for architectural and other professional practices. Some interesting points of law beyond the scope of this discussion are still to be resolved in the courts, as more and more firms seek to reconcile the readily incorporated retailing practices of former decorators with the legal and ethical responsibilities (as well as the prerogatives) of bona fide professionals. (See Chapter 5 section on corporate practice.)

The following general characteristics of the practice of interior design are some that architectural firms should take into account in their approaches to in-house organization.

1. It is vastly detailed in every aspect. There are no areas of massive and readily specified emplacement of major components or systems that can absorb unexpected expenditures of design time on detail in other areas. Therefore, the accounting system for personnel time must be more rigorous than many architects are accustomed to.

2. The number of product categories and variations of color, finish and quality is virtually infinite and changes daily. Some arrangement must be made for sophisticated product information storage and retrieval with a place and designated responsible personnel for sample and catalog storage and updating. For any volume of business much above the break-even point, this can be a full-time librarian operation.

3. Specifications for such diverse items as a ribbon or a chair can be unbeliev-

Interior of the Bank of Houston by
Wilson, Morris, Crain & Anderson
Architects. The banking room is an
all-glass, column-free space designed by
the architects, which contains the officers'
area, public space and teller space.
Alexandre Georges photo.

ably complex in special language and technical detail in any custom furnishing document. Expertise is required.

4. Dealings with a vastly increased number of manufacturers and suppliers
   are usually more direct than they are in conventional construction. The
   architect may have to be prepared not only for a new role in shopping but
   an expanded supervisory if not directly active role in purchasing and
   quality control as well.

5. Clients for interiors tend to have strong opinions in the designer's own professional area, but to vacillate in their decisions as to particulars of execution. Further, their capacities for visualization of a design goal from verbal
   description, swatches, chips or catalog tear sheets are often, if unadmit-
   tedly, limited. Organization can do little to correct these idiosyncrasies, but
   should prepare for added emphasis on presentation techniques and extra
   care and completeness in all letters of agreement as to scope of services,
   schedules, fees, extras, penalties, prepurchase deposits, deliveries, taxes,
   and every possible bone of future contention.

The influence of building type on practice organization

Most architects could sit down and postulate the differences in design approach to the interiors of houses, churches, schools, stores and office buildings. Why, then, do so many interior design ventures by architects founder on the shoals of those differences? Because the obvious differences of shape and form and function with which architects are accustomed to deal obscure the basic—although perhaps simpler—differences that affect the business of handling and charging for the job.

Differences in size and scale, for example, introduce the well known (but seemingly contradictory and often overlooked) stipulation that smaller jobs call for larger multipliers in the fee structure and proportionately more executive time in disciplines of the schedule and budget.

The following observations have been made by various practitioners regarding the organizational implications of two building types—residential and business. They underscore differences at these two ends of the scale, but are by no means a complete guide. The special requirements for other building types also call for specific measures in organization for practice.

RESIDENTIAL INTERIORS (i. e., for houses and apartments, but not necessarily including hotels or dormitories) call for seemingly endless discussions of small matters. The organization should provide for more or less gentle reminders that the designer is a professional and his time is a direct charge to the job. The letter of agreement provides an opportunity to be specific on these points and should be detailed and explicit about the scope of services.

Preliminary interviews are a special hazard in residential work. It is a sad fact that prospective clients have been known to go from office to office picking the brains of responsive architects and designers who are too quick to reach for sketch pads and catalogs before the agreement is signed. The prospect leaves to think it over and finally goes home to a do-it-yourself design project.

The main lobby of the new addition to Stamford Hospital in Stamford, Connecticut by interior space designers ISD Incorporated features long curved walls. The outside wall is hung with white vertical louvers, and the inside wall is paneled in teak-stained red oak, used throughout the building interiors. A rust and beige tweed carpet is used with dark brown leather Scandinavian chairs and sofas covered in green nylon fabric. They are grouped around low Travertine marble-topped tables. Exposed metal is brushed chrome.
Bill Rothschild photo.

Another burdensome feature of residential work that needs organizational attention is the fact that the architect's purchasing function is likely to be more direct, is often piecemeal, and encounters informal business practices on the part of the client in matters of delivery and documentation. The architect's own records have to be extremely well kept to cope with these conditions. And it can hardly be called a dilution of his professional standing if he writes in a percentage handling charge item by item—so long as the client is aware of this procedure.

OFFICE INTERIORS, specifically those large and varied spaces designed to accommodate all phases of business enterprise, present two very large problems for the organization of design practice. First is the fact that the design must follow a voluminous and vastly detailed program which business clients are increasingly calling upon experts to prepare. The development of these programs involves familiarity with commercial business practices and a penetrating study of the particulars of the client operation. It is characteristic of this kind of program that it must be unrelated to physical arrangements (the province of design), but must at the same time take into account the flow of commerce and communication within the client organization.

A whole new profession of specialists in this field has grown up. It has sprung largely from the experience of design firms who have watched the problem of programing grow as their own practices became more and more involved in business space design. Programing capability, therefore, is frequently set up as a service within the design firm. It is a separate and demanding service, however, and must be organized accordingly.

The second paramount problem in organization for business space design is one of degree. That is, the spaces involved are frequently extremely large, the clients are sophisticated and demanding in businesslike practices. And the varieties as well as the quantities of furnishings and interior construction have nurtured a whole new industry called contract furnishings. Parallel to this, of course, the scope of work for business firms has provided opportunities for furniture design by architects.

At least one of the complications architects encounter in organizing for business interior design practice has developed out of the rapid growth of business itself. The manufacturers and suppliers of contract furnishings were not slow to respond to a demand for some sort of planning and layout service. They set up to provide that service with departments of varied capabilities—some of which have demonstrated a high order of competence. Most of these firms now work cooperatively with architects when the occasion demands. But on some other occasions, they must be recognized and dealt with as competitive with professional design practices.

The client group for business interiors divides into categories that will affect especially the promotional aspects of organization. Building owners are a major category which embraces two kinds of work. One is for those owners who are fairly large business firms and occupy their own buildings. This work has a substantial programing component. The other kind of work is for those building owners who want to prepare space for tenants. This may limit the scope of work or at best introduce a block between the designer and the program—which should really fit the needs of the tenant rather than the owner-client.

Tenants themselves form another large category of client. Some design firms have organized to aid in the search for suitable premises. In general, the tenant group tends to underestimate area requirements. A consulting competence to advise realistically in these matters may be an asset in a well developed professional design firm.

Real estate developers are another kind of client that may need special handling. In boom building years in New York, for example, some of these firms offered "free" interior design as a sales point for prospective tenants. They were not always sensitive to the ethical ground rules of professional design practice, but they have improved in this regard and are not only valued clients but are also a good source of contact with tenant prospects.

Some very large business corporations have developed their own interior design departments, which handle their far-flung premises with trained competence if not professional flair. While they are not often prospects for outside professional design, they are sometimes aware of the limiting effects of the one-client practice of their own captive departments. They are then prospects for outside consulting services.

Fee structures for interiors need further study

Architects' provision of interior design services and the special programing requirements of some aspects of this work are listed under the heading "Additional Services" in AIA Document B-131, the standard form of agreement between owner and architect drawn up on a basis of percentage of construction cost. Stipulation is made that these "additional services" shall be paid for separately by the owner, but no figures are suggested in the document as a basis for that payment. The assumption is that for these services, as for basic building design the various professionals will accommodate fee scales to particular conditions.

The multiplicity of detail associated with interior design practice is such that the accustomed percentages and multipliers for building design work are frequently inadequate for interior design. The survey reported on the following pages underscores this assumption.

Architects can work successfully in interior design at a fee nominally stipulated as 10 per cent of construction costs, but the interior construction cost figure to which it is applied must contain a considerable factor for the kind of administration expense that is conventionally contained in the base cost as part of the building contractor's bid. In interior work, it is normally an additional expense directly to the architect because he is more consistently involved in administration of the contract.

Similar increases in normal multipliers applied to direct personnel and technical costs should be considered. The amount of executive time is disproportionate in interiors commissions. And at the other end of the scale, the clerical and technical time devoted to the details of the work greatly exceeds that required for other architectural services. This means that either the methods of recording time must be more stringent or the multipliers must be raised to cover the different norm.

Architects experienced in successful interior design have observed that if the figures for all categories of time, materials, and overhead are accurate and include a provision for profit, the interior design is bound to make money—provided, of course, it proceeds at a reasonably predictable or at least controllable pace.

Survey of architects draws profiles of interior design practice

A survey of architect-readers of *Architectural Record,* selected to provide a representative cross section of U.S. practice, shows that about 64 per cent of the architects surveyed practice interior design as part of their professional service. Of those who do design interiors, 63 per cent find the business profitable. Three quarters of the firms practicing interior design intend to expand that

Clyde's Bar and Restaurant in Georgetown, Washington, D.C., by Hugh Jacobsen, architect, seats 250 people. All woods are clear white oak. The unusual barstools are tractor seats from the John Deere Museum. The brass-plated supports were designed by the architect.
Robert C. Lautman photo

service; some, obviously, in an optimistic attempt to move the operation into the profit columns.

Table 1 shows a summary of replies to some of the survey questions worked out as percentages of those firms now practicing interior design. The following is a summary of findings not reportable as percentages or not readily apparent in the table.

■ About a third of the firms doing interior design in 1969 had been in that field for less than five years.

■ Slightly more than half of these relative newcomers say the practice is profitable.

■ Among those who did not mark the practice as profitable, the predominant reason given is that the service is provided as part of the overall architectural service and is not separately identified as a profit source.

Exterior remodelling and interior design for a Women's Fashion Store for the Joseph Magnin Company, Walnut Creek, California. Design architects and store planners were Chatham & Schulster. Robert Brandeis photo.

■ Others found that work on small projects of interior design entails more detail and internal cost than was anticipated in fee structures.

■ Only 22 per cent of architectural firms who practice interior design have set up a separate department to do so, and of those only one in seven have it separately incorporated.

■ In a representative 100 architectural firms of all sizes who practice interior design, the staffing for interior design was reported as follows:

	Full time	Part time
Registered architects	29	104
Architectural graduates	26	52
Others	30	90

■ The range of size of interior design staff is from one to 50, and it is notable that in the smaller firms the proportion of architects and graduates is higher.

■ In those offices which design interiors for more than 50 per cent of the buildings they design, the likelihood of profitability is markedly higher than among those who do interiors for a smaller proportion.

■ Of 47 firms who design interiors for 25 per cent or less of their own buildings, 38 per cent reported the operation not profitable—often because no profit was sought.

■ Among those reporting no profit, about half included interiors as part of the overall design, characterizing their interior work as an "extra service" done to retain total design control.

■ Other reasons given for lack of profit were: insufficient size and volume of projects to cover research or to keep files current; too time-consuming; inadequate fee structures.

■ Of architects charging 8 to 10 per cent of materials and construction costs, 40 per cent did not realize a profit.

■ Of those charging 12 to 15 per cent, only 14 per cent reported no profit.

■ Those few (four per cent) who charged 20 to 30 per cent of construction costs made money.

■ On another fee basis, the most frequently charged multiple of direct personnel expenses was 2.5, a figure commonly used in general architectural practice.

■ But 45 per cent of firms who operate at 2.5 times direct personnel expense realize no profit for their interior design efforts.

■ Occasionally architects opted to negotiate fees on the basis of a multiple of 2.5 to 3.0 times an estimate of expense plus overhead, but again the method is reported to be unprofitable in nearly 50 per cent of the cases.

■ In a separate mailing of the same questionnaire to a list of presidents of AIA chapters, the profile of practice was virtually identical to that drawn by the larger, statistically random sampling of architect-readers of the *Record*.

Fee structures vary but generalizations are possible

A sampling of comment on trends or problems volunteered by some architects in the space provided on the questionnaire is as follows:

Interiors done in the office of the designing architects for the building help to control the "total project."

Problem—convincing clients that all interiors should be coordinated with the building design.

Problems of conflict of interest—I feel that no retailer of merchandise should give interior decorating service, and vice-versa; all furniture should be billed directly to owner, following designer's approval; designer should not purchase material in his own name ever; and he should not be forced into this position by the manufacturers.

Here (in a major Southern city) the designers are owned by suppliers; with state work there is more flexibility in bidding practices (but with) political interference.

Need for better "systems" approach to aid architectural designer (i.e., "how to do-specify-order, etc."). Organized source information would help especially to unravel the "mystery" of cost.

Biggest problem is overcoming client tendency toward "decorating" rather than designing. Client tends to think of interiors as something divorced from the building.

I see a trend toward interiors being included in architectural work.

Retail establishments are cornering interior design activities due to their free design services!

I see a trend in closer relation and more integration between architects and interior designers.

Problem: Interior designers who claim they serve for nothing and make a fee on materials.

Problems: Lack of definition, professional ethics and standards; manufac-

Comments on trends and problems

TABLE 1. ARCHITECTURAL RECORD SURVEY OF INTERIOR DESIGN PRACTICE

The following is a summary of answers to those questions in the survey (described in the text) which could be worked out as percentages of those architects in the statistically random sample who do include interior design as part of their professional services.

1. *Is your interior design practice profitable?*
   Yes 63   No 28   Varies 6

2. *Do you hope to expand your interior design practice?*
   Yes 73   No 20

3. *Do your interior designs include design and/or selection of movable furnishings?*
   Yes, design 75   selection 87

4. *Per cent of firms reporting a separate department for interior design: 22*
   Department separately incorporated: 3

5. *For what per cent of buildings you design do you complete interior designs?*
   5 to 25% of buildings: 45   30 to 60% of buildings: 27   70 to 100% of buildings: 15

6. *Please check the types of interiors you have designed.*
   offices 90   theaters 20   stores 39   museums 4
   dormitories 20   schools 43   libraries 24   banks 54
   apartments 42   hospitals 23   restaurants 37   houses 59

7. *Who are your major clients for interior design?*
   other architects 3   real estate developers 23   commercial tenants 43   building owners 85

8. *Who purchases the furnishings you specify?*
   Architect does, 37   client does, 81

9. *Do you work with interior designers retained by the client?*
   Often 9   Sometimes 72   No 19

10. *If so, do you approve or otherwise control material specifications on behalf of the client?*
    Yes (at least sometimes) 55   No 17

turer-dealer relationships and policies; need for interior furnishings contractors.

Biggest problem is keeping up with all the newest items.

First the problem is to obtain a qualified interior designer with a background in architecture—then you have to expand so that you can keep him busy.

Frankly we haven't been able to cut the line between "architectural services" and just where "interiors" begin. Just for the record: where do floor finishes, wall coverings, colors and lay-in ceiling patterns actually fall—notwithstanding actual "furnishings" themselves?

Quality standards need to be established in some easily digested form.

The problem as I see it is that too many interior designers attempt to narrow down their scope of design choices by establishing arbitrary and artificial "rules" regarding interior design. This allows them to practice with a minimum of talent and imagination; frequently with none at all. The other problem is that too many architects regard interior design as "window dressing," rather than as an integral part of the total building concept.

Inability to purchase certain lines of furnishings when manufacturers protect franchised distributors creates a problem. Also the general requirements of keeping showroom space to maintain maximum discounts from manufacturers.

We are architects. Our selection of materials and furnishings reflects our architectural design concept of the building and is somewhat more architectural than that of interior design firms.

Unless a client employs a reputable space planner or his architect, the end product usually ends up a complete disaster. Also, when the client moves his load of has-been furnishings into a new space, the game is lost.

Architects initiate interior design in planning buildings. To offer comprehensive services to clients and to control total design, it is mandatory that we be expert in inteior design as well as other services.

Interior design should be done by interior designers, not architects—we're not trained for it.

Interior contractors are taking professional designers' plans and competing on a "package deal" direct to the client. It is still cheaper for the client to send interior work out for competitive bids.

Lobby of the L'Enfant Theater and Communications Center, part of the L'Enfant Plaza complex in Washington, D.C. The architectural firm of Jan Hird Pokorny planned and designed the theater and all its interior spaces. The lobby's primary light source is hundreds of clear five-inch incandescent globes that run in strips across the ceiling like a sparkling theater marquee.

Competition of office supply companies doing interior design (for free) is a problem. There is definitely a trend toward architectural firms having their own interiors department. But I think that this can only be practical in large companies with many jobs because of the very broad field of interior design.

There is need for licensing of interior designers.

Finding good bidders for contract work is a problem. We also feel all alone in attempting to set up really good specifications—particularly for carpeting.

We will very likely depend more frequently on consultants.

Fees create a problem. Interior design should be contracted for on a separate basis. Architectural firms performing this service should be compensated for on a multi-rate basis or some other equitable arrangement.

The day of the interior decorator selling merchandise for his fee is fast ending. Interior design can stand on its own two feet today as a design service paid for by the client on a direct fee basis.

Franchises in limited areas are poor for open bidding work. And manufacturers' control of carpet installation is harmful.

Most architects—including ourselves—are terribly inexperienced about this. We must become involved—the AIA does not seem to recognize it as far as providing contract documents, etc.

Interiors take much more time than we are equipped to handle. Many clients of buildings now want interior design along with building design—particularly for banks and small office buildings.

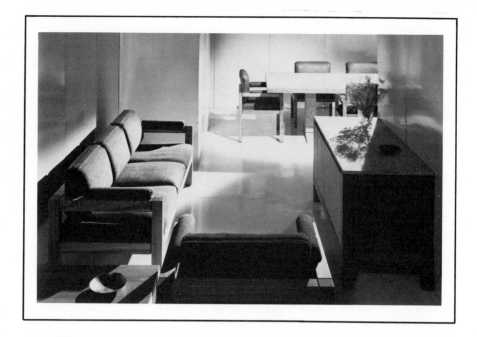

Trend is toward a softer look in furniture, but not to the "cute" or merely "decorated." Problem No. 1: convincing the public that experienced architects are well qualified for interior design. Problem No. 2: convincing more architects

Architect Warren Platner created a
collection of furniture for CI Designs. The
line possesses the unity of character,
consistency of scale and forthright use of
materials which characterize distinguished
architecture. The materials are ash,
granites, leather and other coverings. The
joinery is a logical use of these materials.
Tables may be had with stone, wood or
leather tops. Cabinets have stone, wood or
leather doors and tops. Seating pieces
include a dining-conference chair, lounge
chair, sofas of various lengths and large
and small ottomans and benches.

that they must become proficient at, and practice, interior design to maintain
the integrity of the buildings they design.

Interior design should be included in project design and both worked through
together.

There must be a closer relationship in the basic architectural development of
spaces, functions, etc. Interior designers should develop designs for specific
furnishings (i.e. custom designs for furniture, textiles, lighting and graphics).

Practice problems in remodeling

Architectural commissions for preservation, remodeling, renovation, restoration and (in some cases) expansion of existing buildings are the bread and
butter of many small-to-medium-sized offices—and the agonizing loss leaders
of others.

Why?

Because the special conditions of practice in this field are rational, solvable
and remunerative when they are understood—and fraught with pitfalls when
they are not.

Many of the special conditions of practice for work on existing buildings
can be itemized by merely thinking of the problem; others can be determined
by inquiry; still others are brought home by experience, sad and otherwise.
Following are some of those conditions gleaned from recent interviews, reports
and surveys.

**Budget and fees
are the first problem**

In general, the architect's work on existing buildings calls for more pre-design research, both in the field and in pertinent archives and codes, than is normal to new-building work. Therefore, the architect should be sure his compensation for at least that phase of the work is charged on a basis that covers the extra detail and services.

Where the compensation cannot be charged on the basis of a multiple of direct personnel expenses (plus any special consultation, laboratory work or other charges inherent in alteration work)—i.e., where the compensation cannot be negotiated, but must be on a basis of a per cent of construction cost—the per cent rate should be considerably higher than on new-building work. Curves developed by the New York State Association of Architects show a suggested increase of three to six per cent above the new-building rate for buildings in the middle and upper ranges of complexity and for jobs in the $500,000 to $1 million cost range. Smaller jobs, of course, call for higher premiums on the new-building rate.

Another general problem in alteration work is the fact that conventional modes of establishing the budget and relating it to the program do not apply.

Where the budget is a fixed amount in the client's pocket, and the program is a wishful dream, the architect had better insist on relating the dream to the pocketbook—and charge for that service—before he enters into a design contract. At least he should prepare the client for additional pre-design service charges and, in effect or in fact, participate in development of the program.

The relationship of budget to program is highly specialized in alteration work. Unless the architect has certain and current knowledge not only of the hidden detail of existing building systems but also of the costs of demolition and of any non-standard materials that may be required, he should insist upon paid consultation in these matters. Contractors who specialize in remodeling work are a resource in this area—and should be paid for their consultation accordingly. Contractors who are not familiar with remodeling work should not be consulted.

Special knowledge of applicable code requirements is also a requirement, although it is not necessarily beyond the scope of the architect's own homework. For example, a change in the type of occupancy after alteration of a building may invoke a whole new section of code requirements—or remove a pre-code building from any exemption that might apply without such an occupancy change.

Lewis and David Slingerland of New York's Slingerland, Booss & Fakas (an architectural and engineering firm that seems to thrive on remodeling work in a demanding milieu) tell of the case where a church took advantage of generous ceiling height in one of its buildings to install a mezzanine classroom. They were suddenly in costly violation of a number of structural, mechanical and fire-exit code regulations that applied to this new layering and occupancy.

**Problems of the building
as form and/or function**

The building itself and the objectives of the alteration work have an obvious bearing on how the work is handled—although some of these effects are not so obvious as might be supposed. For example, Chapter 21 of the *Architect's Handbook of Professional Practice,* covering "The Architect as Preservationist," defines the objective of architectural preservation as: "to conserve those buildings and sites which contribute to our environment and culture by their historical or architectural significance. Preservation projects may involve individual buildings or groups of buildings requiring various architectural approaches. When completed, all should serve a useful, economically feasible, contemporary purpose, since few buildings warrant preservation in order to exist as museums or static exhibits.''

Reasonably, the notion of preserving a building of ''architectural significance'' for a useful contemporary purpose might extend the definition of architectural significance to many well-designed buildings in addition to those of historically notable façade or technically interesting structure and materials. The preservation of *any* sound building for economically feasible contemporary use might be considered a sound architectural objective. The difference between such broad objectives and strict preservationism would be, of course, in the wider extent of acceptable remodeling and in the increased degree of architectural freedom from the requirement to *preserve* the appearance and identity of the existing structure.

The building upon which work is to be done under any of these terms poses characteristic problems of complexity, desired occupancy and the degree to which existing documents reveal an accurate record of location of hidden mechanical, electrical and structural elements. A change in occupancy may not only involve code restrictions as previously described but may also call for structural reinforcement that may or may not be possible with existing foundations.

These are the conditions that impose a real necessity for research and field testing of existing conditions as well as consultation with skilled remodeling contractors during the programing and pre-design phase.

Decisions and procedures regarding preservation or remodeling are affected by the nature of the client as are also the forms of the commission contract and the negotiations for compensation.

Problems of the client are more complex

In general, the procedures and documentation can follow the basic practices that prevail in new-building practice. Standard documents, however, must be considerably modified at key points to accommodate the special conditions of the work. Some of these points have to do with special services and payment schedules as will be apparent in this discussion, and legal counsel is advised.

The individual client for smaller jobs, such as houses and stores, is probably the most expensive to handle per dollar's worth of work put in place. He is also the most likely to be dismayed at the architect's compensation rates that must be charged to handle that work. While the extent of historical and legal research is likely to be less burdensome in this category, the hours of client consultation and the limited degree of client sophistication more than offset this lighter burden.

There are elements of competence and salesmanship that assume added importance for the architect in remodeling work, and those elements cannot be conveyed by written instruction, but only by experience and confidence. Further, the temptation to diminish the degree of documentation on the grounds of seemingly easy communication among client, architect and contractor should be curbed. The contractor may very well understand objectives and provide the skills for their execution, but the client is likely to find small (or large) matters for post-completion discomfort and even legal action that might be avoided by thorough documentation and explanation.

An interesting example of how one small firm got its start in this area of individual residential clients and parlayed the experience into larger, more diversi-

How one firm grew with remodeling work

fied work is reported in the following extract of a communication from Samuel A. Anderson, III, of the Richmond, Va. firm, Glave Newman Anderson.

"Starting out life six years ago in a converted downtown stable loft in Richmond, Glave Newman Anderson has gone on to make a profitable specialty out of remodeling work.

"We found an immediate clientele among pioneers of the back-to-the-city movement in Richmond's Fan District—a multi-block area of substantial but deteriorating old townhouses. Those pioneers were the admirable young couples with turn-of-the-century townhouses, great imagination and little money who fuel half the architectural firms starting practice all over the world. We have done a dozen of these houses, but, from the start, our involvement in the life of the Fan District led to other work than the purely residential. When the Valentine Museum—a venerable institution dedicated to the history of the life and times of the City of Richmond—commissioned us to prepare a long-range development plan, it was no coincidence that the museum director was a Fan District resident. Widespread publicity on this project—which was, essentially, another remodeling job—put the firm's name somewhat in the public eye for the first time and we have stayed busy since.

"Three years ago we outgrew the stable loft and expanded into the stables and carriage house as well. While our present practice includes a high proportion of new construction, we find that much of our most interesting work is still remodeling.

"In our master plan proposals for the 25,000 student urban campus of Virginia Commonwealth University, we dealt at length with that institution's re-use of its existing nineteenth century buildings, and the relationship of its new buildings to the fabric of the residential neighborhoods surrounding it. We are developing plans now for revitalizing left-over buildings in two districts bracketing Richmond's financial and commercial center. These and other projects all have involved coordination of a wide array of para-architectural skills, from long-range strategic planning, to preparation of detailed financial feasibility models, to the packaging of a development syndicate.

"From our point of view, it can be seen that remodeling is intellectually challenging and tends to lead to other work. But most importantly we know it is remunerative, often making the difference between a so-so year and a profitable one. There are pitfalls, however. We have learned how to avoid many of them, and we are at least aware of most of the others.

"Our internal costs are always heaviest at the outset of remodeling projects. In comparison to the generally accepted cost breakdown of 35 per cent Design Development, 40 per cent Contract Documents, and 25 per cent Contract Administration, our design development costs may run as high as 50 to 60 per cent of the total fee. This is largely due, of course, to the complications of working within the parameters of an existing building, but is also a measure of the degree to which we make use of creative and reliable contractors.

"We strongly recommend pre-selection of a general contractor, so that by consultation during the design phase our drawings contain neither more nor less than is actually needed by that particular contractor for that particular project. As everyone knows, a good contractor will contribute significantly to the success of a building project, and in this manner we take full advantage of his ability. At the same time, the work can be so arranged that much of the detail is not essential to the success of the main theme, and this variable can be controlled to fit the pocketbook of the client. Since an unknown or disorganized builder may cost us a disproportionate amount of time in the drawings phase and particularly during construction, we tend to be very selective in our recommendations to our clients.

"It must be clear that we are concerned that the cost of our services remain within the financial reach of small project clients. By some of the methods outlined above, we feel we can keep the time chargeable to a client down to a minimum, but this is only half the story. The unbillable overhead time spent in moving from one small job to another makes up one of the well-known financial pitfalls in remodeling work. Poor time-keeping records contribute to this, and so do endless discussions with an irresponsible contractor. In being selective of the general contractor employed, we do our best to avoid at least one potential high cost situation ahead of time. In another instance of high design cost—that is, client indecision—the simple mechanics of the inexorable monthly rendering of time spent multiplied by the hourly rate tends to produce an acceptable degree of self-regulation on the part of the indecisive client.

"The high front-end loading of the typical remodeling fee contributes to another cost problem which has proven more difficult to resolve—the client who pulls out before proceeding into working drawings or construction and is (I suppose, understandably) unenthusiastic about paying for what has, for him, become an entirely unproductive building venture. Since our uncollected bills can only work to increase our overhead and hence our billing rates, we are actively seeking ways to overcome this problem. In this regard we have found that when a first meeting with a client has indicated any likelihood of a project's untimely demise, the old fashioned retainer works very effectively. But since prognosis of this type often borders on clairvoyance, we are investigating other more mundane methods."

The commercial client, that is, the owner or prospective buyer of an office building, is understandably more hard-headed about the cost of remodeling versus the returns on proposed occupancy. Economic feasibility of the project therefore becomes a double study; first, to weigh the economics of total demolition and rebuilding, and second, to accurately assess the cost of remodeling. Early consultation should be fortified in these areas of feasibility for commercial work with special attention not only to accurate costs but also to the floor loadings and mechanical requirements of proposed occupancy.

Two advantages commercial clients have over some others are: Sophistication in assessment of the economic rationale of proposals, and flexibility in adaptation to appropriate compensation negotiations.

Commercial remodeling occurs over a wide range of project size and the compensation rates vary accordingly. The Slingerland firm previously mentioned reports a range of projects from $500,000 to over a million dollars and a corresponding range of compensation rates that work out to about 12 per cent on the smaller work and about 9 per cent at the upper end of the scale. These are generalizations subject to considerable modification from job to job depending on the complexities involved.

Occasionally, preservation and remodeling occur jointly on some important projects. The $9.3 million commission to Alfred Shaw and Associates for remodeling Chicago's Board of Trade building is a case in point.

The Board of Trade's landmark structure, designed 41 years ago by Holabird and Root, will be virtually re-designed on the inside while preserving the external character and basic structure of the building.

The modernization project, launched in 1970, includes replacement of existing heating, ventilating and air conditioning systems; conversion to an all-electric energy system; replacement of 22 elevators; the creation of two entirely new interior stairwells and the reclamation of 180,000 square feet of waste space for rental.

Simultaneously, a tenant improvement program will transform office space into modern, flexible units offering amenities competitive with any new building in the city.

Virtually the only area to remain untouched is the trading floor, a five-story oak-paneled chamber where $73.3 billion worth of commodities were traded in 1970.

The renovation program has been directed by the real estate firm of Cushman & Wakefield, Inc., which assumed management of the building on November 1, 1969. The program is based on a 16-month study made by Alfred Shaw and Associates, architects; William Meek Associates, Inc., interior designers; DM&L Construction Company; and Environmental Systems Designs, consulting engineers.

Despite the scope and cost of the undertaking, the decision to renovate was made with relative ease, according to Lawrence Blum, a silver trader and chairman of the Board's Real Estate Committee: "We hadn't made any money on office rental in two years. The building would have been empty in another five. It wasn't hard to figure out that by investing $10 million we could almost double the value of the building and bring our gross annual rental income to a profitable level by 1973. Besides (and important to value considerations), the building has become a symbol of this city over the years."

Institutional clients such as hospitals and universities pose the same problems of architect-client relationships that exist in new-building work with the added complication that much of this work is in the form of additions to existing buildings that may require remodeling to accommodate joining of the old to the new. Some examples of this kind of work were shown in the Hospital Building Types Study in *Architectural Record* for September, 1971.

Characteristic of institutional work is the likelihood that the remodeling and additions often occur as an on-going relationship between the architect and the institution. Robert Hegardt of Kahn & Jacobs, architects for the Mt. Sinai Hospital, New York, describes the situation as follows.

"Rather than looking at this ongoing commission as a series of isolated, trying alterations varying in cost from $50,000 to $1.5 million to be sandwiched into the schedule of a large busy general practice in architecture, Kahn and Jacobs treated it as a single continuing task of protecting and enhancing a highly complex, interlocking, specialty real estate investment valued well in excess of $100 million.

"To this end the architects maintain a section of their office which devotes itself entirely to the problems of the Mount Sinai Medical Center. In effect, this group has become an office within an office. It has the flexibility and specialists normally available to the large parent practice. At the same time it provides the client with personal-service architecture of the nature more usually encountered in small office alterations practice.

"Through its continiung knowledge of The Mount Sinai Medical Center, its buildings and its growth problems, this group, in conjunction with the Mount Sinai Offices of Planning and Design & Construction, can and does remove some of the mystery prior to starting an alteration. It cannot, however, remove the perversity, or resistance to change, so often built into original structures as a result of false economies made to meet a stringent budget (short structural spans, inadequately spaced or sized risers, badly located stairs and low floor-to-floor heights). These represent minor first cost savings but are a major factor in increased costs incurred by the inevitable series of alterations that follow. This is one of the major issues to be resolved in establishing long-term institutional client relationships.''

The public client usually operates under a set of procedural constraints that are particularly difficult in remodeling work. First is the widespread legal provision that compensation must be charged on the basis of a legally pegged per cent of construction cost. Second is the common requirement of open competitive bidding on construction work of all kinds. This precludes early consultation with pre-qualified contractors except on a strictly professional basis and by separate commission directly with the client. It also encumbers the pre-qualification of contractors, an important aspect of successful remodeling work. Documentation of public work also is forced into patterns of phasing and approval prior to the start of actual work. This frequently defeats the economics and flexibility of remodeling as a mode of lengthening life for public buildings.

In most remodeling and preservation work, the building itself is a physical component of the documentation of required work. The existence of record or as-built drawings is not only problematical but is frequently insufficient for conventional documentation of the new work. Therefore, the architect in developing efficient modes of remodeling documentation is turning more and more to photo techniques. Some of these involve actual photographs of the existing building, key details, or parts of the mechanical and structural systems on which drawn alterations are superimposed. Another technique uses a photographically shaded set of plans on Mylar or other film systems upon which the designers of the various new systems can work out their changes in solid black line.

Problems of documentation reflect special conditions

The drawings of record of the completed remodeling job also will contain the photographic record, which therefore must be fairly well documented as to date and angle of exposure of each picture.

Where standard forms of agreement between owner and architect are used in remodeling or preservation work, they should be carefully adapted to this special use. The outline of basic services, for example, should be amplified to cover any special research or consultation, not only in pre-design services but also at key points during the schematic, design development and construction document phases. Where AIA document B131 (per cent based compensation) is used, it should be modified to cover these extra services. The previously cited Handbook chapter 21 provides detail on these points in preservation work, and the implications of all of the foregoing should provide legal counsel with some guidance.

Increasingly aware of the importance of remodeling, preservation and restoration as a substantial portion of architectural practice, the RECORD Research Department during 1972 drew up an extensive questionnaire that was mailed to 1,000 architectural firms selected by a sampling method that characteristically

Survey of architects shows most do some remodeling – and find big jobs and big rewards

produces a true national cross section of firms with respect to size and location. There was a surprisingly large and detailed response from 25.3 per cent of the firms surveyed.

The questionnaire began with the following statement: "The questionnaire that follows is about *remodeling.* By this we mean any commission to alter an existing building—whether the project is called *renovation, rehabilitation* or *restoration.*"

Results are summarized as follows.

Response in detail shows active participation

The first question: "Has your firm been involved in building remodeling in the last two years?" Answers revealed that 77 per cent of firms had been so involved, and of those who were not, only five firms declared they would not undertake commissions for remodeling work.

Question 2: "Approximately what percentage of your firm's work is remodeling (as opposed to new construction)?" brought 191 replies, among which 65 reported more than 20 per cent of their work as remodeling; five firms had over 70 per cent of their work in this category. The median firm had about 14 per cent of its work in remodeling of existing buildings.

Question 3: "Are you doing more or less remodeling work than you did, say, five years ago?" brought 190 replies of which 87 per cent reported they were doing the same amount or more than they had done previously.

Question 4 was a two-part question asking whether respondents expected more or less remodeling work in the next two years—and why. Some 35 per cent expect more; 55 per cent about the same and 9 per cent expect less. The reasons given for an expected increase were: the increasing cost of new construction, the prevalence of structurally sound existing buildings and a general tendency to expand existing facilities. Notable among observations supporting an expected increase were those dealing with systems approaches to inner-city rehabilitation and the probability of more school remodeling as local bond issues fail in passage and school expansion needs diminish.

Three of the respondents who expect less remodeling work simply state: "It doesn't pay."

Shift in procedures revealed in key question

Question 5 was another two-part question about whether firms handle remodeling projects in the same way as new building projects.
a. "Do the same people in your firm work on remodeling projects as work on new buildings?" (yes, 94 per cent)
b. "Does your firm write the same kind of specifications for remodeling work as for new buildings?" (yes, 54 per cent; sometimes, 24 per cent; no, 22 per cent)

Respondents who replied "no" or "sometimes" to the question about specifications were asked for comment about what is different. Following is a sampling of comments:
"Special conditions are more varied and complicated."
"We try to define much of the work and materials on the drawings."
"Specifications for remodeling work usually put on drawings."
"Matching or reusing some existing equipment."
"Instructions on how to perform."
"Other headings, processes, etc.—often not bid—but contractor selected at outset."

"Specs vary on alteration jobs. No repeats, at least not too many."

"Description and control at demolition; contractor has more leeway to handle unforeseen conditions."

"All the difference in the world. Scope is always more complex."

"Most sections have paragraphs referring to existing work."

"Revamping and reusing existing items in order to keep costs down."

"More specific in areas of cutting, patching, painting, demolition, etc."

"Demolition, site utilities, shoring, special conditions, temporary facilities, finishes, mechanical and electrical."

"The basic reason is that remodeling work is not the same as new work. Demolition and site investigation are important items. Disposition of removed materials plays a big part, etc."

"On larger work above $100,000, specs are the same type. On smaller, incidental work the specs are on the drawings as much as possible, plus a 'Scope of the Work'."

"Many items subject to specific site considerations."

"In remodeling work you never know for certain what conditions exist until you have the job under construction and changes are apt to occur in specifications as a result."

A substantial market comes to light

The questionnaire probed projects handled in the last two years by each firm. Some 645 projects with a total dollar volume of $242,682, 500 were reported in detail; average value was $376,251 per project. Among these, 232 projects involved major increases in floor area. The principal reasons given for remodeling were change in function of space; improve comfort; bring up to standard; increase profitability; and conform with codes.

The age distribution among 613 buildings reported was as follows:

Under 5 years 19
5-10 years 80
11-15 81
16-20 76
21-25 45
26-30 50
31-35 13
36-40 55
41-45 14
46-50 52
51-60 34
61-70 18
71-80 25
81-90 5
91-100 10
over 100 years 36

Comments summarize experience and reaction

The results by building type are tabulated on page 85. It is interesting to note that the average job cost for houses is about $55,000. This rather high figure is a result of considerable expansion work on some very large and very old houses.

The survey's concluding invitation was: "Would you give us what comments you like on your firm's experiences with remodeling work—how important it is to you—how your firm approaches a remodeling job—what you think is the future of the architect in the remodeling field—your thoughts on the whole subject of remodeling." Following is a sampling of replies received.

■ We feel that remodeling should be approached with the same degree of attention, enthusiasm and idealism as a new project. The challenge to solve existing problems in the most efficient, esthetic and economical manner possible is just as great or even greater due to the investigation and research required. As construction costs continue to rise, remodeling jobs should increase greatly. Architectural firms interested in remodeling and prepared to do it properly should have little trouble in keeping gainfully occupied.

■ Most architects have started their careers with a renovation commission, and those who maintain fairly small general practices will always be involved with additions and remodelings of some type. This is an important area of service, as it should achieve the same goals as a new structure for the client. Many older buildings are in too good condition to be razed but need to be updated. Architects will always be called on to render this service and should treat it with the same respect shown any commission.

■ Remodeling is a way of life with clients who are constantly expanding existing facilities and acquiring new markets. Our specific endeavor is with the airlines industry. There is continual change at existing airports and remodeling is the byword for most architectural engineering work even when new facilities are constructed. Existing outdated facilities are revamped for another use.

■ Remodeling is a very important part of our practice. Some of our most satisfying significant work is remodeling. Remodeling work is highly challenging due to the additional limits imposed. Our approach is complete modernization, not "make-do."

■ Most often exteriors of existing buildings are completely usable and often are too expensive to duplicate. Approach is substantially same as for new building. Design is often simplified by having a set of boundaries—floor area, heights, etc. Remodeling is a great challenge and for the most part interesting work.

■ In our work remodeling is not a separate field, but is done either in connection with an addition to a building or for an owner for whom we have done new building work—a "regular client" who wants to update and improve an older building.

■ As far as our firm is concerned, remodeling and renovation work is important. We are primarily engaged in the design of hospitals and for the last four or five years approximately 75 per cent of our work has been expansion programs for hospitals which we originally designed.

■ We find an increase in remodeling work, thus are spending more time investigating new products and architectural solutions for this type of work. Generally, we have been able to satisfy the client's requirements, sometimes with better results than could have been achieved with new construction. Our firm has experienced great success with minor capital improvements programs for schools and hospitals. The greater portion of this work is remodeling. Many facilities require updating of old buildings while the newer areas are constantly revised to accommodate expansion and/or new programs of occupancy.

■ We do mostly custom residential work and from this experience I believe there will be a great need for residential remodeling due mainly to the high cost of property and heavy construction. I believe new materials are helping to save money on remodeling. As for commercial work, of which we have none at the moment, I believe there will be a greater surge.

SUMMARY OF BUILDING TYPES REMODELED (by 253 representative architectural firms)					
Building type	No. of projects	Total value, $ million	Average proj. cost $ thousand	Median bldg. age years	Per cent involving expansion
All buildings	645	243	376	28	36
Office buildings	103	23	222	28	19
Houses	106	6	55	23	57
Schools (K-11)	71	101	1,423	36	44
Msc. commercial	59	13	217	20	39
Religious	42	4	101	37	38
Stores	38	4	94	33	16
Factories	30	22	722	12	47
Banks	30	6	209	29	17
Hospitals	30	34	1,116	16	57
Public buildings	23	3	129	40	26
Social & recreational	34	10	288	40	32
Msc. institutional	16	1	815	30	25
Apartments	12	3	222	37	25
Warehouses	11	2	158	27	27
College buildings	10	3	338	18	30
Hotels, motels & dorms	10	2	235	42	20
Msc. non-residential	20	7	332	22	40

Management
of
the
Professional
Firm

Why and how to plan professional firm management

Success in the design professions, however it is measured, rarely happens by accident. Most successful firms have luck and talent to help them, but luck and talent alone are never enough, as clients of this writer's firm can attest. (Bradford Perkins prepared this section of the text when he was with the consultant firm, McKee, Berger, Mansueto. He has since joined Llewellyn-Davies Associates.)

Several years ago one of our clients asked us for a one word summary of what we found to be the common denominator for success. Our answer was "planning." The same concept which architects, engineers and interior designers attempt to promote among their clients has equal validity in the development of their own practices.

This article, and the several following in this chapter, will attempt to discuss how firms can develop and implement successful plans for many of the major business aspects of their practice: business development, organization and staff, financial planning and control, and many other critical aspects of all design professionals' practices.

Careful planning is the foundation for successful handling of any of the above areas, and the first step in the planning process is the development of a precise statement of the firm's goals. On the surface, of course, this sounds like something one does only for promotional brochures and to justify to one's friends and relatives why he is in business for himself working 16 hours a day for not much money. In fact, however, if done properly, a statement of objectives is the important first step in preparing a meaningful program for the firm's development.

Why it is important to outline objectives can be seen by examining the typical small young office's goals. Take, for example, an office of ten men headed by three equal partners a few years out of a large local office. If you asked them to list their goals, they would probably respond with the following:

1. To become respected by the profession and by the public as a leading design-oriented office.
2. To have an interesting variety of projects and thus, to avoid having the firm's practice limited to specialities in one or two building types.
3. To achieve a size large enough to undertake large projects but to be small enough to permit involvement by the principals in the design and client relations of every project in the office.
4. To make enough money for the principals to have a comfortable income.
5. To attract a group of bright, talented employes and to be able to pay them well.
6. To retain ownership of the firm among the current principals.

Consciously or unconsciously many firms seem to be pursuing goals like these. Admittedly, they are better detailed than one client firm's expressed goal. "Work like hell and get ahead." But what firms with similar objectives often do not realize is that some of the inherent contradictions in the above goals may prevent achieving any of them. Specifically, the major problems with these goals are the facts that it is difficult today:

1. To achieve a major reputation or comfortable income for both principals and key employes without some steady growth beyond a ten-man office.
2. To grow without both an able staff and some consistent means in the firm's business development program to differentiate the firm from all of its competitors for new projects. This latter point normally implies some specialization.
3. To attract and keep a good staff if the principals retain full ownership and control of all major project activities.

Thus, the next step in the development of a plan is the redefinition of the firm's goals in a form that eliminates the major contradictions. This redefinition should also be as specific as possible (i.e. how much growth, how much profit, etc.).

Having related its goals, a firm must then make a careful analysis of its strengths and weaknesses. The obvious purpose of this self-examination is to identify those factors which will help and those which will hinder obtaining the firm's objectives.

Every firm is different, of course, and, thus, each has a unique combination of strengths and weaknesses. Typical strengths are a demonstrable expertise in one or two building types, a principal who is a particularly good writer and speaker, and/or demonstrable expertise in an important area such as construction documents or construction cost control.

Identifying a firm's weaknesses can be even more important, but it is often more difficult to do, for it requires both experience and objectivity. In our experience, the most common shortcomings in the typical design firm are: one or two major gaps in the capabilities of the principals (usually business development or business administration); a weak project-manager level; little or no demonstrable basis for differentiating the firm from its competitors in a new-client presentation; inadequate financial control to permit planning or controlling the firm's profitability; and a staff which is not organized, trained or managed properly to achieve maximum productivity.

Following this self-examination, the next step is preparation of a plan that will guide the firm toward its goals by exploiting its strengths and eliminating or minimizing its weaknesses. Although following sections in this chapter will discuss the major segments in a business plan in more detail, some of the important points from each area will serve as illustrations of what must be considered in every plan.

A management approach to business development

The first step in most people's minds is obtaining a sufficient volume of work. Accomplishing this involves far more than meeting people or getting invited to enough presentations. In the simplest terms, it usually involves implementing what is known in other industries as the "marketing concept."

The marketing concept has been best defined by the simple statement "Find a need and fill it." Every client has needs which he expects the architect he commissions to fill. In some cases the overriding need in the owner's mind (particularly for facilities such as hospitals or schools) is to have a building that meets his functional goals. In others a more basic need is paramount, such as developing an acceptable facility within a tight budget for occupancy before a certain date. Even politically-oriented selection committees prefer to choose someone who they think is the safe choice—in other words, the easiest to justify on some reasonable grounds rather than political pull.

The most successful firms in terms of business development are consciously or instinctively aware of these needs and structure their efforts to reflect the appropriate client needs. The average firm (which does not have the advantages of a national reputation, principals who can spend their full time meeting clients, or hundreds of completed projects) must be even more careful to channel its business development efforts so as to achieve a maximum impact at each client contact.

In the management plan, the principals must decide the type of projects they will concentrate on developing. Shotgun approaches rarely work. Project goals might be defined by building type, by locality, by client type or some other classification. Care must be taken to select potential project groups which the firm has a realistic chance of obtaining. One friend of ours recently came close to having to close his practice because he concentrated on two building types which he did not have the marketing muscle to penetrate.

The next steps involve researching how to contact the selected target groups, analyzing their needs, and structuring the firm's presentations, staff and operations to meet these needs. There is a way of developing leads for every client type. All clients have needs, and the needs have definite implications for the design firm seeking work. Major hospitals, for example, are normally very concerned with performance, and thus, expect their architect to understand their operational requirements. As a result most firms that have been successful in obtaining hospital work have been able to talk about hospital administration problems and medical care concepts as well as bricks and mortar during their interviews. A firm hoping to enter this field usually must gain this working knowledge through research, by associating with a firm with previous experience in the field, hiring hospital specialists, and/or careful structuring of presentations to reflect the concerns of specific medical facilities clients.

The one trap that all design firms must avoid is the assumption that inherently superior design ability will somehow be rewarded with continuing commissions. To use another marketing buzz word, this introverted "product-orientation" (as opposed to "client orientation") is the one thing a business development plan must avoid. If the firm's design ability, however that is measured, really is superior, find some way to demonstrate it in an owner's terms on a regular basis to potential clients.

How to develop organization and staff

A firm with work must, of course, be correctly organized to handle it. The number of possible basic organizational structures is limited, and every office must choose the organization which is most appropriate to its practice.

Firms that handle only large, relatively simple projects such as office buildings can have a limited number of principals who draw on a generalist staff pool. On the other hand, offices with many small complex projects must have many more principals (or at least qualified project managers) and may choose to organize the office into specialist teams.

Staffing, too, is a critical planning concern. A firm should always be searching for staff that has the experience and capabilities to increase the firm's strengths or eliminate its weaknesses. For example, one firm's huge hospital practice can be traced directly to the hiring of a former hospital administrator (and architect) to head that segment of the practice. Prior to that time they had not been able to get a single major medical facilities project. What functions should be performed by which consultants (as opposed to in-house staff or subsidiaries), whether out-of-town work should be performed by a branch office or one central office, what personnel policies should be employed, and other questions should also be answered in the plan.

Even the legal organization of the firm—corporation, partnership, proprietorship or some combination—is important for reasons other than tax considerations. Each of the legal forms of organization should reflect the way decisions are made, and a corporation with one president implies a different relationship among the principals than a partnership—even if it is not an equal partnership.

How to go about financial planning and control

The AIA has been very active in recent years promoting intelligent financial planning and control. This is, of course, one of the most important aspects of any plan. What can the firm afford to do? How much money do the principals want to earn? What fee volume will be necessary at break-even? What will be the source of cash to maintain the firm's operations? These are all questions that must be studied and answered. The techniques for answering these basic questions are all contained in the AIA publication *Profit Planning in Architectural Practice.*

The result of this planning process should be a comprehensive budget for at least the next year of operations and a method for measuring performance versus the budget. This involves decisions on the structure of the accounting system (accrual vs. cash, what coding, automated or manual, etc.), cash management procedures, methods of compensation (percentage, lump sum, etc.), payment of consultants, and other financial concerns.

All of the above areas and other aspects of the firm's operations should be studied on a regular basis, and it is worth committing each plan to writing. But once written they should not be put in a drawer and referred to on rainy Friday afternoons. Instead, they should be internalized so that the plan becomes an active guidance system for management.

This then leaves the final step—implementation. Obviously, this is the most difficult, for the first law of implementation is that it takes at least three times longer than anyone expects.

Moreover, there will be a continuing need for flexibility. In spite of all this planning—nothing goes exactly according to plan, and, thus, it must be administered flexibly. New projects, staff problems, and many other factors will all require adjustments in the plan. Few developments in the firm's practice, if any, need make the plan obsolete, however, as long as management uses the plan as a general guide rather than as a detailed road map.

One development that can call for a detailed reevaluation of the plan is growth. A firm changes radically as it grows and management must be prepared to deal with these changes as they occur.

As with all other aspects of a firm's operations, the exact changes differ from firm to firm, but general guidelines still apply. The most traumatic change takes place when a one-man office becomes a two-man firm. At this point the firm takes its first step away from merely being one man's services toward becoming an organization with a personality of its own.

The personality changes and becomes more formal when the staff reaches eight to twelve. By this time the technical staff are employes and projects are worked on by teams rather than individuals. As a result the firm has to have personnel policies, a steady volume of work, financial controls and the other business trappings.

At twenty-five to forty staff members, the principals must decide whether they wish to continue growing or level off. They are no longer able to be directly involved in every important aspect of every project. A group of competent project managers must be employed and the principals have to develop a more refined sense of priorities so that they can manage by exception. With the introduction of a second management level the firm has become too large not to have all of the most important management tools of large firms: a full-time aggressive business development program, a real accounting and financial control system, a personnel policy program, a formal organizational structure, etc.

By the eighty to one hundred staff level, the firm has wittingly or unwittingly made the decision to grow and it is already a big firm. It probably has shifted from teams to departments and already has added one or more in-house capabilities normally provided by consultants. But this size is an uncomfortable middle ground or "tweener" size. It is too big to have the flexibility of smaller firms and too small to support all of the specialized functions required by large offices. Therefore, it usually must continue growing or return to thirty to fifty.

At four to six hundred, staff reaches its peak, for the personality of the organization achieves domination over the combined personalities of the principals who built the firm. The men who developed the firm as an extension of their own capabilities and interests are gradually replaced by a group of professional architect managers.

At each of these points as well as at many points in between, every principal has to ask himself: is the firm prepared for the changes that are taking place, is it ready for the next stage whether it be growth or a new service, is it still moving toward the most meaningful objectives? If the answer is ever "maybe" or "no," the time has come for another thorough examination. Should the plan be changed or should steps be taken to bring the firm back in line with the plan?

Financial management of the professional firm

"Profit has no place in the practice of architecture!" That was the lofty sentiment repeatedly expressed in response to a recent national survey. But sentiment, unhappily, does not provide the cash required for extra research and design effort, nor the working capital required for growth and for large projects, nor for the salaries currently demanded by both principals and employes. The question should not be *whether* to make a profit but rather *how* to make a profit sufficient to those needs.

Since the various aspects of financial management—profit planning, fees, accounting, management controls, taxes, and cash management—have been covered in detail in a number of full-length books, this article will concentrate on providing a brief overview and setting the general guidelines for answering the "how?" of financial planning and control.

The key steps to profit planning

The first steps, as noted in the previous section of this chapter, are (1) a statement of goals and (2) a plan for their achievement. The process of profit planning is discussed in the AIA publication *Profit Planning in Architectural Practice,* but the essential elements are: a clear definition of the firm's and its principals' financial goals, a budget for every area of the firm's operation and an understanding of the cost-volume-profit interrelationship.

There are no correct or incorrect goals, but typically design firms try to allocate 20 per cent of their accrued fees as pre-tax profit over and above the principals' base salaries. As several AIA studies have shown, however, most firms are actually able to achieve only eight to ten per cent allocation. But according to the published profit achievements of some firms, there is no reason why 20 per cent should not be an achievable goal for most offices.

The percentage objective will, of course, vary somewhat with the second financial goal—the salary target for the principals and staff. Outside of the large firms in the major cities, most respondents feel $20,000 to $30,000 salary plus profit sharing is reasonable compensation for principals. Staff salary targets are, of course, considerably lower even for key personnel. Considering the education, effort, skill, liability, responsibility and investment required of a principal, prevailing small-office targets are too low, and the salaries paid to employes are often absurd even from the selfish management viewpoint of morale and turnover control. More reasonable objectives will, of course, not change this situation overnight, but as a guideline for change, they are an important first step.

Other factors which also have a significant impact on the appropriate profit target are growth plans, client types, and related factors. For example, a firm with ambitious growth plans should achieve a high level of profits to support its increasing working capital requirements, but it also has to spend more in business development, research and other areas to stimulate the growth.

A firm that does most of its design work on large commercial or industrial structures should be able to set a higher profit target than one specializing in single-family homes. Inherent profitability varies significantly, from one building type to another, with degree of complexity.

With these variables in mind, look back through last year's expenses and, based on this record and expected changes during the coming year, develop a realistic twelve-month projection for each area of expense. This analysis should distinguish between direct (project related) costs and indirect (overhead) expenses.

The analysis must then be tied to a budgeted fee volume, for the essential concept in a profit plan is the interrelationship of cost, volume and profit. In the most basic terms this concept can be summarized as follows: a firm makes a profit when the sum of the gross margin (the amount left after all direct project costs) of all earned fees (the amount of the fees earned on all projects whether billed or not) exceeds the firm's indirect costs. In other words, a firm with a constant overhead can make a profit by either having a low volume with a high gross margin, a high volume with a lower gross margin, or, of course, a high volume and high margin.

A firm's profit plan should be a flexible guide for determining at various points during the year which of three basic actions should be employed to keep the firm on target: 1) cutting direct costs to increase the margin, 2) cutting indirect costs to lower the overhead, and/or 3) drumming up new commissions, even at lower margin as in residential projects, to provide the necessary volume. This may seem very basic, but most firms still think that to win the battle of profitability on every project is the only way to win the war of profitability for the firm as a whole. It is one way, of course, but widely fluctuating volume is as great a threat to profitability as is narrow margin.

Fee structures are part of business development

Having developed a set of goals and a plan, the next step is obtaining the required workload. Although the basic guidelines for business development are outlined in subsequent sections on marketing, one essential aspect, not always considered as a part of business development, needs separate emphasis: establishing an appropriate method and level of compensation.

More than 80 per cent of design professionals' fees are set on the basis of a percentage of construction cost. Among the many shortcomings of this method is the fact that it is so arbitrary that it often does not represent an equitable (to either the owner or the architect) compensation for the services provided. As a rule of thumb, many good clients pay too much and most bad ones pay far too little.

Architects are finding now that an increasing number of clients are receptive to many of the other methods discussed in another AIA publication, *Methods of Compensation for Architectural Services*. Of the dozen ways outlined in that book, we strongly recommend the professional-fee-plus-expenses approach developed in accordance with a careful analysis of how much work and associated cost will be required by the project. If the client insists, a guaranteed maximum should be established at least ten per cent above any acceptable lump sum or percentage fee. The argument here, of course, is that the fee-plus-expenses method provides the client with an opportunity to save on the architect's fee if he helps the job run smoothly; but the price of this opportunity is a protective cushion for the architect if the client and project prove unusually difficult.

The current economic slowdown has also re-emphasized one more argument for a method other than the percentage of actual construction cost. Projects are once again coming in under the budget and design firms are finding their expected income seriously cut.

Even when the project cost runs over budget, many clients will refuse to pay the increase. Further, if the architect's consultants are also on a percentage, overruns on their part of the project may also seriously reduce the architect's expected gross margin. Even if the client is not sophisticated enough to analyze the full consequences of a proposed method of compensation, the design professional should be able to explain them.

Accounting and management controls can make the difference

Assuming that the firm has work, and has established equitable fees, the major problem remains how to control the firm's own operating costs. Good accounting and controls do not make money for a firm, but they can be just as important as a successful business development effort in preventing losses.

There are two basic aspects of this area of financial management controls; one is procedural and the other is a matter of firm policy. The procedural aspect is covered in sufficient detail in still another AIA publication, *Financial Management for Architectural Firms—A Manual of Accounting Procedures.* Although every firm has some unique requirements that will lead to deviation from this recommended format, the AIA book's basic accounting procedures will be adequate.

What the AIA book does not cover are some less technical aspects of accounting such as who should do it, how much should it cost, and when should it be automated. The answers to each depend, of course, on the firm's long-term objectives, the complexity of its operations, and, most of all, the quality of personnel involved.

Some rules of thumb are: 1) A small firm (less than ten) probably should use an outside accountant coordinating with a combination secretary/bookkeeper within the firm. 2) If a firm plans to grow much beyond ten, it should plan on hiring an experienced full-time bookkeeper who can draw support during peak periods from a secretary/bookkeeper and advice from a local CPA. 3) If the firm intends to grow beyond 25, it should consider a business manager of at least associate status supported by a full-time bookkeeper and an automated accounting system.

The financial management in large firms should be directed by a full partner with extensive management education, experience, and interest. Again, a very rough guideline for cost would be that the total cost of the financial management area of the firm would run between four and eight per cent of the firm's gross volume. This guideline does not vary much with the size of the firm, for there are few efficiencies of scale. The larger the firm, the more formal is the reporting required.

As a firm's size increases, an increasing amount of the accounting burden should be transferred to a computer. The exact timing will depend on the quality of the firm's staff—the better the staff, the later automation is appropriate. But a growing firm should seriously consider automation when it sees that it will eventually have more than twenty-five employees. The basic reason for this change is that the principals begin to lose their once-intimate feel for all aspects of the firm's operations at about this point, and, therefore, must rely on reports in addition to personal observation in order to continue effective management.

Most of the new reports that will become necessary at the twenty-five man level are management controls rather than basic accounting records. The two AIA publications on Profit Planning and Financial Management also cover this subject—as does one of the American Management Association's better books, *Management Controls for Professional Firms.* While all of these publications have slightly different formats or emphases which reflect the management style and requirements of different firms, there are a number of basic elements common to all control programs. The most important of these can be summarized in brief as follows:

1. *A monthly, accrual basis, profit and loss statement.* Most firms do not get such a statement or if they do it is on a cash basis. Cash-basis accounting is adequate for very small firms, taxes, and cash flow purposes; but it is a dangerously misleading basis for management reporting. For example, on the cash basis the firm usually loses money while it is growing, makes abnormally high profits when it first levels off or whenever a big check comes in, and appears profitable during the first months of decline—all because cash income is out of phase with cash expenses. Therefore, if a firm maintains cash-basis books for tax purposes, it should make the appropriate accrual adjustments when it develops its monthly statements.

2. *The balance sheet.* Most firms do get this report on a regular basis but it is rarely useful as a management tool.

3. *Income projections.* All firms should maintain at least a twelve-month projection of their current backlog of signed contracts to help in manpower and business development planning. One of the most common management shortcomings among professional firms is a failure to foresee and take corrective measures for impending peaks and valleys in the workload.

4. *Project cost controls.* The most commonly discussed but least understood tools are the project cost controls. As was pointed out earlier, job profit—except on a gross margin or "contribution"—basis can be a misleading factor. Therefore, the important thing to control is direct project costs—payroll, consultant fees, travel, reproduction, etc.

   The first step in direct cost control is the establishment of a budget for each project phase. Just as with the project fee, the budget should reflect a realistic evaluation of the time and expense involved. The calculation should not be some arbitrary allocation in accordance with some formula. Many firms, for example, use the AIA phase-payment breakdown, but this tends to front load the income for most firms and, thus, makes the later phases look even worse than they normally would.

   If someone, such as a project manager, is to be held responsible for the budget, he should be involved in its preparation. If he is not, he will claim that any overruns were due to the fact that he had to live with an unrealistic budget which he did not set.

   Once the project is underway, the control system should provide a monthly summary of the phase costs for the most recent month, costs to date, a calculation of the cost to date divided by the budget, and an estimate of the per cent complete. If the cost-to-date/budget calculation exceeds the per cent complete, the project may be in trouble and should be watched.

5. *Indirect cost controls.* By themselves, direct cost controls are not fully effective if they are not accompanied by indirect or overhead cost controls. Each area of indirect expense should be budgeted for a twelve-month period and monitored on a monthly and year-to-date basis. Any overruns or variances from the budget should be noted and followed up.

   The important monitoring consideration is that the reports should highlight the variable expense items—telephone, employe downtime, travel and entertainment, etc.—for most indirect expenses are fixed and as such do not require much monitoring.

Profit and management decisions can be affected by tax laws

Assuming that the firm sets the right goals, maintains the project volume and controls costs, it will make a profit. Because of the existing tax rates, however, as much as half of that profit can be spent on taxes. Therefore, it is extremely worthwhile to have a thorough understanding of the current tax implications of both the firm's operating profits and major decisions such as acquiring another firm, adding a partner, establishing a pension, buying out a principal, or incorporating.

A complete discussion of these matters is far beyond the scope of this chapter, and should be done with an experienced tax attorney or accountant. Tax law is so complicated that seemingly logical or innocent decisions can have severe tax consequences. Even the old rule of thumb that incorporation will save taxes is not necessarily true anymore because of recent changes in the laws. Expert counsel should be able to provide an ethical plan to guide this and all other actions with potential tax implications.

The basic elements of cash management

Ultimately, the goal of all of the planning, control, tax analyses and related effort is to end up with enough cash to operate the firm, pay good salaries, etc. To achieve the desired level of solvency requires still one more planning and control effort. The basic elements of this effort are the following:

1. *Cash flow projection.* AIA publications provide guidelines for this and the other controls noted below. This particular projection is most important when there is any question about the adequacy of the firm's cash resources over the next six- to twelve-month period. It also is a good basis for making application for a back-up line of credit, long-term loan, or a short-term investment plan for excess cash. This last point is important for many firms have short-term cash peaks, but do not realize that their banks can arrange for a no-risk thirty-day investment so that the money does not sit idle in a checking account.

2. *Accounts receivable and accounts payable; aging schedules.* Each month the financial manager of the firm should have a list of accounts receivable and accounts payable spread by age to use as a basis for follow-up calls and short-term cash planning.

More important than any of the above mundane benefits of profitability, positive cash flow, tight control, etc. is that it is a great deal more fun to run a profitable firm. Morale is better, it is easier to concentrate on the important aspects of the firm's practice, i.e., the client's design problems.

Personnel practices in professional firms

The ongoing surge toward unionization of architectural firms and chronic high turnover in men are two symptoms of a major problem within the profession. While architectural firms are as dependent as other enterprises on the work and actions of their staff, this dependency has not been generally reflected in the personnel practices prevailing within the profession. Therefore, the following is intended as a general guide for the acquisition, care and management of architectural staff.

As with the other aspects of architectural management covered previously in this chapter, personnel management cannot be dealt with in a vacuum. A firm's staffing is a function of what it can afford, how it is organized, the type of work it has and hopes to have, and many other factors. Therefore, the planning process, which is the foundation for effective management of any aspect of the firm's operations, should be applied to the area of personnel management. The personnel management plan must, of course, be developed within the context of a profit plan, defined organizational structure, and the many other parts of a comprehensive management plan discussed in previous sections.

The first step is the identification and employment of the capabilities that the firm needs and can afford. In well managed firms this analysis is derived from a balancing of the demands of current workload projections, capabilities required to back up the marketing plan, the expense limits outlined in the profit plan, and the gaps identified in the organizational analysis. The result of this analysis should be a set of careful position descriptions that outline the functions each person will perform, where he or she will fit in the firm, what qualifications are required, a proposed salary range and any related considerations, including future potential.

Even the limited number of firms that do make this analysis often ignore the basic employment procedures which translate employe-need identification into a superior fit of the candidate to the job description. Such procedures should include: an aggressive search; several interviews by at least three members of the firm; and, most important, obtaining references from *all* prior employers. Most firms settle for the results of one or two advertisements or phone calls, a single interview and no reference checks.

Termination is typically even more poorly handled. Few firms cut dead wood when they should, have equitable termination policies, or even find out why the employes did not work out or why they resigned. As a general rule, firms should clean house at least semi-annually, not keep employes working once they have been terminated, provide at least two weeks' severance (or one week for each year of employment) plus accrued vacation, and conduct an exit interview with all staff leaving the firm to identify the reasons for the termination.

Once a staff member has been employed, another set of parameters must be considered in the firm's comprehensive plan—i.e., the employe's needs. One way of organizing a firm's response to these requirements is to relate them to Abraham Maslow's famous "hierarchy of needs." According to Maslow the typical employe looks for the job to satisfy a succession of personal requirements which could be grouped into five categories:

Consider the hierarchy of employes' needs

1 *Physical needs*—usually defined as a living wage and adequate working conditions;

2 *Security needs*—that is, the benefits and policies which bear on health or security;

3 *Social needs*—working conditions and factors with a bearing on communication and morale;

4 *Egoistic needs*—where the employe's self-image becomes an important part of management consideration; closely related to—

5 *Self-realization*—An employe's highest level of needs is self-fulfillment—the realization of personal growth.

Clearly no personnel policies can be related to a single one of these needs nor is any staff or individual employe concerned with only one need at a time. Therefore, an effective personnel management plan considers all five levels.

The wage and salary administration plan

The first aspect of an effort to meet employe needs should be a carefully administered wage and salary administration plan. This, of course, involves far more than a living wage. All salaries within a firm should be carefully related to what is being paid for similar positions by other firms in the area (verified periodically by a few phone calls), other salaries within the firm (there must be a clear logic to the differences in salary), the individual's importance to the firm, what the firm can afford, and what the employe feels his salary should be. All of these factors should be part of a formal semi-annual review of the performance of all employes.

Unscheduled raises between reviews should be avoided unless there is a change in the person's position in the firm. All salary adjustments, promotions, terminations, or other changes resulting from these reviews should be approved by the principals of the firm, but responsibility for the review and recommendation should come from each employe's direct supervisor.

A review of the benefit structure

After wages, most employes are affected by and concerned with the firm's benefit structure which may represent a 15 to 40 per cent addition to their base income. Most of the basic benefits are already provided to some extent in the majority of established firms. In spite of their commonness, however, most firms continue to have to re-invent answers to the basic personnel policy and benefits questions. Some of the most common policy problems are noted as follows:

1. *Vacations*—The common policy is two weeks per year for the first five years of employment, three weeks for the next five and four thereafter.

2. *Holidays*—Few firms give more than two or three days more than the basic local holidays.

3. *Sick leave*—There is no such thing as a good sick leave policy, for some employes use it as extra vacation while others never take it. The firms that have had reasonable success, however, have taken one of two very different approaches. Either they provide a minimum number—usually five or six days per year—and then are flexible about granting more days in case of serious illness, or they have a firm policy of ten or twelve days and permit the employe to accumulate unused time as insurance against major illness.

4. *Other paid leave*—Paid time is often granted for jury duty, registration exams, death in the family and a few other special circumstances.

5. *Overtime*—Over and above requirements of the law, it is generally considered appropriate to pay overtime to staff who have no control over the cause of the overtime requirement. Professional staff that are responsible for the satisfactory completion of a project, rather than performing individual tasks assigned by others, normally should not be paid for overtime. Moreover, all overtime staff work should be authorized in advance and supervised.

6. *Work week*—A small number of firms are experimenting with the four-day work week (four either nine-and-one-half or ten-hour days with Monday or Friday off for all or half of the staff) and appear to be pleased with the results to date. Ellerbe Associates has also placed a ban on inter-office calls and meetings during the first two hours to let the staff get well into its work before routine interruptions begin.

7. *Group insurance*—This area of benefits has become increasingly important to most employes. It is also the most complicated because of the

myriad differences between the many available plans. As a rule of thumb, you get what you pay for. So set a budget, decide what benefits are most important to your firm, and then ask several reputable companies to make proposals (including the state AIA plan, if any). It is important to discuss any proposed plan with key employes—especially if the employes will have to pay part of the monthly premium. (In most firms with plans, employes pay 25 to 50 per cent of their own and 50 to 100 per cent of their dependents' premiums.) The major available features of most of these plans are the following:

Group hospitalization—coverage for all hospitalization where some of the major variables are the amount deductible (typically $50 or $100), the maximum coverage ($10,000 to $50,000), whether the maximum coverage is cumulative or per case and, of course, all of the coverage limits, special coverages, and exclusions.

Major Medical—for major medical expenses is the most common and most important element of all plans.

Dental coverage—is relatively new but increasingly common and is extremely expensive.

Life insurance—other than the $2,000 "burial coverage" in many hospitalization plans is usually set at one and one-half times the employe's salary in the limited number of firms providing this benefit.

Long term disability—plans are often overlooked in spite of their relatively low cost and important protection.

8. *Retirement and pension plans* are extremely rare except in the form of deferred profit-sharing plans. Because of the large postwar crop of architects who are over 45 (and many other factors), this gap in most plans is becoming a major concern in many older offices.

9. *Performance benefits*—Many firms have experimented with a variety of performance rewards and incentives. The most important are the following:

Bonuses are only effective if they are clearly related to performance. If they are allocated in accordance with a formula, most employes regard them as part of their salary. Therefore, in well-managed firms, they are usually limited to senior, key employes.

Profit sharing is usually on a deferred basis, but it is often not regarded as an important benefit by many employes because of the small amounts usually contributed to such plans.

Stock or other ownership purchase plans are often an effective incentive to key employes—even if the percentage purchased is small.

10. *Miscellaneous policies and benefits*—Many or most firms now also provide a dinner allowance for salaried employees working overtime; permit leaves of absence without pay; supply drafting equipment and free coffee; pay 10 to 15 cents per mile when the employe uses his personal car for company business; and pay semi-monthly or bi-weekly. It is usually best for firms to put all of their policies in a brief manual which also includes the firm's history, goals, and other major policies to be given to all new employes.

None of the above benefits will, of course, compensate for a bad working or "social" environment. Alienation and low morale contribute more to many firms' problems than any other single cause. The most common causes are the

How to keep up employe morale

boredom, insecurity and rumors that accompany a long, slow period; a physical and psychological separation between the principals and the staff; general employe lack of a clear understanding of their individual roles, reporting relationships, and perceived performance by their superiors; lack of opportunity for advancement or part ownership; low salaries and non-competitive benefit structures; and, of course, the disillusionment that affects many young architects when they are exposed to the harsher realities of the profession.

The counteractive responses that are most often effective are the following:

1. Early cuts of the obvious dead wood prior to any major slow period and encouragement of rumor-squashing meetings with the remaining staff. If there are any faults that almost all firms share, they are an inability to fire and a failure to communicate basic information to their employes.

2. Continuing principal visibility, participation and employe contact even after the firm grows to where it has a middle management level. One prominent West Coast firm defeated a unionization attempt by initiating a regular meaningful series of meetings on personnel management problems and recommendations with its whole staff participating.

3. Clear organizational structures and reporting relationships. The majority of employes do not like unstructured environments (although some do) and, even more important, they prefer to have what is expected of them clearly spelled out. The Harvard Business School devotes almost an entire personnel management course to the concept of providing all employes with clear objectives and then measuring performance against these goals. On the other hand, formal written job descriptions are rarely useful.

4. Regular semi-annual performance evaluations and, where appropriate, special notice (often in the form of a note, a small cash bonus, a dinner for the employe and his wife on the company, etc.) for exceptional performance in the line of duty.

5. Clear opportunities for growth and advancement.

6. Organization of the technical staff into teams or groups of a size that the employe can identify with once the firm grows beyond 20 to 30 employes.

7. And, of course, competitive and equitable salary and benefit structures.

Obviously, many of the above points relate back to more than the employe's "social needs." Some of them are directly related, for example, to the employe's perception of his own importance. Traditionally, architecture has been long on ego-satisfaction and short on most of the other needs, but this is changing as more architects become employes of large organizations. In such cases, seemingly unimportant things such as titles, recognition of performance, working relationships with the principals, etc. become important substitutes for the ego-satisfactions of the one-man office.

This same theme carries through into the area of self-realization. Few, if any, employes will stay highly motivated if they do not see their work helping them achieve whatever personal goals they have set for themselves. As a result, this is just one more reason why the common denominator for successful personnel management is the firm's recognition and sincere attempt to meet each employe's unique set of needs.

Marketing architectural services

Any architect who wants to achieve a steady or a growing volume of interesting projects (we've already pointed out there is an organizational difference between "steady" and "growing") has to seek new clients and convince them that they should commission his firm. Even those clients who come to him "over the transom" must have had some presentation other than the yellow pages of the telephone directory. A previous job, perhaps? In some way made known?

We have already emphasized the need for developing and following a plan for all aspects of a firm's practice, including business development. What follows is a more detailed introduction to the development and implementation of a marketing plan.

The importance of a successful business development effort was memorably summarized by H. H. Richardson. A wide-eyed mother implored him, one day, to advise her son who aspired to be an architect. "What," she asked, "is the most important thing in architectural practice?" "Getting the first job!" Richardson replied. "Of course that is important," she agreed, "but after that what is most important?" "Getting the next job!" was Richardson's gruff response.

The "how" of business development is not something that can be taught as a series of tricks and pitches. Professionals are selling a service, not an encyclopedia or vacuum cleaner. Each firm has to be extremely creative in developing that approach which is exactly right for it, because a successful professional business development program is one that is molded to the unique personality of the firm.

The first steps in this molding process, as was pointed out in the section on management planning, are an internally consistent statement of the firm's goals and an objective analysis of the firm's strengths and weaknesses. Certain offices may want only prestige projects, the lion's share of which are obtained by what Morris Lapidus has labeled the "ivory tower" firms. But if that is the firm's objective then the architect must chart a realistic business course that will eventually bring his office to a point where he is the logical choice for these commissions. A firm cannot expect to be chosen until it knows how much and what type of work it wants, as well as how to build the strengths and minimize the weaknesses that will affect its selection.

The most important guide in this process should be what is known in other businesses as the "marketing concept." This concept, if it is well developed, can be used effectively not only to help sell professional services but also to improve the quality of the service sold. In simplest terms, this concept has been defined as "finding a need and filling it." Every client has needs which he expects the architect and engineer he commissions to understand and to fill.

How to identify the client's needs

Each client's needs are somewhat different, of course, but there are certain general if not universal expectations. The typical client wants an architectural firm that considers all aspects of the job—function, cost, schedule, esthetics, etc.—and designs effectively to meet the project's schedule. While meeting these practical requirements, the firm is still expected to produce attractive facilities.

Increasingly in today's complex milieu, professional firms are expected to deal effectively with the many management problem areas that affect so many projects. In addition to the normal and familiar procedural areas of management, clients are beginning to expect more and more of the professional's participation in such areas as community relations, prequalification of contractors, project financing, etc.

It is less simplistic than it sounds to say that clients want a professional who is easy to work with. The day of the prima donna has passed and corporate clients especially are accustomed to dealing at well defined levels of authority with the various aspects of their projects. So the professional firm must not only sell its over-all capacity and specialized capabilities to carry out the project, it must also set up those capabilities in a way that will assure the complex client that the project will get the attention of the most senior and most qualified personnel available at key points in the procedure.

While the exact needs of particular projects differ from client to client, groups of potential clients do share roughly similar categories of emphasis in their needs. For example, hospital clients typically consider an understanding of the facilities' operational requirements as paramount. Others, including many industrial clients and developers, rank project cost and schedule as their primary concerns.

Identify the target— then shoot straight

As part of its initial planning effort, the firm should select and concentrate on several potential client and building types. Some concentration is necessary, for as even the largest, most diversified firms know, the broadside approach rarely works. The selection of target building types will naturally be guided by the principals' and staff's interest, the firm's long- and short-term objectives, the competition, the projected volume, whether or not the firm is or could be qualified to handle the project type, profitability, and many related issues.

Part of the process of narrowing the field down to two or more target groups (no firm should concentrate on just one because of the risk) will be research into the major problems facing each group: i.e., financing, operating methods, the need for flexibility, growth potential, siting problems, etc. Also, the firm should find out as much as possible about the strengths and weaknesses of other firms in the field, their presentation methods, the design selection process, and, of course, the target group's basic level of sophistication in construction programing and management—since all of these factors will affect the architect's own costs and methods of doing business.

While all of this research will have the effect of narrowing the field of target groups, *it should not be regarded as simply a search for the easiest windfalls.* The most fertile ground may indeed lie among clients with the most difficult or the most neglected problems. The search, in fact, is for a market for services within the professional's most outstanding potential.

As we move from the general to the specific, the question becomes: "How does one identify and contact prospective clients within the target group?" Many professionals do not seem to realize that there are usually at least three routes to each client: The architect contacts the client; an intermediary contacts the client; or the client contacts the architect. Virtually every successful firm uses all three, and there are neither eithical nor business reasons to favor one over another.

To illustrate typical approaches, let us look at one client group—hospitals. Many people know about a hospital's building plans long before the architect is selected. To name a few: hospital consultants, regional health planning agencies, government (federal, state and local) health agencies, local newspapers, and, of course, hospital administrators.

Aggressive firms interested in hospital work might contact all of these sources directly to ask if they know of any proposed building plans and to express an interest in being of service if and when there is a need for the firm's capabilities. This, of course, implies those capabilities exist and are in some way documented. The direct approach requires backup by direct response to any client's expression of interest. There is another kind of backup implicit in and supported by more indirect approaches, such as attending the conventions every target group has, joining the group's associations and participating in its committees, etc.

One way to expand the potential use of intermediaries is through association with other firms. Several large firms, for example, have made a successful career of lending their national names and impressive experience to local architects who may have certain contact advantages but limited staff credentials for major projects.

The best and most frequently used intermediaries are friends and past clients. All firms should maintain close contact with as many people as possible—especially past clients. To quote one principal of a 600-man firm: "Everything leads somewhere."

The third category, that of client-initiated contacts, is the most desirable but, of course, the hardest to achieve. Most firms who enjoy a large number of unsolicited contacts received them as a result of satisfied clients and one or two well known projects. In fact, virtually every successful "design-oriented" practice can trace its reputation back to one or two early successful projects.

How to get the client to come to you

The impact of many of these projects can be assisted by an effective public relations program. Articles in the trade journals of the target client groups, newspaper features, places on client convention panels, etc. are the most effective. Too often a firm's public relations program is aimed at the design profession's trade journals, which are useful in building a firm's general reputation, but other architects are not clients. So if your building is published in an architectural journal, see that the prestige of that event is made known to the client group as well as to your peers.

One further note on public relations: Robert Townsend in *Up the Organization* noted, "We eliminated the P. R. staff. And we called in the top ten or so people in the company and the telephone operators and told them they were the P. R. department." The same advice applies to architectural firms. Outside consultants are worth their fees if—and only if—they write well, understand design and construction, and know a target client group well. Used carefully, however, to achieve specific tasks—such as writing and placing key articles, advising on the firm's marketing plan, or securing key introductions for speaking engagements—a firm of qualified consultants can be used to supplement the efforts of the firm's own staff.

Whatever the route to a client, the next step is to convince the potential client to select your firm for a project. Although, unhappily, a few projects are awarded on the basis of contacts and pressures rather than qualifications, most are not. In fact, most clients try to choose on the basis of some rational criteria.

Let your presentation show your wares in clients' terms

The major purpose of a firm's marketing and sales planning is to prepare itself to satisfy these criteria better than any other firm. The successful architectural business development effort must achieve this in order to provide the firm with a consistent means of differentiating itself from the many other offices competing for the same project. In other words, if you believe the firm should be selected for a project, find some way to demonstrate it *in the client's terms.*

Each client presentation and its support material should be specifically structured to give easily understood answers to each of the client's primary needs. Leading school boards, for example, want to be reassured on the chosen architect's understanding of educational concepts, his ability to control costs and to have the new facility open for class at the beginning of the school year, the experience of the proposed project architect and principal in charge, etc. If the firm's demonstrable capabilities and experience do not provide these ready answers, then it must work to build its marketing strengths. Some firms do this by such techniques as hiring senior experienced staff; using strong consultants; and preparing special presentation materials. Several can trace large numbers of projects to their decision to take these steps. This is the "marketing concept" applied to architectural practice.

The various client contacts must also take into account who in the client's organization is listening. The late D'Orsey Hurst, management consultant, noted that since fewer commissions are being awarded by a single individual, it is important to distinguish

1. "initiators" who establish the first contact,
2. "influencers" whose goodwill is important but who don't make the final decisions,
3. "permitters" who can narrow the list of firms under consideration,
4. "deciders" who make the final selection decision.

All of those are important, and the contacts with each must be fitted to the client's particular needs. If, for example, one or all of the above are a committee, remember that many committees look for the "safe" decision. As one architect noted, selection committees—both corporate and public—"are as concerned with protecting themselves from criticism as they are in selecting the best firm. If the project is a doghouse, many committees will prefer to award it to a firm that has done eighty previous doghouses, for no one can criticize them for awarding the eighty-first." A firm that best meets all of the client's needs as well as makes itself the "safe" decision will consistently get its share of projects.

Exactly how the effective message is transmitted—by oral presentation, slides, brochures or skywriting—depends on the client as well as the architect's own presentation capabilities. As long as it is relevant, expressed in the client's language, and demonstrates an understanding and interest in the project, it is likely to be generally correct. In spite of how obvious these points are, however, it is a constant source of wonder to us that most firms use the same brochure, slide show, consultants and other "point-of-sale" material and approach for every client contact.

Marketing (the overall planning) and sales (the implementation of the plan) must be a dynamic process. Each project, presentation, new staff member, etc. should contribute to the firm's next project. As a result the firm must continually learn from the answers to such questions as why it was chosen for or lost a project, what does new staff add to the firm's knowledge of a client type, or what changes are taking place in the firm and its potential clients.

How much effort and cash investment should be devoted to all of the above steps will, like all other aspects, vary in accordance with the firm's objectives. A firm with national aspirations will typically spend more than one wishing to stay local and small. Typically the amount spent, including salaries, will range from five to eighteen per cent of the firm's income. Whatever it is, it should be carefully budgeted and then managed in accordance with careful planning and control.

Computers as automated practice aids

How to use automated practice aids, especially the computer, is one of the major management questions facing professional firms today. An architectural firm in the midst of deciding whether or not to use computers in its operations is faced with a bewildering maze of alternatives. To date this maze has been made all the more difficult as a result of the seriously misleading claims put forth by many writers for time-sharing companies, software firms and others who have been promoting automated practice technology.

Some computer applications are feasible in many firms, large and small. Thus, the purpose of this article is to provide an outline guide to answering such typical questions as: should we use a computer; what applications, of the many now available, are feasible and cost-effective; how to obtain use of the best applications available, how to select the right hardware, how much will it cost and how much will it save; and what personnel and organizational impact will the computer have on the firm?

The first question for a firm to answer is, of course, whether or not it should ever use a computer. There are no strict, quantified guidelines. Many small offices have used automated practice technology effectively while some of the largest have not. The rules of thumb identifying those who probably can or cannot use it effectively, however, can be listed:

1. The firm's size is an important factor. Engineers talk of a firm being able to justify approximately $50 to $70 per man per month in computer-related costs. Architectural firms typically cannot justify as high an average figure because of the smaller number of available and relevant applications. A few architectural firms spend in excess of $80 per employe per month, but most cannot justify more than $20 to $30 unless a significant portion of their routine business accounting is automated.

2. The firm's scope of services is also a factor. Very specialized firms—such as those designing only one or two building types—are often able to automate far more than general firms. Those with in-house engineering and other services with high computer utilization potential are also likely users. In general, the greater the number of cost-effective uses a firm has for automation, the more likely it is that it should be using the computer.

3. Since it can be expensive for a firm to first set up to use a computer, many computer applications are restricted to those firms with some spare personnel and financial resources.

4. A firm's geographical and/or business location can also be important. If it is in an area with a service bureau with design-firm experience or if the firm can share a computer facility with one or more other design offices, it is more likely to find automated techniques cost-effective.

5. Individual projects at times justify one-time uses of automated techniques. For example, a large, hospital project can justify special applications in space planning, equipment selection and other areas while an equally large project of an another building type might not.

6. Probably the single most important factor is whether or not there is someone in the firm sufficiently interested in automated practice techniques to take responsibility for making a chosen application work within a firm. Computer utilization—in particular the first few applications a firm tries—is almost never successful unless a senior member of the firm is really interested in making it so.

As the above list indicates, the common criteria for computer use do not exclude the majority of architectural firms. Moreover, by this time there are available automated practice tools for a great many aspects of architectural practice. Unfortunately, the overwhelming majority of the tools available have not been cost-effective nor have they achieved the expected results.

Therefore, a firm's second question should be "what computer applications and automated practice tools are cost- and quality-effective?" There are many applications which meet this test, but it is helpful to remember another rule of thumb: The computer is best used to make large numbers of repetitive calculations or to manipulate large quantities of simple data. It operates as an immensely rapid sorting file.

An integrated process improves cost-effectiveness

Each phase of the plan-design-build process has relevant applications. To date only a few firms have begun to integrate them into a comprehensive architectural system. While ultimate integration is a reasonable objective, individual parts also have proved to be valuable tools for many firms. A review of those with some general applications may provide clues as to where a firm might start.

■ *Architectural programing and planning.* Most of this group of applications require large machines and experienced operators and, thus, are usually only cost-effective if used through a consultant or on large, complex projects that can warrant a major investment. Among the specific applications are traffic analysis, mapping of census data, optimization of land-use within the context of a local zoning code, statistical analysis, space requirement projections, and storage and manipulation of standard functional area data. There are other areas such as gaming and simulation which are occasionally justified as adjuncts to other programs. One important initial planning application open to all firms is financial feasibility analysis. These programs, which test various programing assumptions for privately financed projects, are easy and inexpensive to use and increasingly popular among clients.

■ *Conceptual design.* Very little has been done in this area beyond a variety of space allocation, building optimization and limited perspective applications. By themselves, these tools are rarely cost-justified and are only effective when part of a large group of applications. This is the case because of the cost of the hardware and software required and, in some cases, the need for considerable sophistication in data input by the user.

■ *Design development.* Again this is an area where very few firms have been able to use the computer effectively. There are a number of increasingly sophisticated applications including ones for selecting the structural and design modules, storage retrieval and manipulation of standard room designs, site cut and fill calculations, elevator selection (if not done by the mechanical engineer), and a few other applications. Again, by themselves, these applications usually require too much user sophistication in both staff and hardware to be justified except through a consultant or as part of a larger group of applications.

■ *Contract documents.* A few firms use the computer as a draftsman, but beyond firms with practices that consistently involve projects such as large repetitive multi-family residential, motel, subdivision, and possibly office building programs this area is not cost-justified.

Even automated specifications have not yet proven themselves on either a technical or a cost basis. As in so many other areas, differences in approach between firms, the relatively small incremental savings that can be achieved through any single automated practice application, and the general resistance to change have all combined to minimize the widespread acceptance of automated specifications.

Certain other related applications are also expanding computer usage in these latter design phases. They include equipment and furniture schedules, manufacturers' data retrieval and other data storage, retrieval and manipulation programs.

■ *Construction management.* As has been published in many articles, the most talked-about construction management application—computerized budgeting and estimating—is still in the development stage. The programs exist, but the data for many building types do not. Because of the massive data required, this is one of the areas that should be bought rather than developed internally. No single firm can justify the large expense required. Other construction management applications, such as critical path method scheduling, are widely used through service bureaus and on in-house hardware. And recently, this tool has been integrated with project cost controls to provide integrated construction controls, automated progress payment requisitions, change order control, shop drawing schedules and other tools for construction phase management.

■ *Office management.* This has been and will continue to be the largest application area in design firms. The available applications include financial management (accounting, job cost controls, cost management, etc.), manpower scheduling, and miscellaneous data such as address lists, Christmas card mailing lists, etc. Of these, financial management is the most important and the easiest to solve, but to date no one has. Even the new AIA system, which is one of the best available, is missing some important pieces and is priced in such a way as to limit its cost-effectiveness. Moreover, few firms are willing to adjust to a standard system and, thus, architectural firms use hundreds of slightly different financial management programs. This is a logical application area, however, and should be followed in accordance with the guidelines noted in the section on Financial Management of the Professional Firm.

Manpower scheduling, address lists and other miscellaneous office management applications are only justified in large offices or during unusual peak periods. One final guideline: all of the office management applications combined will not justify any significant in-house installation. If the firm does not have at least an equal number of non-office management applications, it probably should use an outside service bureau.

The somewhat negative tone running throughout the above summary should not be interpreted as meaning firms should not use the computer. On the other hand, it should be interpreted as a warning to be realistic about what areas are really appropriate and cost-effective.

All of the above applications are commercially available. Unfortunately, in spite of their availability too many firms decide to reinvent the wheel. For example, the three-volume Computer-Architecture-Programs abstracts by Teicholz, Stewart and Lee published by the Center for Environmental Research in Boston includes as many as 25 versions of some programs. In engineering, some applications have been written at least 50 times.

This duplication of effort is appallingly wasteful of technical manpower in a field where so much remains to be done. There are many firms that specialize in making this software available and in providing instruction in its use. In many cases, programs that cost up to $20,000 to develop are now available for a small fraction of their original development cost.

Whether the software is developed in-house or outside, architectural users must remember another important rule. The computer program that performs the calculations or sorts the data or projects and moves an image on a cathode ray tube is typically a relatively inexpensive and minor part of the user's problem. This problem is almost always overshadowed by cost and complexity of defining the problem, developing and organizing the data, and integrating the system into the operations of the firm. The cost of solving the latter problems can often run more than ten times the cost of the software itself.

Preparing to use computers can be a major investment

The above costs also typically far outweigh the hardware investment. Nevertheless, it is still important to carefully control the hardware costs. Most design firms have four major options:

1. A service bureau is the most commonly selected option because so many firms already have their accounting done by an outside consultant. There are problems in computerizing these operations, however. In most cases architects are small accounts. Moreover, the service bureau's operations and programing staff is likely to be unfamiliar with the special needs of design firms. The combination of these two factors—as well as others—has led to considerable dissatisfaction on the part of many architect users.

    In response to this, several service bureaus are developing specialized services for the design professions. These firms are usually staffed by design professionals and are often affiliates of major design firms.

2. A few people share computer facilities with several other firms. In spite of the cost-sharing advantages of this approach, it is still a rarely followed option.

3. Some firms use typewriter terminals tied to large time-sharing installations. This can be the most economical approach if the firm makes limited but fairly regular use of large machine applications such as space allocation, information retrieval, and financial feasibility analysis—which require rapid turnaround. The most common mistake made here, however, is to think that the cost of this option is only the $130 to $220 per month for the typewriter terminal and some amount for each time a program is used. There are many other charges such as connect-time, storage charges, program rental charges and others which often are not fully understood until the first bills begin to arrive. It is not uncommon for firms to spend as much on time-sharing as they do for a modest in-house facility.

    A more expensive version of time-sharing involves remote batch entry terminals. These terminals, which permit a firm to quickly enter large input problems such as CPM accounting, detailed cost estimating, and specifications, rent from $800 to $1,800 per month. Thus, they are not typically cost competitive with a local service bureau unless a firm has a very large volume of large machine, batch-oriented problems.

4. Some of the larger architectural firms—as well as a large number of engineers—have gone to in-house hardware. IBM hardware—in particular the 1130 and recently the System 3—is by far the most common. These are predominantly batch-oriented machines suitable for specifications, accounting, scheduling, information sorting, calculations and similar large applications. They are not typically suitable as architectural design tools—even if they have a plotter attached—because they are not interactive. That is, there is not a continuous man-machine interplay.

These installations range from a minimum configuration costing approximately $2,000 per month to installations of a few large plotters, larger memorexes, faster printers and other peripheral equipment that can cost about $4,500 per month.

One firm that has committed itself to the upper end of the in-house hardware expenditure range has helped develop an in-house installation that is also a design tool. Perry Dean and Stewart, in cooperation with the software firm Design Systems and the hardware manufacturer Digital Equipment, have put together a hardware/software combination that permits the designer to interact with a design image on a cathode ray tube. This installation, which costs approximately $4,000 per month, is commercially available but requires a user willing to make the extensive financial and organizational commitment necessary to modify, expand and integrate the system into his operations.

Hardware and software are, of course, only two of the three major considerations. The third is personnel. Not only can the computer require a considerable commitment of staff resources, but also it can have a significant organizational impact. Both must be evaluated.

Most architectural applications and computer installations do not require a large staff. The essential staff are usually one chief—a senior member of the firm committed to overcoming the many potential roadblocks to the successful introduction of the first applications—and one technician—an individual with some programing sophistication, interested and able to deal with the large number of day-to-day problems of implementing and operating any computer application.

How design firms should approach government agencies

A primary key to getting federal or other government A/E work is the formidable but potent Form 251. The following tips on how to fill out and use this form are extracted from the b.i.d.s. Jobletter *for December, 1972, a monthly business acquisition newsletter, copyright, 1972, Building Industry Development Services, Washington, D.C.*

Many knowledgeable architects, engineers and planners are convinced that government bodies at all levels—city, county, state and national—will be the primary targets for business development efforts within this decade. One reason for this conviction is the increasingly important role of government in the financing of design and construction projects, whether or not the governmental unit is the primary client.

The principal of a large East Coast A/E firm suggests that the unhappy alternative to quick adaptation by professional firms to the intricacies of the paperwork, rigid fee schedules and the bureaucratic pitfalls of government work is a full-scale return to in-house design staffs in government departments and agencies. Before 1938, for example, all A/E work for the Department of Defense was done in-house by the Corps of Engineers, unless the employment of an outside design firm was specifically authorized in the legislation funding the project.

While government design projects can be frustrating, subject to unconscionable delays and not very profitable, the fact remains that, if they are to become the biggest if not necessarily the only game in town, one must learn to cope. The first step in coping is to apply for the work. And the first step in applying is to fill out the ubiquitous Standard Form 251. This is the U.S. Government Architect-Engineer Questionnaire and is perhaps one of the most forbidding of government forms, from the standpoint of graphics, general esthetics and length.

A shorter, four-page Standard Form 254 was in proposal phases of development at press time for this book. It was to be supplemented by still another form, SF 255, related to requirements of specific projects. While these forms may in time phase out SF 251, the following will be useful and current for many years.

Tips on preparing U.S. Government Form 251

The first step is to get a supply of blank sets of Standard Form 251. The basic form consists of nine pages, but the completed questionnaire may run to several hundred sheets in some cases. The blank forms may be obtained from government agencies or the headquarters of most professional societies. They also are available in pads of 20 sets from the Government Printing Office in Washington, D.C.—price $1.00 per pad.

The information asked for in Form 251 concerns key staff members and principals, associates and consultants, current and past (completed) work, types of projects for which the firm is particularly qualified and a few miscellaneous questions on such things as security clearances and location of branch offices, if any.

While it is acceptable practice to merely fill in Form 251 and Xerox a few copies for distribution, as long as the basic format is followed and all of the questions answered, there seems to be no real limit to the modifications and innovations a firm may incorporate into its 251.

Where a firm uses a brochure "system," the 251 is usually given a front and back cover to make it fit in with other brochures in the series. The assembled Form 251 may be top- or side-bound with tape or plastic spiral binding.

Even when the 251 is not intended to match or complement other system brochures, a distinctive cover is often used. Some of the most effective covers are lightweight cardboard stock and feature a photograph or drawing of an

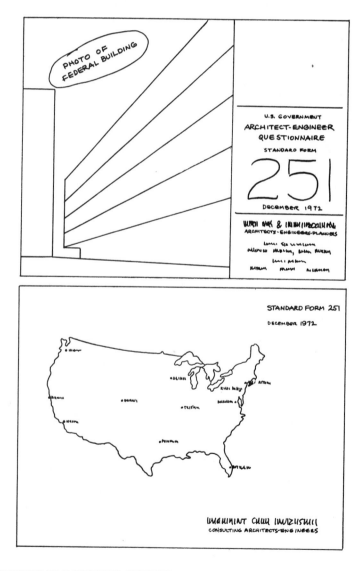

important project, the firm's name and date. If a project photo is used on the cover, it should show a government job. This may seem obvious but some firms who should know better have used office buildings of corporate clients, stadiums and even condominiums to dress up the 251 cover.

One consulting firm uses an outline map of the United States showing the location of its several offices and laboratories; an A/E firm uses the same kind of map to show where it has done work for various Federal agencies around the country.

A few other practical additions to the Form 251 are a table of contents, tabbed dividers to index the several sections of the questionnaire and photographs of completed projects. Surprisingly few firms incorporate photographs into the 251. Among the instructions for completing the Form (Section 20) appears this statement: "Unless specifically requested, submission of photographs is optional. Where submitted, furnish one exterior and one interior photograph of five examples of completed architectural work that are listed in items 18 and 19. (This refers to the list of completed projects.) On the back of each photograph give the following information: 1) Name of your firm; 2) Name and address of client; 3) Type of structure; 4) Location of structure; 5) Cost of specific structure. Photographs of electrical or mechanical facilities and other components of a decided engineering character are not necessary."

Question 13 asks for an indication "in order of precedence, using '1', '2', '3' etc., the types of projects in which your firm specializes." Personnel of Federal agencies who use the information in Form 251 files as a basis of selecting designers and consultants point out that any number other than a "1" by one of the 28 categories listed will normally cause the firm to be rejected for a specific project. In other words, there is nothing to keep a firm from placing second, third and even fourth rankings by some of the categories, but it is a rather futile exercise in getting new business from the government.

Immediately following Question 13 is a block 9½-inches wide by ¾-inch deep (Question 14). Here one is asked to "indicate the scope of services provided by your firm without use of outside associates or consultants on types of projects indicated in Item 13."

Be specific about services of your firm

Far too many firms answer this question with something like "normal architectural services" or "Regular engineering services." Others, feeling that the space allowed for this answer is too confining, say "See attachment" and then use a page or two of inserts to explain in great detail the scope of their services.

Neither of these approaches is guaranteed to accomplish much in selling your firm, although the second method is far better than the first one. Here are examples of how two A/E firms answer Question 14:

1. "We are a total service organization, encompassing all of the pre-architectural and engineering phases, architectural and engineering professional services, and advanced methods of construction management and building techniques."

2. "The firm provides all services within the disciplines of architecture and engineering needed to define and execute the requirements of a building program. These include: complete architectural; landscaping; interior design; mechanical; electrical and structural engineering; planning; estimating; inspection; value engineering and construction management."

Other troublesome blanks in the 251, because they are often overlooked and omitted, are:

1. The box for the date (unnumbered) in the top righthand corner of Page 1. There is another space for the date on which the 251 is submitted under Question 23 on the last page, and both blocks should always carry the date.

2. Signature of the person responsible for the information in the Form 251, attesting that the information therein is a true statement of facts. Strangely enough, many 251's get sent out without this signature.

3. Pages 5 through 8, which ask for current and completed work of the submitting firm. At the bottom of each of these pages is a block asking for the number of projects listed on the page and the total of the estimated construction costs represented by the projects. If these figures are not supplied, as is the case in an unbelievable number of 251 submissions, then someone at the agency must do the compilation if the form is among those being considered for a specific job. As might be imagined, this chore is not calculated to endear the offending firm to the Civil Service employe who has to complete your job.

When the Questionnaire becomes a booklet—as in the case of some large firms—it is worthwhile to include a table of contents. Some offices use lightweight stock dividers to separate the various sections of the 251. Full-sheet dividers usually have index tabs along the right side, which should earn that firm a vote of thanks in government selection offices.

Use normal judgment in submitting Form 251 in connection with a specific project in a governmental agency. If it is a Veterans Administration facility, for instance, you know that the client's primary interest will be in the firm's experience with medical facilities—clinics, hospitals, medical schools, rehabilitation facilities, doctors' office buildings and nursing homes. Always try to put yourself in the potential client's position in preparing any special brochure; then customize the brochure to fit the client, project and special circumstances.

Remember that some of the larger agencies and departments have literally thousands of copies of the Architect-Engineer Questionnaire on file at any given time. Anything you or your firm can do to make the selection process easier and more pleasant will never hurt your chances for serious consideration. Because of the quantity of 251 Forms most government offices must deal with, occasional personal visits are desirable—even necessary—to keep agency personnel familiar with your firm and its qualifications.

Make it a point to revise the Form 251 on a regular basis; schedule the revision for a specific time period. Most agencies automatically clear their files of all 251s over a certain age, on the premise that the information is outdated after a year or so. The preference seems to be for six-month revision, and no firm should ever allow its 251 to get over two years old. This is a primary reason for including the date in a prominent spot on the cover; it is a constant reminder to the firm to revise and re-submit the Architect-Engineer Questionnaire.

A few Federal agencies have begun using a supplementary page 2a to the Form 251. This extra page is to allow easy computerization of the material in block 13. This is in the form of a numbered tabulation by discipline and project types. It should be supplied to all agencies, whether or not specifically requested, because the progress toward computerization may overtake your 251 without prior notice.

After the Form 251 is completed, sufficient copies should be printed to enable a firm to supply all of the Federal offices, agencies and departments to which it might look for work. Make up at least 20 extra copies to use for governmental bodies other than Federal, and for clients to whom you want to give a complete listing of your work over the last 10 years. Used as a companion piece to the regular brochure, the 251 often works as an excellent supplement.

When distributing copies of Form 251 to government agencies, err on the side of over-supply. If an office should get more than one copy, the extra ones can be disposed of, but if there are no copies on file then the design firm is nonexistent as far as the Federal office is concerned.

In summation, there is no prohibition against an application of good design, pleasing graphics and organization in completing the U.S. Government Architect-Engineer Questionnaire—Standard Form 251; a typical, deadly, all-text form which may be vastly improved by a little applied imagination.

Following is a partial list of government offices where current Form 251's should be kept on file.

DOMESTIC PROJECTS: Departments of Agriculture, Commerce, Defense (Office of Chief of Engineers, Director of Military Construction), Health Education and Welfare (Facilities Engineering and Construction Agency), Housing and Urban Development, the Interior, Justice, Labor, State, Transportation, Treasury.

U.S. Postal Service, Atomic Energy Commission, Environmental Protection Agency, General Services Administration, National Aeronautics and Space Administration, Tennessee Valley Authority, Veterans Administration.

INTERNATIONAL PROJECTS: Some of the agencies primarily involved in foreign project development and financing require a form similar to Standard Form 251, but adapted to their own information needs. A.I.D. and the I.-A.D.B. are two examples of agencies with their own version of the 251 Form. A.I.D.'s form, aptly enough, is called "Exception to S.F. 251." Following are typical agencies: Agency for International Development, Inter-American Development Bank, Export-Import Bank of the United States, Overseas Private Investment Corporation, International Bank for Reconstruction and Development (World Bank), U.N. Development Program.

Slide presentations

For many years architects have been asked to make presentations to describe their services to potential clients, school boards, or other public agencies. By utilizing slide projection as their means of visual communication some architects have achieved surprisingly successful results.

When you decide to give a slide presentation for the first time some advance planning will be in order. First, you must determine the size of your audience, and some of the physical aspects of the room you are going to use, and finally, the size of your budget. With these in mind you are in a position to carefully plan and program your approach.

The visual aids that accompany most talks are either difficult for an audience to read or cumbersome to move about. They are generally quite inflexible. Slide presentations, on the other hand, are so versatile as to encourage the use of many diverse elements to tell the story. In short, slide presentations can become a totally creative tool in the hands of an imaginative person.

Planning the storyboard

You can begin to plan your show with a device used for many years by the movie and television industry, called the storyboard. This device makes it possible to plan an entire show in any amount of detail and for any number of slides prior to shooting.

First you will need a master sheet to guide you in programing your show. The best way to make one is to rule off a sheet with two- by two-inch frames and draw within these frames both the horizontal and vertical slide formats.

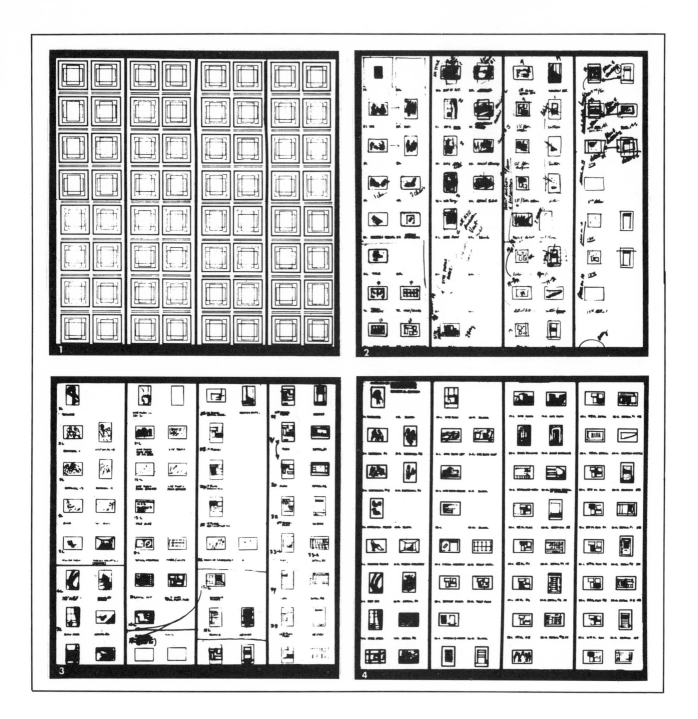

With this as an underlay sheet, begin to plan your show. Start with the opening sequence—for the most important parts of the show and the most difficult to plan are the opening and closing sequences. Then fill in between. Once you have completed a rough storyboard, you will see slides that can be changed around and some that should be eliminated. The storyboard shown here was set up for a double image projection shown side by side. Therefore, the storyboard was laid out in pairs of slides and each frame could be planned in relationship to the other. This storyboard also facilitated the numbering of the slides for their respective left and right projectors, and for writing and keying of the script.

Planning the script

Your script is the mortar that will hold your slides together. Before you actually begin writing, project all the slides in the order you plan to show them. Look at them alone the first time through. Then ad-lib a commentary about the slides as you project them. This will get you involved with the material, and you will begin to see how long each slide should be left on the screen. At this stage, the overall pattern of your show will begin to emerge. All this should take place before you have written a word.

There will be times when you will not want, or need, a caption for a particular slide. Once you have all the captions written, read the script aloud. It will sound choppy at first. Smooth out the writing by analyzing the slides as you read. Strive especially for clarity and continuity.

Building continuity

There are many ways to achieve continuity. Perhaps the most effective is to build a series of slides revolving around a central idea. Shown here is a series of plans depicting various stages of development of a multiple-use land development. The series includes the existing contours and trees, new grades with proposed landscaping, a land use plan showing dwelling units, and a parking diagram. Finally, two stages of a presentation model were shown. These were all in full color using lap dissolve projection. The entire sequence, including commentary, took less than two minutes of a fifteen-minute program.

Creating a story

Behind every good presentation is much experimentation, some selective analysis, and a lot of imagination. For when these shows are brought before the

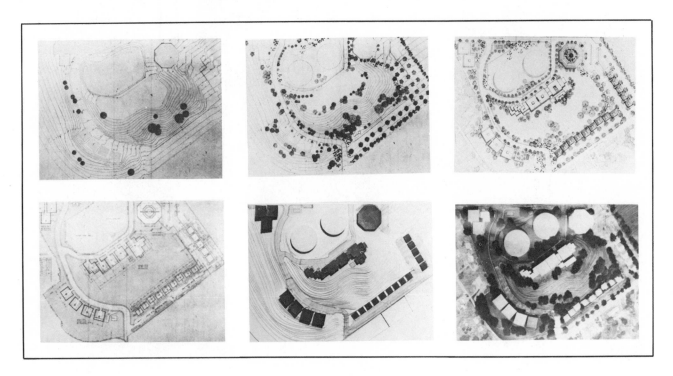

public they must be polished to meet the occasion. The story line must be clear, concise, and convincing. There should be an introduction, a statement of ideas, a development of these ideas and a conclusion.

Preparing the artwork It is always a good precaution to prepare a sample of artwork at a reduced scale and have it photographed to determine how the art will look when enlarged. Any defect on the original, or in the slide itself, will be greatly enlarged upon projection. Lettering on architectural plans will be too small to read. The plans should be reduced to 11 by 14 inches and larger lettering applied on that size. The slides must be very carefully photographed—as out-of-focus, poorly cropped or improperly exposed slides are of course distracting. It is important to work out a shooting schedule early in the program, by working backwards from your presentation date. However, unless you allow time at the end for re-shooting, editing, reviewing and rehearsals, you will be in a rush at the end.

Presenting the show In planning a slide show to present before an audience be sure you are familiar with the physical arrangement of the room. All equipment should be in good working order and the operation of all systems should be second nature. It is a wise idea, when possible, to rehearse your show in the same room a few hours

Façade

Slide Presentation 289

before presenting it. An unrehearsed program will be full of minor flaws which can embarrass the speaker and upset the audience.

The slide presentation "Façade" was designed for entry in a competition. Therefore, competition rules dictated its form. The subject matter was selected for its timeliness in the ever-increasing war on community ugliness. It depicted the story of a group of buildings slated for destruction and the eventual construction of new buildings to take their place. To portray this amount of material on the screen would have required multiple projection, but the competition rules did not allow this. Therefore, all the photographs selected were prearranged, cut out, and mounted on black cardboard. Then the composite was rephotographed onto one single 35mm frame. This allowed up to 250 pictures to be shown on 80 single 35mm slides. Certain parts of the slides were carefully masked to crop off any area not wanted on the composite slide. The end result was a multiple-image presentation using a single projector and a single slide each time. The possibilities of combinations using this approach are endless.

This section on slide presentations is adapted from "Architectural Delineations: A Photographic Approach to Presentation" by Ernest Burden, McGraw-Hill Book Company, 1971, 320 pages. Used with permission of McGraw-Hill Book Company.

Multiple projection made easy

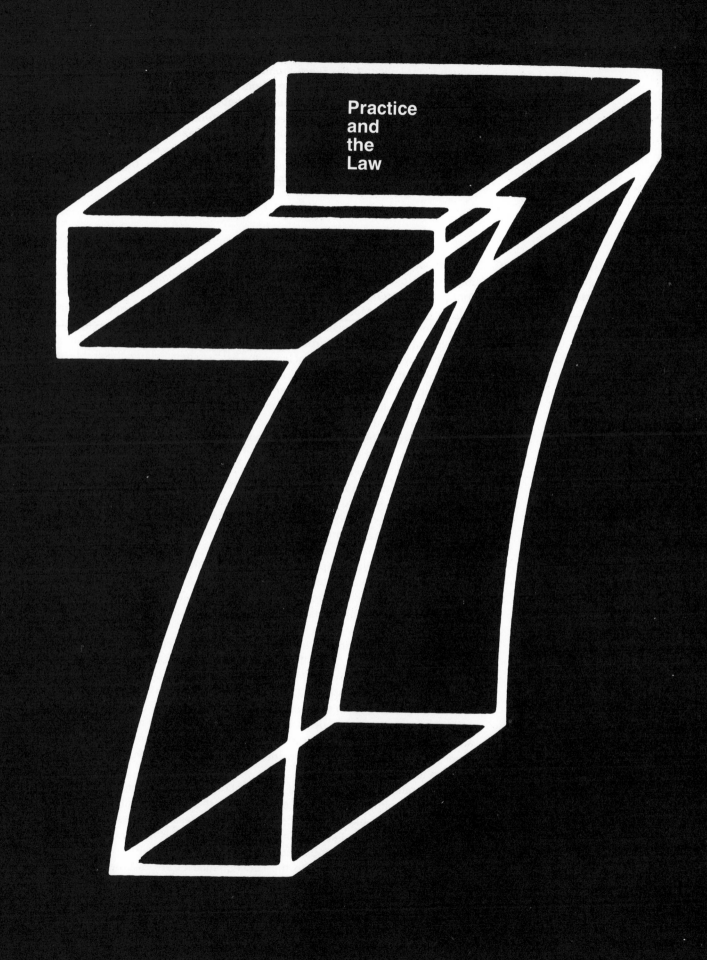

Practice
and
the
Law

Every architectural organization is a structure framed by documents that have precise legal implications. Every architectural commission is a contract with equally precise documentation. The perils of professional liability are all too familiar in these times. For all of these and other reasons, professional legal counsel is an essential element in any architectural or engineering practice.

The following sections on practice and the law clearly cannot substitute for legal counsel. They do, however, review sensitive areas of practice where a little knowledge can prevent costly error—even though that knowledge merely tells the architect when to call in his lawyer.

Legal pitfalls flagged in book for architects and engineers

The following is extracted from the book, "Legal Pitfalls in Architecture, Engineering and Building Construction," by Nathan Walker and Theodor K. Rohdenburg. McGraw-Hill Book Company, Inc., New York, N.Y., 1968, used with permission of McGraw-Hill Book Company. In litigation, common words take on an inflexible precision of special meaning that can leave an architect or engineer with unexpected burdens of liability. The word *including,* for example, is a limiting word in such contract language as: ". . . acts beyond the architect's control, including fire and flood." On the basis of such phrasing, courts have found architects liable for acts other than those following the word *including.* The phrase should have read: ". . . including but not limited to . . ."

That is perhaps the simplest sort of tip contained in this book on legal pitfalls, but it illustrates the authors' unusual sensitivity to language barriers and special meanings. The book is not written in "legalese" but conveys the sense of precision and awareness of legal thinking that can be even more useful than the wealth of detail as to court interpretations that it does in fact contain.

Information is easy to find. Chapters contain logical categories of pitfalls, and virtually every numbered point is listed in a 10-page table of contents backed up by a subject index. Part two offers special forms of contract provisions.

The late Nathan Walker specialized for many years in the law of architecture, engineering and construction, serving as counsel to the New York chapters of A.I.A. and C.S.I. and to the Architectural League of New York. Theodor Rohdenburg, a practicing architect, is associate professor of architecture at Columbia University.

At the risk of losing in condensation some of the exact comprehensiveness which is a virtue of this book, the following extracts of Chapter 1 may provide a useful summary of some of the pitfalls in the owner-architect agreement.

PROFESSIONAL RESPONSIBILITIES IN GENERAL   Each professional (architect and engineer) has an obligation to protect the interests of a larger segment of society than that made up of his clients. In addition, he must be guided by an inflexible sense of fairness in his relationships with contractors and with other professionals and must provide society in general with buildings which are safe and stable.

In preparation of his plans and specifications, and in the supervision of the job as well, if either architect or engineer has the requisite skill and does not use it, he is chargeable with negligence; and if he does not possess the requisite standard of skill, he is liable because of the lack of it. However, these professionals are not held to absolute accuracy in performing their professional duties. They may be charged with the consequence of errors only where such errors have occurred for want of reasonable skill or reasonable diligence.

In soliciting work, or in accepting a commission, each professional represents: 1) that he possesses the requisite skill; 2) that he will use reasonable care and diligence; 3) that he will be guided by his best judgment; 4) that he will be honest. Should he fail in any one of these areas, and injury to person or property results, he may be liable under the law for any damages sustained.

The professional's most obvious and immediate duty, of course, is that established by contract or law. The client has a right to rely on his professional adviser to provide a building which will meet the standards set by the community in order to safeguard life, health, and property. Although the appearance of his buildings is a matter of primary concern to the architect, he does not guarantee to produce a design endowed with beauty, nor one which will be in accord with his clients' esthetic tastes.

IMPORTANCE OF WRITTEN AGREEMENT The right of the architect or engineer to compensation presupposes that there is an express or implied contract between him and his client. Ordinarily, the contract may be verbal. However, in certain jurisdictions (and under some circumstances) the contract must be in writing. The writing is merely evidence of verbal understanding, as a note is evidence of a debt; the indebtedness exists quite apart and independent of the note itself.

CLIENT MAY ASSERT THAT SERVICES WERE FREE The principal reason for insisting upon a written contract is that an oral agreement may not leave both parties with the same understanding of its terms.

One young architect arranged to provide plans and specifications without having a written agreement. Before construction was completed, a difficulty arose, and the architect was discharged. Forced to sue for payment for preparing plans and specifications, the architect testified that his client had expressly agreed to pay him well for his services. However, the client testified that the architect had solicited the job, saying that it would be a great help to him in starting out in his business, and had offered to do all the architectural work without any charge whatsoever. Though the architect was awarded judgment, there can be no assurance that under comparable circumstances the same favorable result would follow. Each case rests upon its own factual foundation.

DEATH OF CLIENT MAY BAR PROOF OF ORAL AGREEMENT Another important reason for a written agreement is that in certain jurisdictions, a partisan witness is prohibited from giving his version of a transaction with another who is deceased, since when death silences one, the law will silence the other.

DANGER IN STARTING WORK BEFORE CONTRACT IS SIGNED A more common mistake, also resulting in a loss to the architect, is to start work on a commission before an agreement has been signed. A single instance, except in detail, is typical of many: An architect sent a written agreement to a prospective client for a large residence, meanwhile starting work on the basis of an oral authorization. Although several reminders failed to evoke more than promises to return the signed agreement "as soon as I find time," the architect completed the preliminary drawings and asked for a conference to discuss them. The client requested deferment of the conference, pleading his wife's illness. It finally appeared that the wife's illness was more severe than had been thought, and the client decided not to build at all—and not to pay his architect, as no written agreement had been signed. Such instances occur so frequently that the architect is well advised to say, "No, I have not started sketches yet, but I am anxious to start. Will you please send back the signed agreement so that we may begin to study this interesting project?"

NECESSITY FOR STIPULATING COMPENSATION Where there has been no request for services, the architect or engineer may not recover compensation unless his services are accepted. One who officiously prepares sketches in the hope of securing employment is regarded in the eyes of the law as being a mere volunteer who may not claim compensation unless his services subsequently are accepted by the client. A request by an owner for services, followed by the rendition of the services, creates an obligation to pay. In the absence of any understanding regarding the specific amount of his compensation, the law will imply an obligation on the part of the client to pay the reasonable value of his services. If the reasonable value of his services is disputed, he would be obliged to entrust the duty of appraising the value of these services to the sagacity of a judge, jury, or arbitrator.

EXTRA COMPENSATION FOR ADDITIONAL SERVICES MAY BE CHALLENGED Is an architect entitled to additional compensation for extra services when his contract is silent on this point? At least one court has denied such compensation under these circumstances. In another case the architect was awarded further compensation for extra services despite the absence of any express agreement to compensate him therefor. The architect agreed to prepare plans and specifications for a building and superintend its construction for a stipulated sum. After accepting plans and specifications prepared under this agreement, the client ordered new plans for an entirely different building on the same site, but on completion of this extra work, refused to pay the architect more than the original sum stipulated in the contract. In this case, the court held that the architect was entitled to additional compensation for the extra work.

In order to avoid any question as to whether the changes involve merely an alternative of the original design, it is apparent that the contract always should include a provision for additional compensation to cover changes of any nature. The standard form of agreement contains such a protective provision.

UNENFORCEABILITY OF AGREEMENT TO AGREE The profession's written agreement or any other document of agreement with the client should state specifically the compensation. If perchance it is not reasonably possible to agree in advance upon the compensation, it should never be stated that "the fee shall be such sum as the parties hereafter shall agree upon," for such an understanding is nothing more than an agreement to agree and usually is considered so indefinite that it is legally incapable of enforcement. But an agreement which is silent as to the amount of compensation is considered in exactly the same light as one which expressly fixes the standard of measure as the reasonable value of the professional man's services, and thus is enforceable.

AGREEMENTS WITH CORPORATIONS AND PUBLIC BODIES Even a written agreement clearly indicating a meeting of minds will not always insure the payment of compensation. Particular care should be taken when entering into a contract with a private corporation. First, the legal right of the corporation to enter into contract should be verified. Corporations are formed for certain specific purposes, and legally they may do only those things which are authorized by their charters. Second, even though it is determined that the corporation has a legal right to make a certain contract, the right of an officer to sign for the corporation should be verified, since in the final analysis it is the directors who normally must approve contracts. Given the opportunity, the professional should obtain a certificate from the secretary or assistant secretary of the corporation, certifying that the officer signing the contract on its behalf was authorized to do so by the directors. If this is not possible, every effort should be made to obtain the signature of the president, rather than a lower ranking officer, since it is usually presumed that the president of a corporation has the authority to enter into ordinary contracts on its behalf with express authority of the directors.

Similarly, caution should be exercised when entering into a contract with a public body; agreements which do not come within its charter or enabling act may not be enforced by law, and often the expenditure of public funds must be approved by the voters.

The foregoing sampling from *Legal Pitfalls* covers less than half of chapter one, which goes on to take up such topics as maximum-cost construction agreements, accuracy of estimates, determining compensation, extra work, etc.

The continuing rise in number and size of liability suits against architects and engineers is generating defensive response at all levels, professional and inter-professional. While professional associations, insurance companies and concerned legal minds research modes of alleviating an over-all condition that now approaches crisis, many architects, for one reason or another, continue to sign contracts and letters of agreement that have astonishing and seemingly simple errors of omission. As a reminder for current use, it may be helpful to review some simple points of contract and liability law, already well established, that architects and engineers should bear in mind.

A summary of legal precautions

Concluding notes to eight chapters of the book offer lists of "don'ts" that provide such a set of reminders and underscore the tricky simplicity that leads many to overlook their importance.

Owner-architect (engineer) agreements

1. Don't neglect to have a written agreement signed by the client before beginning work or undertaking additional or extra work.

2. Don't fail to state in the agreement the amount of the professional's compensation, or the method of computing it.

3. Don't enter into a contract with a private corporation, or a public body, without verifying its right to make the contract and the authority of the signing officer to represent it.

4. Don't use unqualified contract words or phrases to which your client may attribute a meaning other than the one you intend.

5. Don't permit a cost limitation to be established in your agreement, either expressly or by implication, unless you are willing to accept the responsibilities involved. If you are, be explicit.

6. Don't fail to restrict your obligation when it is necessary to include in the contract a reference to cost limitation, but it is recognized that you are not to suffer any penalties if actual cost exceeds the limitation. Be sure the contract says so.

7. Don't guarantee construction costs or permit a guarantee to be implied.

8. Don't overlook the importance of neutralizing unfair contract stipulations making your compensation subject to conditions beyond your control.

9. Don't select a basis for the professional's compensation which is inappropriate to the project at hand.

10. Don't fail to include specific rights and remedies to safeguard you against possible default in payment of compensation, especially in contracting with a foreign client.

11. Don't fail to be definite regarding compensation for prolonged contract administration.

12. Don't neglect to provide for appropriate payments to the professional in the event of abandonment of the project.

13. Don't fail to exercise the most advantageous remedy in case the client repudiates the agreement.

14. Don't forget that, unless specifically anticipated, a change in the member-

ship of a professional partnership may dissolve an *existing agreement with a* client.

Owner-architect (engineer) professional services

1. Don't forget that, because of the technical knowledge imputed to the professional, he should proceed upon the assumption that he is expected to:
   a. Provide a design which is suitable for its intended purpose.
   b. Question the validity of conditions reflected in basic documents such as surveys, when lapse of time dictates a need for review of the contract.
   c. Provide a design which conforms to the governing legal requirements.
2. Don't fail to check and recheck all contract documents to make absolutely certain that no conflicting instructions exist.
3. Don't neglect to have the contracting parties identify, by initialing each page, all contract documents, at the time of signing the contract.
4. Don't assume that the architect is relieved from the duty to exercise his technical knowledge and judgment merely because he makes use of standard contract forms.
5. Don't include in specifications language having no force, but don't delete language necessary to avoid confusion.
6. Don't specify methods of doing work if results are to be guaranteed by the contractor.
7. Don't fail to define all specifications terminology which may prove to be a pitfall for the unwary reader.
8. Don't assume, gratuitously, responsibility for the work of others by incorporating their findings in your own drawings; and when making them available for inspection, don't forget to disclaim responsibility as to their accuracy and completeness.
9. Don't forget that claims of contractors for extras may be successful if the architect's instructions by plans and specifications are incomplete or ambiguous.
10. Don't issue to the contractor instructions that are a material departure from the contract documents, without the owner's written approval.
11. Don't withhold a certificate of payment for any reason not specifically contemplated by the contract documents.
12. Don't neglect to visit the job site as frequently as may be necessary, and to prepare detailed records of these visits for the owner.
13. Don't rely solely on representations of manufacturers as to suitability of materials. Responsibility for selection is yours.
14. Don't serve two masters at the same time.
15. Don't change insurance companies without being assured of continuity of coverage for errors and omissions.
16. Don't fail to ascertain which risks are covered and which are excluded by your professional liability insurance policy.

Responsibility of the professional to public

1. Don't perform professional services, or even offer to perform them, in a state in which you are not licensed, even if the statute merely protects the title "Architect."
2. Don't perform professional services as a partnership in any state, unless every partner is licensed in that state, unless you are positive that you are not violating the law by doing so.

3. Don't forget that the professional may be adjudged liable to anyone who is injured as a result of a hidden defect in his design.

4. Don't forget that an architect or engineer who prepares a faulty plan may be responsible to a third party for any injury caused thereby.

5. Don't forget that an architect or engineer who negligently supervises construction likewise may be liable to a third party who is injured as a result thereof.

1. Don't forget that the architect may be liable to his clients for the negligence of his consultants. **Intraprofessional relationships**

2. Don't neglect to carry professional liability insurance, and to require it of your consultants.

3. Don't overlook the advantages of including the consultant and owner in the same arbitration proceeding.

4. Don't be lax in providing for every foreseeable contingency in partnership and joint venture agreements.

5. Don't fail to define the circumstances under which a joint venturer or partner may or may not act unilaterally.

6. Don't overlook the fact that, despite the absence of a contract between architect (engineer) and contractor, the professional may be given a direct right of action against a contractor by so stipulating in the general conditions or specifications.

1. Don't start work without a contract, in the belief that the starting constitutes the necessary acceptance of an offer. **Owner-contractor relationship: contracts**

2. Don't fail to consider the need for protection against claims resulting from delays for any reason.

3. Don't fail to include in the written agreement every oral understanding.

4. Don't forget that "including" is a word of limitation unless followed by such words as "but not limited to . . . " or "without limitation."

5. Don't rely on a mistake by the other party to a contract to give you an advantage.

6. Don't depend upon custom to establish your right to interim payments; if the contract does not contemplate interim payments, the work must be completed before payment can be required.

7. Don't forget to stipulate that orders for extras, changes, or alterations must be in writing and signed by the proper party.

8. Don't confuse "extra work" (not contemplated in the original contract) and "additional work" (necessary for the completion of the original contract).

9. Don't forget that a contract performed according to only one of two inconsistent or contradictory conditions may be said to have been performed.

10. Don't provide for a guarantee of results and then contradict the intent of the guarantee by other words and phrases.

11. Don't rely upon your own interpretation of a contract to establish your intent, if the contract language clearly establishes a contrary one.

12. Don't change the terms of the original contract until after the relet contract is entered into, if excess cost is to be collected from the original defaulting contractor.

13. Don't forget that a subcontractor, having no direct contract with the owner, is not liable to the owner for breach of contract.

14. Don't forget that the submission of unit prices requires the contractor to do the work for those prices.

Owner-contractor relationship: performance

1. Don't think that performance of a contract becomes impossible simply because it becomes exceedingly expensive, inconvenient, or even absurd.

2. Don't omit to define adequately those conditions beyond your control which would excuse delay or nonperformance.

3. Don't forget that a contractor may recover for partial performance if contract requirements prevent full performance.

4. Don't overlook the fact that a contractor will not necessarily be relieved from his guarantee by owner's changes, and that if the contractor contracts to do the impossible he may be held to his promise.

5. Don't fail to arrive at an understanding regarding who shall bear the loss in the event of a calamity resulting in damage to or destruction of a building being built, remodeled or repaired.

6. Don't fail to be definite regarding whether the contract is entire or severable.

7. Don't fail to arrive at an understanding regarding who shall pay the additional cost arising from a subsequent change in building department requirements.

8. Don't forget that assumption by owner of joint responsibility with contractor involves risks.

9. Don't neglect in disputes under contracts with the government to follow specifically and carefully the avenue for relief stipulated in the contract.

10. Don't rely upon the owner's taking possession as a waiver of his right to damages for defective work.

11. Don't forget that the injured party must make all reasonable efforts to minimize the loss resulting from a breach of contract.

12. Don't blame the contractor for defects arising out of faulty instructions given to him.

13. Don't rely upon acceptance by FHA as proof that the building necessarily conforms to FHA specifications.

Precautions for the contractor

1. Don't forget that by engaging a subcontractor, the general contractor may not avoid duties imposed upon him by statute.

2. Don't hesitate to exercise such general superintendence as is necessary to see that the subcontractor performs his contract. However, in exercising such superintendence, don't control and direct the manner in which the work shall be done.

3. Don't give instructions involving the safety of subcontractor's employes.

4. Don't forget that it is the duty of a general contractor to provide a safe place to work for all workmen, no matter whose employes they may be.

5. Don't assume that engaging a subcontractor relieves you from your responsibility to protect the public from injury.

6. Don't forget that you may be held liable for injury sustained long after completion and acceptance of the work.

7. Don't fail to consider the need for products liability—completed operations insurance, to protect you from liability for damage or injury occurring after completion of your operations.

8. Don't agree to indemnify anyone unless you fully understand the scope of your undertaking and are prepared to assume all of the risks involved.

9. Don't overlook the fact that an indemnity agreement may be so broad in scope as to make you an insurer for the negligence of others.

10. Don't forget to secure contractual liability insurance to protect you in case of liability to the owner under an indemnity agreement.

1. Don't fail to incorporate into a subcontract all of the relevant and material terms and conditions of the prime contract.

2. Don't forget that a general contractor should make provisions in his subcontracts to protect himself in case the prime contract is terminated.

3. Don't forget that the problems relating to temporary heat are such a frequent source of discord that extreme care should be exercised in specifying the rights of the parties under all circumstances.

4. Don't neglect to verify that provision is made for adjustments in the contract price to operate upward as well as downward.

5. Don't forget that the term "when, as, and if" ultimately may mean "never."

6. Don't abandon performance because the other party is no longer a good credit risk, unless your contract expressly permits you to do so.

7. Don't confuse "delay" and "abandonment," or fail to provide for both contingencies.

8. Don't expect to hold your subcontractor responsible for damages for delay if you, also, were at fault.

Relationships of the several contractors

Following are two essays by Justin Sweet, professor of law, University of California, Berkeley. Each suggests a different mode of group action on the part of professionals and others in the building design and construction fields. Both are timely against a background of increasing group activity, not only among professionals in their attempts to solve liability insurance problems, but also among labor unions which are gaining wider experience with both local and national legal cost insurance programs.

Professor Sweet's first essay proposes just such new methods for securing legal services for architects and engineers, not only against the crisis situations of "third party suits" so hazardous today, but also for firm organizational matters, contractual agreements, tax advice and other items for which small firms, especially, may have had misgivings as to the cost of legal service.

The second essay offers another approach to reduced liability, also by the concerted action of professionals, but in this case as organized citizens seeking amendments to Workmen's Compensation laws to preclude third party action by workmen against multiple participants in construction projects, including architects and engineers.

Professor Sweet is author of the book, "Legal Aspects of Architecture, Engineering and the Construction Process," West Publishing Co., 1971.

New approaches to liability and legal service costs

Some recent case decisions have held the architect liable for construction-connected injuries resulting from unsafe construction methods. Liability is rested principally upon the architect's power to condemn defective work and

Reduce nuisance claims by amending compensation laws

stop performance. To meet this expanded liability, the architectural profession has included in its contract forms language which attempts to make it clear that the contractor has the responsibility for construction methods.

Whether such contractual attempts will succeed is uncertain. Another process to reduce liability has been ignored by the architectural profession.

Most victims of construction accidents are workers on the project. An injured worker usually recovers workmen's compensation benefits from his employer's compensation insurance company. Often he sues any persons *other than his employer* whose action or inaction in some way caused the injury. For example, an injured employe of a subcontractor often sues the prime contractor, other subcontractors, the architect, the engineer and the owner. In addition, if his injury appears to have been caused by defective material or equipment, he often sues the manufacturer or supplier of the material or equipment.

The multitude of defendants causes a complicated lawsuit. The legal action becomes even more complicated because of indemnification. Typically, an owner who is sued will seek indemnification from the architect and the prime contractor. The architect often seeks indemnification from the prime contractor and sometimes the owner. The prime contractor often seeks indemnification from the subcontractor. The result is a hopelessly complicated lawsuit.

Note that the injured employe *does not* sue his own employer. To understand the reason for this, it is necessary to review briefly the history of Workmen's Compensation laws.

Prior to the enactment of these laws, injured industrial workers had great difficulty in recovering for their injuries. The worker had to establish negligence on the part of his employer, often a difficult thing to do. Even where the worker could establish negligence, he would lose if it could be established that he had knowingly assumed the risk of the injury, or was guilty of contributory negligence, or if the injury occurred because of the negligence of a co-employe. As a result, many injured workers were uncompensated.

Workmen's Compensation laws were designed to give the injured industrial worker a quick and certain compensation for work-connected injuries. He only had to show that he was injured in the course of his employment.

Workmen's Compensation laws often involved legislative compromise. For example, to compensate the employe for taking away defenses employers had prior to the enactment of Workmen's Compensation, these laws typically limited the employe to his Workmen's Compensation remedy against his own employer. The injured employe could not bring a tort action based upon negligence against his own employer. In addition, those who developed the Workmen's Compensation system wanted a closed system which would keep such matters out of the courts.

But despite the desires for a comprehensive or closed system, workers were permitted to sue *third parties* whose negligence or defective products caused the injury. The industrial worker has difficulty finding third parties he can sue. Perhaps he can sue the manufacturer or supplier of any defective material or equipment involved in his injury, but third party claims have been uncommon in industrial accidents.

On the other hand, the injured construction worker finds a more fertile field for third party actions because of the number of different parties involved in a construction project. While laws affecting the results vary somewhat from state to state, the injured construction worker usually has the option of suing other contractors on the project, the architect, the engineer, the owner and suppliers or manufacturers of defective material or equipment. The only person he cannot sue is his own employer.

In some states, injured employes of subcontractors cannot sue the prime contractor. This is because of "subcontractor under" statutes. Such statutes make the prime contractor "the statutory employer" of subcontractor employes. The injured subcontractor employe often can bring a Workmen's Compensation claim against the prime contractor under these statutes. The corollary is that in some states the statutory employer cannot be a defendant in a third party action.

Indemnification further complicates workmen's compensation claims. Typically, there is a chain of indemnification clauses starting from the owner and ending with the smallest subcontractors. Through such indemnification the employer of the injured employe may have to ultimately bear the loss in the tort claim despite Workmen's Compensation laws precluding the injured employe from suing his employer.

A few states preclude third party actions against those in a common employment. For example, in Massachusetts, ordinarily an injured employe of a subcontractor cannot bring a third party action against another subcontractor or the prime contractor on the project.

Employe claims can be substantially reduced by amending Workmen's Compensation laws to preclude third party action against participants in the construction project, including architects and engineers.

Proposals of this type would encounter opposition. Lawyers who make their living from third party injury claims would oppose curtailing such actions. Also, some believe that Workmen's Compensation laws do not provide an adequate remedy and that third party claims can supplement deficient awards in order to adequately compensate the injured worker. For this reason any proposal for limitation of third party rights must be accompanied by legislative change which would make Workmen's Compensation awards adequate.

Architects and contractors, the main defendants of third party actions, should join forces to make an adequate and fair Workmen's Compensation program the exclusive remedy for construction injuries to workers.

New methods of securing legal services

Law and legal institutions play an increasing role in the professional lives of architects and engineers. Professional liability is expanding. A troubled economy means a greater likelihood that an architect will have to use the legal system to collect his fee. Mechanics' lien laws, public land use controls and licensing laws often require contact with the legal system. It is important that architects and engineers obtain quality legal services at a cost they can afford.

Traditionally, professional people seek legal advice only when they are in trouble and feel they cannot handle the matter themselves. While lawyers do play a significant role in planning, i.e., drafting and reviewing *important* contracts, partnership agreements and incorporation papers, generally architects and engineers seek legal advice when they must go to court.

This reluctance to consult lawyers except in a crisis often is due to the fear of high fees. Young architects whom I have taught often tell me that I taught them when they *should* seek legal advice, but they simply cannot afford it. Fear of high fees is not always justified. Architects may not realize that some lawyers base their fee on ability to pay, with the expectation that when the architect is more prosperous he will continue to use them. Yet it is clear that many architects do not seek needed legal advice.

There is another reason why architects often hesitate to use a lawyer for organizational services. When an architect is sued for a specific sum or sues for his fees, he knows what is at stake and he knows not only that he must have legal service but that the stakes are high enough to justify the fee. However, in organizational matters, such as drafting partnership agreements or professional service contracts, it is difficult to know how to place a dollar value on the legal services.

Finally, architects are fearful that the unscientific way a client often selects his lawyer (by reputation or through the yellow pages) will bring them an attorney who does not understand their problems or is not skilled in the matters vital to them.

We need more efficient methods of furnishing legal services to architects and engineers. Modern methods of obtaining medical services are a useful analogy.

The medical clinic, with a high degree of specialization and efficiency, provides the patient with almost complete service. Also, there is an increased use of large scale group health plans under which the subscriber pays a fixed monthly amount plus a small amount for each visit.

Finally, the medical profession is at last recognizing that far more general benefit can be accomplished by a comprehensive program of preventive medicine through public health controls than by occasional spectacular operations. We admire the skill by which highly specialized doctors perform operations that have never been performed before. Yet such operations affect a small number of people and come at an extraordinarily high cost. Some of that cost might be better spent by comprehensive use of public health to reduce or eliminate disease and accidents.

There have been modest changes in the way the legal profession has performed its work. For example, many large institutions are finding it more efficient to have salaried lawyers on their staff who are close at hand, are familiar with their problems and can perform fast and efficient service at a calculable cost.

Legal service to the poor is another illustration of a shift in legal services. One interesting aspect of this type of practice is the increasing tendency to periodically use communications to inform the poor of their legal rights in terms they can understand.

Groups of clients with similar needs and resources can be the instrumentality by which better legal services can be obtained. For example, suppose a group of architects or engineers banded together to secure legal services. Such a group could enter negotiations with a law firm with the present or potential expertise in legal matters most relevant to architects and engineers. Such negotiations would culminate in a "master" or "group" contract for furnishing legal services. This contract would encompass the types of services to be performed and methods of financing these services.

The law firm would provide group members with well trained personnel who would assist them in drafting or reviewing partnership agreements, incorporation papers, standardized and specialized contracts and give them advice in tax matters.

A vital aspect of group practice would be the periodic audit. The analogy to the medical profession is again useful. There is an increasing tendency for group health plans to provide a low cost, yearly physical examination for all its members.

An audit could be done once or twice a year. It could consist of the auditing team reviewing agreements used by the client. The team could check selected files to see if matters were and are being handled properly. The team would check for compliance with the multitude of laws applicable to architects who have employes. For example, architects and engineers often get into difficulty because they do not pay their employes time and a half for overtime under the Fair Labor Standards Act.

The auditors would also look to see whether the group member has adequate public liability insurance, professional liability insurance, property damage insurance and workmen's compensation insurance.

The group members could pay specified monthly amounts for these services. The amount could be determined by the gross billings of the firm or by the number of the employes. Such a monthly payment would enable the firm handling legal matters for the group to develop an adequate library, to build and train an adequate staff of lawyers, and to provide for the overhead which such service would entail.

In addition to the monthly fee, group members would pay a designated amount for specified legal services such as reviewing contracts, handling litigation, providing periodic audits, etc. The monthly amount, if large enough, could mean that certain types of services will be provided without additional charge. If the amount specified for the monthly fee is small, then this would mean a higher charge for designated services. Much depends upon the size of the group and range of services furnished to it.

We must broaden the service and planning aspects of legal services and provide a financing mechanism which will enable group members to receive these services at a cost they can afford. (Some labor unions are starting to use a prepaid legal fee insurance with payments deducted from their wages.) Interested architects and their professional associations should take the lead in developing such a group legal services program.

Let's clear up laws on copyright of plans

Although not mentioned expressly as a separate category in the statutes, architectural plans, drawings and models are clearly copyrightable under the present copyright laws under the specified class of "drawings or plastic works of a scientific or technical nature." This is recognized by regulations promulgated by the Copyright Office which has, in fact, made many registrations of copyright claims of architectural plans.

The basic difference between a common law copyright and a statutory copyright is that a common law copyright exists solely in unpublished works. Statutory copyright (with certain specific exceptions) exists only in published works. Common law copyright protection is automatically accorded to all unpublished works from the moment of their creation. The mere act of publication (submission for bids) will not automatically grant statutory protection to a work; there must be, in addition, strict compliance with the statutory formalities. Common law copyright protection is perpetual. Statutory copyright is for a term of years. Common law copyright is regulated by the several states. Statutory copyright is solely a matter for the Federal Government.

If someone infringes your copyrighted plans, he may be enjoined from the making or sale of the infringing plans and his copies may be destroyed, and he may be compelled to pay damages to you, the copyright owner. These damages include the damages you have suffered, as well as any profits the infringer may have made as the result of the infringement. In lieu of these actual damages and profits, the court may assess certain statutory damages. This amount is not less than $250 or more than $5,000. In addition, there are criminal penalties provided for infringement. An infringer may be liable for imprisonment up to one year and a fine of $1,000. This same fine may be levied against anyone who fraudulently inserts a copyright notice on plans which are not copyrighted or who fraudulently removes a copyright notice from a copyrighted work.

If someone infringes your copyrighted plans, how soon must you take action against him? You should institute your action as promptly as possible but you must bring the action within a three-year period. However, you are expected to take all reasonable steps to minimize any loss you may suffer. The best rule is to act immediately.

Once you get your plans copyrighted, the copyright is good for 28 years and may be renewed within the year just prior to the 28th anniversary of the date of first publication. This renewal period is also for 28 years, but you must file your renewal or the work then falls into the public domain.

You do not have to register your plans when you publish them, but in order to be protected by copyright, the plans must contain the correct notice of copyright in the proper position. But unless the copyright is registered, you cannot go into court and protect your rights against infringement. You cannot renew a copyright unless you secure an original registration.

In the event that you do copyright your plans, you can protect yourself, and you should, by inserting the required copyright notice on the plans prior to filing them with any building department. It is no hardship to do this, and there is really no excuse for failure to have a copyright notice on your plans. This copyright notice serves as a warning to the public that the plans are protected by copyright, and such notice prevents innocent persons from being guilty of copying a set of plans which are claimed by the owner to be protected by his copyright. The copyright notice serves the further purpose of informing the public of the date of first publication, which in turn determines the duration and extent of the monopoly granted by the statute to the proprietor of the copyright. The case law indicates that the publication of plans with notice of copyright is the essence of compliance with the copyright statute, and publication of the plans without such notice amounts to a dedication to the public sufficient to defeat all subsequent efforts at copyright protection. *Sieff vs. Continental Auto Supply,* D.C. 39 Fed. Supp. 683.

Copyright of plans is not an exclusive right to build

You should remember that the protection extended by Congress to the proprietor of a copyright in architectural plans does not encompass the protection of the buildings or structures themselves, but is limited only to the plans. The Copyright Act is silent on this point. However, it appears to be the unanimous view of respected text writers that under the current copyright laws of the United States, the architect does not have the *exclusive* right to build structures embodied in his technical writings. Ball, in his work on copyrights, says that a close analogy exists between an "architectural work of art" and a case involving a copyrighted catalogue containing illustrations of dresses, in which it was held that the protection did not prevent the copying of dresses and did not even prohibit their illustration in another catalogue after they had been copied. *National Cloak and Suit Co.* vs. *Standard Mail Order Co.* 191 Fed. 528. This interpretation as applied to architect's plans would permit the copying of a constructed building and the subsequent use of plans which might closely resemble the originals. Protection would be limited to the unauthorized copying or use by another of the original plans themselves. In the case of *May* vs. *Bray* (30 Copyright Office Bulletin 435), the court permanently enjoined the defendant's printing, copying, use or imitation of the plaintiff's copyrighted architectural blueprints for a certain type of ranch house. The court held that the plaintiff's copyrighted plans had been infringed by the use by the defendants of the drawings, and that the defendant had constructed houses in a tract, which were so similar in appearance to the plaintiff's copyrighted plans as to mislead the public into thinking that they were genuine houses of the plaintiff.

This view is further substantiated by a study published by the United States Copyright Office where, in summary, it is stated that copyrighted architectural plans are not now protected against their use in building a structure with the possible exception of a structure which would qualify as a work of art. Various revision bills introduced in Congress between 1924 and 1940 contained provision for the extension of the protection afforded to architects, but so far none of these bills has been enacted by Congress.

What are the rights of the parties where the structure is copied from a plan? In *Muller* vs. *Triborough Bridge Authority,* D. C. N.Y. 43 Fed. Supp. 298, it was held that the design, plan, construction and operation of the approach to the defendant's bridge did not infringe the plaintiff's copyrighted drawings "of a scientific or technical character" which depicted a "novel bridge approach", originated by the plaintiff "to unsnarl traffic congestion". The system of ramps, viaducts, loops, and traffic lanes, jointly described as a traffic separator, comprising the approach, took care of the traffic at the Rockaway Beach end of the bridge, so that all lanes of traffic could move without crossing or being interrupted by other lanes of traffic at that point. The court first found that although the plaintiff's drawings and the design of the defendant's bridge approach were similar, the defendant had not actually appropriated any part of the plaintiff's copyrighted work, saying that the design for the defendant's bridge approach was independently conceived and executed by the defendant's engineers.

You may need a patent instead of a copyright

The court said, however, that even if it were assumed that the defendant actually used the plaintiff's copyrighted drawing in designing and constructing the bridge approach, the plaintiff would nevertheless be without any remedy, under the principle of the cases deciding that a copyright does not protect against use of the system, method of operation, invention, discovery, or idea described in a copyright work. Thus in this case, the court said that the plaintiff's copyright did not prevent anyone from using and applying the system of traffic separation set forth in the drawing. Accordingly, the complaint was dismissed. The whole point of the opinion here was that the only way the plaintiff could secure adequate protection to the art which he sought to protect was to obtain a patent, rather than a copyright. The court based its view on *Baker* vs. *Sullivan* 101 U.S. 99, wherein the court held that a claim to the exclusive property in a peculiar system of bookkeeping cannot be maintained under the law of copyright by the author of a work in which the system is exhibited and explained. The Supreme Court said that protection was the function of letters patent, not copyright. The claim to an invention or discovery of an art or manufacture must be subject to the examination of the patent office before an exclusive right can be obtained and it can only be secured by a patent from the government.

In 1962 in *De Silva Construction Corp.* vs. *Herrald* (1962 D.C. Fla. 213 Fed. supp. 184) it was recognized that the protection which is extended to the proprietor of a copyright in architectural plans is limited to the plans themselves and (with the possible exception of a structure which would qualify as a work of art) does not give the architect the exclusive right to build the buildings or structures embodied in the plans. The court pointed out that a building is not a copy of the plans for the building, and that to build a structure from the copyrighted architectural plans is not an infringement of the plans themselves. The court further stated that the law is clearly contrary to the position that an architect who has copyrighted his plans is entitled to the same protection as authors of musical compositions and dramatic works who have copyrighted their works.

In commenting upon the case of *Muller* vs. *Triborough Bridge Authority* mentioned earlier, the court said that the underlying rationale of that case seemed to be that a copyright on a drawing or a picture of a nonartistic object of utility does not preclude others from making the three-dimensional object portrayed in the drawing or picture. The court observed that the situation was analogous to the trade catalogue cases deciding that the copyright in the picture of a product is not infringed by making the product depicted. The court further said that it could not read into the copyright laws something which was not there; and that until Congress should decide to extend the protection afforded to architects, there was no basis in law to grant such an extension.

All this, as you can see, is very discouraging when it comes to really protecting your rights in your plans by copyrighting them. But fortunately in 1967 a case was decided which may give some future hope for the value of actually copyrighting architectural plans. This is the case of *Scholz Homes Inc.* vs. *Maddox.* 379 Fed. 2nd 84. In that case, while the plaintiff was not successful because the court found that neither defendant utilized the plaintiff's copyrighted plans, nevertheless the court had some constructive views which may prove pertinent in subsequent litigation. The court indicated that copyrighted architectural plans should be treated differently from copyrighted books, and that the principles enunciated by the Supreme Court in the *Baker* case should be held inapplicable to copyrighted plans. The only protected category into which the Supreme Court could fit the treatise on bookkeeping, the subject of that case, was that of "books", and it was obvious to the court that the book in question had been written for the purpose of instructing others in the art of bookkeeping. It is far less obvious that architectural plans are prepared for the purpose of instructing the general public as to how the depicted structure might be built. Rather, they are often prepared so that they may be used in the building of unique structures, or at least structures limited in number. If the copyright statute protected purely against the selling of plans instead of against their unauthorized use, it would therefore fail to afford a form of protection architects might strongly desire. This protection would most effectively be provided by holding the unauthorized construction of a building according to a copyrighted plan to be an infringement. If, said the court, the *Baker* case is to be followed to the extent of holding that the possession of the copyright on the plans gives no exclusive right to construct the building, then protection could be provided by declaring the making of unauthorized copies of the plans to be an infringement in itself.

State when your plans depict a work of art

If the architectural plan or drawing is copyrighted as a work of art under Section 5(g) of the Copyright Act, rather than simply as a scientific or technical work under Section 5(i), the copyright proprietor is given the exclusive right to complete, execute and finish it. Hence, it would seem to follow that one who wrongfully builds a structure from plans copyrighted under Section 5(g), would infringe the designer's "completion" and "execution" rights. In *Jones Brothers Co.* vs. *Underkoffler,* 16 Fed. Supp. 329, wherein a cemetery monument was deemed properly copyrightable under Section 5(g) as a design for a work of art, the defendant's construction of a similar monument from the copyrighted plans was held to constitute an infringement. The court said that the test of infringement in such a case is whether the defendants have made an original, independent production or a copy of the plaintiff's work. The court noted that the testimony showed that the work of the defendant was not original but that it was copied, with several changes, from the copyrighted work. The evidence showed that the design from which the defendant's monument was made was traced from the copyrighted design.

Architects should seek opportunities to point out to legislators that plans are neither publications nor commodities, but represent unique designs for which protection is required by clarified or new laws.

Drawing
and
Drafting

Architectural drawing for printing processes

The drawing medium controls the processes by which it can be reproduced. Black line on white is simplest. Gray shades require halftone reproduction. Full color requires a much more complex process of film separation and superimposed reproduction.

Drawing has two modes: one that is conceptual and free-hand; and another that is precise to the degree necessary for construction documents. Both of these modes are likely to require reproduction, sometimes at greatly reduced scale, in order to make them effective in their primary role—communication.

Scale is no strange concept to architects. And yet the simple knowledge that a fine line on a large drawing becomes super-fine to the vanishing point when normal reduction to page size is required too often escapes the attention of the renderer.

Or again, the exquisite detail, endlessly repeated, consumes inordinate time in a hand process that modern techniques could shorten without loss of quality. Those are some of the considerations of this section by Mildred F. Schmertz, AIA, a senior editor of Architectural Record.

If drawing is the language of architecture, the means by which conceptions yet to be built are communicated and made real; if these conceptions must be duplicated many times and widely disseminated for architecture's sake; if the art of printing serves other languages well, then more architects should learn its secrets and begin to draw according to its demands.

Like a medieval scribe, absorbed in the creation of a manuscript page, choosing to ignore Gutenberg's movable type, and preferring to perfect his calligraphy, an architect will make a beautiful drawing to show a client, without giving a thought to its subsequent usefulness in a magazine, newspaper or brochure.

The disappointment he so often experiences when he sees his work in printed form could be avoided if he were to consider the published appearance of his drawing while he is doing it, making it compatible with the available printing process and the specific size requirement in such a way that it would be *at its best in print*. A different version of the same basic drawing could of course be developed in another manner to be shown as an original to impress the client.

The architect will argue with good reason that neither he nor his staff has time to make one set of drawings to overwhelm the client, another set to look just right in a brochure, and hopefully a third to suit the specific requirement of a professional magazine about to do a feature story on the project. He will then put all his effort, time and money into one set of originals for the client, and hope that, if necessary, they can be reproduced some way. And of course if money is no object they *can* be reproduced, in the manner best suited to them, beautifully, in all the original colors or black and white, in a handsome size on splendid paper. As a general rule, however, drawings which are too expensive to reproduce, don't get reproduced. Although Frank Lloyd Wright survived to his 90th year, he didn't live long enough to see his colored pencil renderings properly printed. The luxurious book, "Frank Lloyd Wright Drawings for a Living Architecture," financed by the Bear Run Foundation and the Edgar J. Kaufmann Charitable Foundation, appeared shortly after his death and finally did graphic justice to his masterly hand.

There are three simple ways out of the dilemma of how to draw for both client and printer, while trying to save time and money. The first way is to do as many architects do and make use of a good tempera and wash renderer. These artists, while working in full color to please the client, carefully control their tones in terms of the gray scale, so that their productions reproduce fairly well in an 8-by 10-inch black and white photograph which is then made into a halftone. Photographs of this type of drawing are usually included in press releases and appear in the newspapers and the news sections of the professional magazines. Unless exceptionally well done, these drawings lack character and quality in printed form and have very little vitality on the page.

Drawing for halftone engravings will be discussed more fully in a subsequent section. The methods described here are all intended for line engravings. In halftones the entire drawing including the lightest and darkest tones is screened into a series of dots. It is possible for the engraver to drop out the light tones

Portions of drawings by Ara Derderian shown full size here and greatly reduced on opposite page.

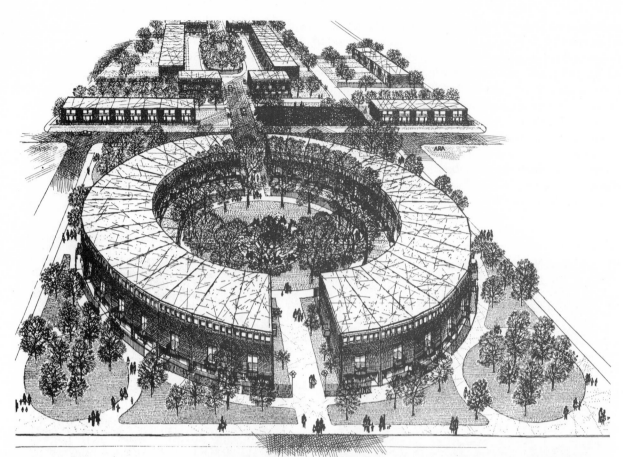

Above: Drawing showing an early scheme designed by I. M. Pei for Webb & Knapp's Hyde Park, Chicago development. *Right:* Lincoln Center. Both drawings are by Ara Derderian. The degree of reduction in each can be seen by examining the full size portions on page 137. Line weights and cross hatching were made bold enough not to fuse into black or disappear in extreme reduction. Included in the Lincoln Center drawings are Philharmonic Hall by Max Abramovitz, The New York State Theater by Philip Johnson Associates, the Metropolitan Opera House by Wallace K. Harrison, the Vivian Beaumont Theater by Eero Saarinen and Associates, and the Juilliard School of Music by Pietro Belluschi and Catalano and Westerman

Drawing for a presentation booklet for the Gehag Redevelopment, West Berlin. The Architects Collaborative International Ltd., Architects.

to read white and intensify the darkest tones to read black, but each of these steps is progressively more expensive. In line cuts blacks are black and whites are white and grays are made by patterns of black. Line cuts are generally simpler and cheaper to make. Techniques suitable for halftone reproduction are: line and wash drawings, pencil studies, wash drawings and tempera techniques. Those suitable for line cuts, all of which are demonstrated in this article, are: pen and ink line drawings, brush drawings in ink, lithographic crayon on Ross board, scratchboard drawings, and pen and ink line drawings with shading tints added.

The second way to draw for both client and printer is to do what very few architects do: make an *adaptable* black and white drawing, one which at the original size is handsome enough to show the client, but which is drawn with sufficient strength and separation of line to look well at a number of different reduction sizes. Ideally, a drawing should be twice final reproduction size or at most, three times. The book, brochure or magazine presentation of a project, however, may not be offered to the architect until several months or years after he has completed the presentation drawings, and he can rarely be asked to make another set according to strict size specifications. (If he *is* drawing for a specific printing job, he should ask the responsible person, whether it be the editor, art director or printer, for an approximation of the final printed size. There is no excuse for furnishing an out-size drawing in these circumstances.)

Paul Rudolph's drawing technique is extremely successful from the point of view of art directors, engravers and printers. He has mastered the change of scale involved in reproducing his drawings and understands the basic graphic processes. His clients see immense drawings in black ink on tracing paper, yards long. The line weights, cross hatching and lettering sizes have been carefully studied through a reducing glass, however, and these bold perspectives, elevations and plans look extremely well even when printed quite small.

The drawing of Lincoln Center, and the drawing of I. M. Pei's early proposal for townhouses as part of Webb & Knapp's Hyde Park Redevelopment Project in Chicago, both by Ara Derderian, have been included as examples of the adaptable style.

Left and center columns: Zip-a-Tone patterns. Full size portions of large screen graduated tones. *Right column:* Three commonly used Zip-a-Tone patterns shown full size and reduced one third and one half. Note that further reduction of the top pattern would cause it to disappear.

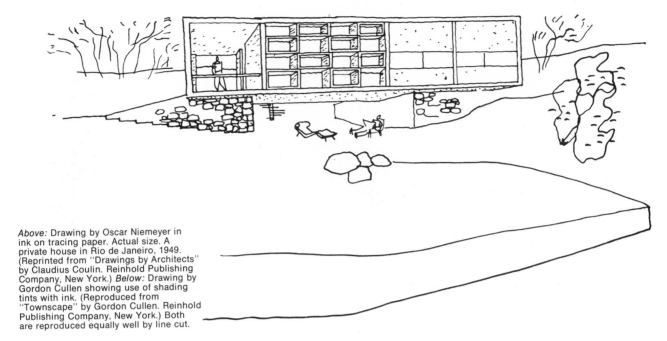

Above: Drawing by Oscar Niemeyer in ink on tracing paper. Actual size. A private house in Rio de Janeiro, 1949. (Reprinted from "Drawings by Architects" by Claudius Coulin. Reinhold Publishing Company, New York.) *Below:* Drawing by Gordon Cullen showing use of shading tints with ink. (Reproduced from "Townscape" by Gordon Cullen. Reinhold Publishing Company, New York.) Both are reproduced equally well by line cut.

The six different methods shown *(above)* and rarely used by architects, probably because opaque paper or board is required, and architects prefer to prepare their drawings as a process of successive tracings on translucent paper, and don't often transfer them to cardboard. It is also possible that these techniques are familiar only to commercial artists and newspaper cartoonists, but not to architects. The first three examples show uses of lithographic crayon and Ross board. Ross board is available in many textures which transform the strokes made by a lithographic crayon into various dot or line patterns which read as gray but are reproduced as line. The fourth example is of scratch board which offers a white clay like surface which permits white lines to be scratched into a continuous layer of black ink. The surface also takes ink lines well. The bottom drawings *(center and right)* show Singletone and Doubletone paper manufactured by Craftint, which are impregnated with shading tints made visible by brushing on special chemicals.

If the strong heavy drawing techniques of the adaptable style are unsuited to the gifts or inclinations of the architect or his staff, the third basic way to persuade the client, yet satisfy the printer, is for the architect to show the client whatever kind of original rendering he thinks will sell the job, but at the same time produce another suitable for printing by one of the many quick drawing techniques. At some stage while large presentation drawings are being prepared, photostats should be made of them as a basis of another set to be drawn for printing. The photostats should reduce the drawings to twice the size they are expected to appear in print. Assuming that they will be reproduced by line cut rather than by halftone, the drawings should be done in ink and shaded by Zip-a-Tone or Craftint. Craftint shading tones are available not only as a pressure sensitive applique similar to Zip-a-Tone and useful where regular edges are required, but in chemical form imprinted on special drawing paper, invisible until transparent chemicals are applied to create a vignetted wash effect. The Craftint Manufacturing Company makes two papers: Singletone, providing one invisible dot or line pattern; and Doubletone, providing two. Both papers offer a broad choice of patterns. After the black and white drawing is made on the special paper, the tone or tones are brought out by the application of a chemical for each.

Ross boards have a range of patterns which can be varied by the surface pressure of a lithographic crayon. All shading tone patterns should be selected with care to be sure that they will not fill in when reduced, thus turning them into blacks.

Only for certain kinds of drawing is reproduction by line the appropriate method. For all other kinds, some type of halftone is almost always required. When the architect who has a knowledge of the graphic processes makes a drawing expressly to be seen in print, he will probably use one of the media suitable for line work. When he considers it most important that a drawing be at its best in its original state, many other choices will determine his use of media, and if the drawing is ever printed, a halftone will probably be essential.

Drawing for halftone reproduction

In black and white printing, the basic difference between line and halftone is in the way each reproduces shades of gray. A drawing to be printed by the line process can consist of no grays at all, merely black ink line on white paper, or in portions of the drawing the black ink is made to enter the gray scale by built up cross hatching or single strokes of varying density and thickness. Shading tints such as Zip-a-Tone which reproduce as line are another way of adding the gray scale. Other drawing methods suitable to line work were discussed in the first section of this chapter.

In the halftone, tiny black dots produce the gray range in proportion to their density on white or light paper. The fewer the dots, the lighter the gray and vice versa. Available for transfer to the half-tone plate, some to remain, others to be etched away, are the 22,500 dots per square inch in a 150-line screen, or the 4,225 dots per square inch in a 65-line screen. There are 50, 85, 100, 110, 120 and 133 line screens with their proportionate number of dots. In letterpress coarser screens (50 to 100) are used to make the halftones which are to print on rough papers like newsprint; 100- and 110-screen halftones can be printed on machine finish or supercalendered paper, but finer screens than this demand coated paper. In photo-offset lithography finer screens do not require smooth, harder surfaced papers, but look well on uncoated stock. Offset is excellent for wash drawings and pencil sketches. Line work, on the other hand, reproduces well on any kind of paper suitable for printing.

It is possible by halftone to achieve a far more subtle gradation of grays, especially with finer screens on expensive coated paper, than is possible by the line process. Tone blends into tone, it is continuous, and there are no hard edges except where wanted. The line method, however, produces a true black or a true white and if the original is a vignette, so is the printed version.

A drawing made in any of the techniques suitable for line reproduction can be duplicated exactly. The ordinary halftone, however, is a rectangular block defined by the screen. The white surface of the paper which is part of the drawing becomes a light gray in the halftone. A vignetted (or silhouetted) halftone in which white areas have the same relations to grays and blacks as they do in the

Portion of black and white drawing by
Helmut Jacoby made of ink line and
Zip-a-Tone shown full size.

The essentials of the three basic methods of printing are shown at left. In letter-press *(left)* ink is received by the raised surface and transferred to paper. In planography, the major commercial application of which is photo-offset lithography, the ink is applied to the entire surface, but because the surface is specially treated with strong light and photochemicals, the result is a plate which is receptive to ink where it is supposed to print, and receptive only to water where it is not supposed to print. This process is diagrammed *(center)*. In the gravure or intaglio process *(right)* ink is transferred to paper forced by pressure into depressed surface containing ink.

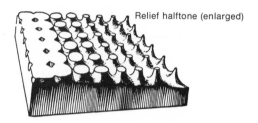

Relief halftone (enlarged)

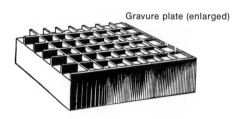

Gravure plate (enlarged)

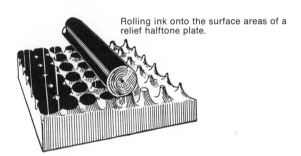

Rolling ink onto the surface areas of a relief halftone plate.

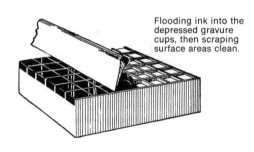

Flooding ink into the depressed gravure cups, then scraping surface areas clean.

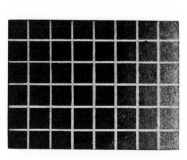

The relief engraving prints only from ink on raised areas; the gravure plate prints only from ink in its depressed areas. The relief dots vary in size; the gravure "ink cups" are of uniform size, but of varying depth. The shallowest carry barely enough ink to soil the topmost fibers of the paper, or none at all. The deepest carry enough ink to soak the paper to the point where the squares run together. Copy to be reproduced is transformed to dots or "ink cups" in the engraving process by the use of screens. (Drawings and captions of printing processes from "Printing and Promotion Handbook" by Daniel Melcher and Nancy Larrick, published by McGraw-Hill Book Company)

Drawings by Jacoby in pencil on tracing paper of Lincoln Center Plaza preliminary design done by Philip Johnson in 1958 and rejected. Although in many cases the best reproduction of pencil drawings requires a "highlight" or "dropout" halftone in which white areas in the original are white in reproduction, these drawings were made with an over-all pencil tone within a rectangle, and lend themselves admirably to printing by regular halftone in the letterpress process. Pencil drawings in which backgrounds must remain white are best reproduced by photo-offset lithography.

original requires special procedures on the part of the engraver. So does the production of a true black.

What is required is that the platemaker alter either the film negative or the plate or both to achieve the true black or white. After the drawing has been transferred to the film negative in the form of a pattern of dots produced by an intervening screen, the negative is affixed to a metal plate treated with chemicals which respond to light. In the letterpress process, where light passes through the negative an acid resisting surface is created. This is the raised surface which prints black. The surface eaten by the acid does not touch the paper. In photo-offset lithography light passing through the negative to the plate creates a surface which will receive ink; that part of the plate unreached by light accepts only water, rejects ink and does not print.

For a true white the engraver must fill in or "opaque" on the negative the dots through which light would otherwise pass to create a printing surface on the plate. He may also "rout out" or "deep etch" unwished for dots on the plate itself. For a true black he must, on the plate before it is etched, alter the areas which are to print darkest with an acid resisting coating to cover the acid receptive dots transferred by the screen.

These procedures double or triple the cost of the plate, depending on how many tricks are involved. Such operations are never used to improve a newspaper halftone, and except in special cases they are not requested by the art directors of the architectural magazines.

A halftone is not necessarily any better for vignetting or reproducing the solid blacks or whites of an original, but where such improvement is possible, only the producers of expensive books, or brochures or advertisements demand it. What does this mean to the architect who is making a drawing to be printed? Simply that he should consider where and how it will be reproduced. If engraving, paper and printing cost is no problem, he should know the full range of possibility which the halftone offers, and take advantage of it. If cost is a problem he should make sure that the quality and punch of his drawing do not depend on effects that will not be captured in the regular halftone. If he knows, for example, that the drawing he is making will appear principally in the coarse screen halftones of the newspaper, he should realize that subtle gradations of tone will be lost and simplify his gray scale tonal transitions and detail.

All the drawings shown as examples are by Helmut Jacoby, the brilliant German-born artist whose work is known to everyone in the architectural field. Except for his work for advertising agencies which is done with color process in mind, he is most frequently asked to make a fine drawing as a thing in itself. His work has been selected to demonstrate how his manipulation of a delicate range of tonal values from black to white makes beautiful use of the resources of the halftone. Jacoby uses color sparingly. He often begins by doing a complete line drawing in black ink on white cardboard. When this is completed it is photographed and from this copy a line cut can be made to fill some future need. Then translucent gray tones are applied to the drawing by airbrush as are translucent colors. The basic ink line remains visible. Like the great draftsmen of any age Jacoby often fully develops in shade, shadow, highlight and color

(Text continued on page 152)

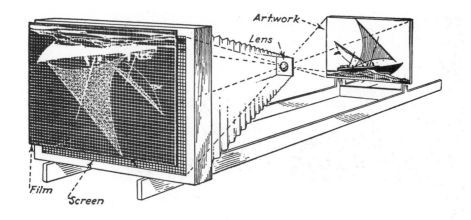

Drawing by Jacoby in ink line and air-brush on white cardboard of house designed by Charles Goodman & Associates, shown as it would appear in a 60-65 coarse screen of the type used for news print, (*opposite page top*); as a line cut where preferred (*opposite page bottom*); as a regular 120-screen halftone (*left*); and as a "highlight" or "dropout" halftone (*below*). The latter costs exactly three times as much as a regular halftone of the same size, and was made to reproduce Jacoby's use of pure white to express the concrete cornices.

Black and white drawing by Jacoby in ink line and airbrush on white cardboard, of the new addition to the Museum of Modern Art, designed by Philip Johnson and completed in 1964. Each sculpture in the museum's garden was photographed from the viewing point at which the drawing was made, printed at the proper scale and pasted in position. The drawing is reproduced here as a regular halftone.

(Text continued from page 147.)

only a part of the drawing, in his case always the building, while trees, people, cars, roads and grass are defined only by the original ink line and the lightest of gray tones.

Jacoby draws in pencil also, and will use black ink and Zip-a-Tone, but he prefers translucent to opaque paints, and avoids tempera which he feels to be too clumsy a medium to express the precisions of contemporary architecture.

It is possible that the more flamboyant uses of tempera by some commercial renderers cause Jacoby and his architect clients to recoil from a medium which, when used with skill and restraint, has long provided a fine way to render buildings. Other halftone media not shown are ink line in combination with wash and pastel.

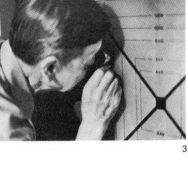

1

2

3

4

5

6

7

1. Ellerbe draftsmen make sharp drawings for reduction.
2. Care is taken with lettering for size and quality.
3. Cameraman checks image on ground glass screen.
4. Full-size drawings are put in holder for process camera.
5. Film is developed and dried in an automatic processor.
6. Offset printing plates are exposed to film negatives in a mechanized contact printer.
7. Equipment includes distortion-free enlarger.

The sheer size and number of architectural and engineering drawings and renderings make them bulky to store, costly to mail, awkward to work with in the field, and expensive to reproduce. Ellerbe Architects of St. Paul is one of several firms who are trying to reduce these problems by using half-size photoreproductions of their normal-scale originals for all distributions.

To maintain consistent quality without distortion, the full-size drawings are reduced to half-size on a 20- by 24-inch negative film using a special process camera. These negatives are then used for contact prints on a variety of film and paper products, selection of which depends upon the job need.

"Major jobs require a large number of drawings," notes Dean Stoven, Ellerbe's office services manager. "One recent example ran up to 300 pages, and the average is 150 or more. When these are reproduced full-size by the diazo

Architectural firm uses half-size drawing system

process, each set will weigh 50 pounds or more, and a construction project may require as many as 150 sets for various phases of the work."

By a conservative estimate, reducing such drawings to half-size cuts at least 25 per cent from the cost of mailing drawings to Ellerbe projects throughout the United States and Canada.

At present, the firm still retains its originals, but Mr. Stoven looks forward to a day when additional savings will be realized through reduced storage space needed for the half-size reproductions—perhaps even further reduced to 35 mm film as legal and retrieval problems are solved. An important advantage of the present half-size sheets, he says, is that they are much easier to handle by crews out on the job. The few initial complaints about readability of the reduced prints have been eliminated by minor adjustments in drafting technique—slightly heavier finest line, slightly larger minimum lettering size, sharper definition, etc.

Ellerbe uses an automatic processor to develop the negatives. The processor eliminates any need for a conventional darkroom and delivers developed and dried films in 60 to 90 seconds. It operates with pre-mixed chemicals and requires a 4-gpm water supply and periodic drainage. The processor handles four kinds of film for Ellerbe's system: a negative, a positive and the projection variants of each. Films are exposed either with the process camera or in a contact frame.

Prints of drawings are produced with a matte finish suitable for pencil and ink additions, corrections and retouchings.

Photo-drafting: time-saving aid to quality

The expanding adaptation of photographic processes to architectural and engineering drafting has been accelerated by development of versatile films, paper and emulsion products in large sizes together with camera, offset and xerographic equipment that can reproduce with dimensional stability over wide areas. For example, polyester film in drafting room sizes comes in clear, matte or opaque finishes on which sharp black line (or tone) can be either erased or washed off when alterations in hand-drawn ink are desired. Sensitized papers and even tracing cloth can be similarly treated.

Savings in drafting time, especially for repetitive, partially repetitive or mirror-image detailing, can be enormous, once the drafting staff becomes accustomed to "thinking photography." The staff finds itself freed for the creative aspects of the drafting process, and both the quality of detailing and the freedom from human error are enhanced.

Improved communication among architects, engineers and contractors for the various trades takes advantage of techniques unique to the photo-drafting process. That is its ability to produce "shadow" or halftone prints of basic plans upon which mechanical, structural and/or electrical systems can be drawn in black line. This permits easier reading of the systems and gives more positive assurance against interference of one system with another.

A 16-step case-study example of how the process was used on one project by Gruzen & Partners is reported on the following pages by Rolland D. Thompson, partner in charge, and Allan Johnson, designer and job captain for the project. The architectural firm worked very closely with Louis DiPaolo, vice president of Reprostat Corporation, in adapting potentials of the photo-drafting process to the stringent time-urgencies of the project.

The architects point out that they made no investment in cameras, light tables or any special equipment or personnel for this project. Most sizable cities have firms well equipped for the photographic and reproduction portions of the process who can work efficiently on a fairly large regional basis. Gains in drafting efficiency and quality pay for the service, and the design professionals do not have to go into the reproduction business.

The example deals with the working drawing phase of a college science building as the phase the most demanding of drafting time and detail. Following is the report by Rolland Thompson and Allan Johnson, based on a slide presentation they have used for both internal and external communication.

16 steps in the photo-drafting technique

Production of the working drawing phase of an architectural project is one of the most costly and time-consuming of any of the project development phases. This plus the fact that today's architectural graduate has little interest in repetitive chore work at the drafting board spurred our own interest in photo-drafting.

Photo-drafting is more than the simple reproduction of drawings by photography. It is the actual production of complete drawings by the photographic assembly of repetitive parts and the improvement of communication by photo techniques of tone and contrast. This is not to say that the draftsman/designer is to be replaced by the camera, but rather that camera techniques must become an additional skill used by the draftsman in order to produce better drawings faster.

For a period of four years, Gruzen & Partners, architects, planners and engineers, of New York City, had been developing photo-drafting techniques suited to the requirements of various projects. As a result of this research, management decided to run a case study on a particular project in order to uncover problems and establish criteria for future projects.

The project selected was the Social and Behavioral Sciences Building at Stony Brook, Long Island. The client, State University Construction Fund of New York, informed the architects that this project was to be a multi-story academic building that would house a minimum of eight different departments of the University. The project was begun on August 26, 1970 with a partial occupancy desirable in the fall of 1972.

The 16 steps that follow represent the organization and planning of this particular project using photo-drafting. These steps serve as a guide in the production of an architectural project and strongly emphasize early planning and decision making in order to use these techniques to their fullest extent. Many of the drawings on the following pages have been cropped to preserve detail at the necessary reduction and demonstrate the method rather than content of the plans. The architect's logo, also part of each print, has been trimmed off for the same reason.

Step 1. Standard sheet is developed using paste-up photography, tape and ink. It is reproduced as a washoff polyester (mylar) film, matte both sides, using a film negative. The negative can be used to print standard sheets by the offset printing process (when large quantities are needed). Note: When using photo drafting techniques (wash-off polyester paste-up drawings), fewer standard printed sheets are necessary.

Step 2. Structural framing grid should be determined by the architects and engineers showing column center-lines and numbers. This grid must be derived from the building plan even if the structural system (concrete, steel or precast) has not been determined pending analysis of comparative cost. The grid should be drawn in ink for better photographic reproduction of the future generations of drawings.

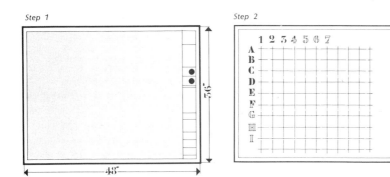

Step 1

Step 2

Step 3

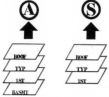

STEP 3. Architect must then analyze the building design to determine the number of different types of floor configurations. In the Social and Behavioral Sciences Building at Stony Brook, these are the basement, first, second through eighth floor and roof plans. The structural engineer must determine the number of floors that he can use the basic grid on which to draw typical framing plans—in this case the first, typical and roof plans. The architect then sends the basic grid drawing to the photographer for solid line washoff polyester films (seven were needed for the SBSB), four to be used by the architect in developing the above mentioned plans and three to be used by the structural engineer in his development of the typical framing plans.

Step 4

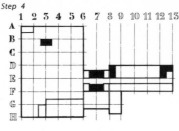

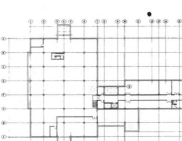

STEP 4. Architect then develops basement plans showing stairs, elevators, mechanical services, exterior walls, interior partition layouts, drinking fountains, fire hose cabinets, columns, and mechanical openings in the exterior walls and slab above. If the mechanical rooms were to be located on an intermediate floor or the roof, the same principal of developing the drawing would apply. At this stage of development the drawing should not show interior dimensions, door numbers, room names or numbers, because this would interfere with the mechanical/electrical and structural developments on the future generations of drawings.

Step 5

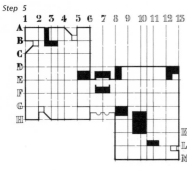

STEP 5. Architect develops first floor plan showing the perimeter architecture including material indication. Stairs, elevators, mechanical services, toilets, and other special items such as wind bracing should be shown at this stage of development. However, no exterior dimensions need be shown on the drawing at this stage. On the SBSB, the first floor plan was given to the HVAC engineer at this stage of development to be used for a typical riser diagram as fan coil units were being used as the perimeter mechanical system.

Step 6

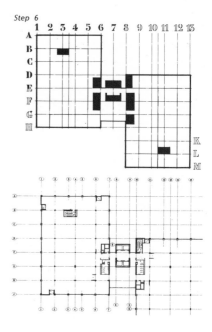

STEP 6. Simultaneously the architect would develop the typical floor plan, the same as in Step 5 above, and in addition, indicate the location of the corridor system.

Step 7

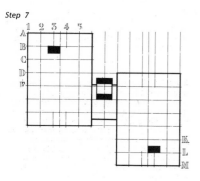

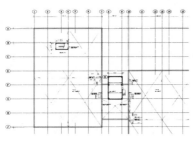

STEP 7. Architect develops roof plan showing parapet, stair and mechanical penthouses and roof accessories. Note: The level of development for Steps 5, 6, and 7 is very important so as not to make the future drawings cluttered when the mechanical engineers develop them into working drawings.

Step 8

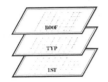

STEP 8. Structural engineer develops the first floor, typical floor and roof plans . . . into typical framing plans for each of these respective levels.

Step 9

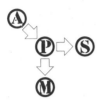

STEP 9. Architect sends the developed basement plan to the photographer for a solid line right-reading washoff polyester for the structural engineer, so that he can prepare a final foundation and footing plan. The mechanical engineer receives four shadow print reverse-reading polyester copies (one for each trade; HVAC, plumbing, lighting and power) for him to prepare layouts of the various mechanical systems. Since all drawings thus far have been photographically reproduced from the same basic drawing, which was drawn by the architect, coordination level is at 100 per cent.

Step 10

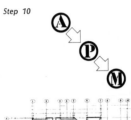

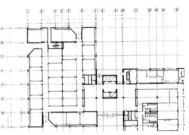

STEP 10. Architect sends first floor plan (which should now show partitions, door swings, drinking fountains, wet columns, fire hose cabinets, and electric panels) and roof plan to the photographer for two sets each of shadow print reverse reading polyester film copies for the mechanical trades to develop into working drawings.

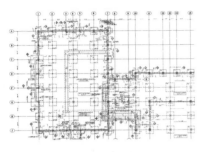

Step 11

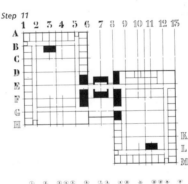

STEP 11. Architect then develops the typical floor plan, showing the interior (partitions, door swings, and the above mentioned fixed items) of the most repetitive offices and various research spaces. This drawing should show no interior dimensions, door numbers, room names or numbers. Note: At this level of development, exterior dimensions can be put on the drawing as it will be photographically repeated the number of required times.

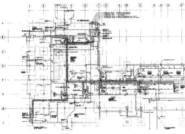

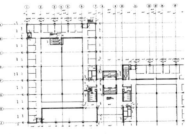

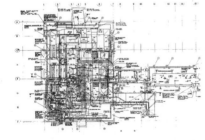

Step 12

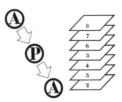

STEP 12. Architect sends the typical floor plan from Step 11 to the photographer who produces seven solid line washoff films and one shadow print reverse reading of this typical floor. Eight will be used by the architect in his further development and one will be used by the HVAC engineer as a typical floor riser diagram working drawing.

Step 13

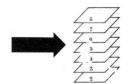

INTERIOR LAYOUTS

STEP 13. Architect develops each plan (second through eighth) into its final interior layout required by the function of a particular department. Note: A minimum of additional partitions and door swings have to be added to each floor in the future development since the basic drafting was repeated by photography.

Step 14

STEP 14. Architect then sends each of the seven typical floor plans showing the department layout to the photographer. The photographer then produces 28 floor plans (shadow prints) for the mechanical engineer, one set of plans for each of the four trades (HAVC, plumbing, lighting and power). The first floor plan was received in Step 5. In addition, the photographer produces three sets each (solid line right-reading polyester copies) of the eight floor plans, one set for the interiors consultants, one set for the telephone company to prepare its departmental assignments. Approximately 60 drawings have been reproduced from the typical architectural plan. The number of drawings that can be photographically reproduced for any one project would be determined by the number of consultants on the team and the number of repetitive floors in the project. The drawings can now be developed into the final working drawings showing room names, numbers and door symbols.

Step 15

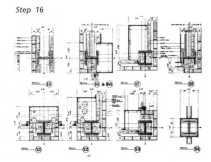

STEP 15. Paste-up drafting, a term that all architects are familiar with in some form, was used as an additional skill in producing the working drawings: This method allows the architect to determine sheet layouts and gives him the flexibility of revising details until late in the project. Specialized area which must be shown at larger scale; i.e., interior and reflected ceiling plans, can be enlarged by the camera into solid line or shadow prints for paste-up use by the architect or engineer. On the Social and Behavioral Sciences Building, the interiors consultant used a large scale blow-up of the lobby for interior design studies. Sepia prints were made of these plans for pasting onto a cardboard model. From this model, presentation slides were made.

Photography was again used in preparing the polyester cover sheet for the set of working drawings by combining a rendering of the project with paste-up titles. The title sheet was also a paste-up using office standard abbreviations and symbols that were on clear polyester film.

Step 16

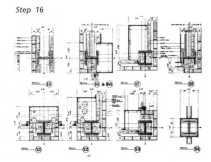

STEP 16. The architect, who is the project coordinator for all consulting engineers, should make it clear to other consultants that photo drafting can also work for them. An example of this is the landscape architect preparing the site plans and having them photographed for use by the site utilities engineer. This step is not illustrated.

Project
Administration
and
Cost
Control

Professional construction management and project administration

The following plea for common sense and integrity in sorting out the braided lines of professional agency, as construction management and project administration take on the dimensions of new professions, is from the book "Professional Construction Management and Project Administration," by William B. Foxhall, jointly published by Architectural Record *and* The American Institute of Architects, *1972.*

Professionalism is an essential and inherent quality of every human process that combines both specially-trained knowledge and dedicated action on behalf of a client. This is so because professionalism in both skill and integrity provides the *only* bulwark against failure or corruption of the process—be it judicial, medical or architectural. Further, the processes that must be served by the professions are the basic ones by which the human condition is uplifted and sustained.

When a creative art is one of the components of professional action—as it is in architecture—the whole process becomes servant to that art; and the requirement for professionalism extends all the way from the pre-design conditions fostering conception through the technical complexities of development and delivery of the finished building.

All of these ideas have had a long history of demonstration in classic client-architect-builder relationships. And in that portion of today's work that can be commissioned as to both scope and cost by one-man clients who can speak with a single responsible voice, the same ideas of professionalism are still clearly identified. But such clients are increasingly rare, even for projects of moderate scope.

Instead, three compelling and confusing conditions have developed over the postwar decades until they have now reached near-crisis proportions in their combined power to obscure the enduring values of professionalism in our time.

First, the ever-larger works of man are now commissioned by the public client, the corporate client, the hospital board, the school board, the development consortium—a hydra-headed host of groups spending the money of other groups to whom they must report and be responsive. The consequences in make-shift checks and balances and in safe-action compromise have accumulated over the years—like the waste products of evolution—to a point where only the muscle of professional management seems capable of cleaning the stables. There are, of course, the positive effects of united action, where again the sinews of management can pull the great projects of today's practice together.

But the elevation of "management" to the realms of magic has many dangers in it. Architectural abdication is paramount among those dangers. Let no architect believe that he is less than the constant and essential professional presence from start to finish of any project. Even the multi-client is entitled to that singular and able presence, that agency, unique in its guardianship of every aspect of the project's values. Then let no "manager" believe that he is more than instrumental to the practical support of that guardianship. Some of the modes of today's business may invite management to usurp the architect's agency where cost and speed are paramount. Individual architects themselves may shrink from the terrors of sheer technical complexity or the wounds of liability. But there is no escape from the classic one-to-one relationship of client and architect; and management is the means of its survival.

The second postwar condition that obscures professional identities is, again, one of proliferation, in that the marshalling of professional and other skills for execution of large commissions entails the directed input of many individuals.

That does not at all mean that only large architectural and engineering firms with an array of in-house specialists can enter into this complex arena. The multi-client and the multi-disciplined commission do indeed imply obvious burdens of clerical and communications tasks that, by themselves, would be beyond the scope of any one-man office. But the small-to-medium-sized office today is no stranger to consultation and joint venture. These are but two of the many modes of marshalling expertise. Two not-so-new ideas or images need constant and confident redefinition in this context: the image of the architect as team leader in design and construction phases of the process; and the image of professional management as an instrument of team accomplishment.

The third compelling condition that pervades all aspects of building design and construction today is inflation—under which the fixed budget (concomitant of the multi-client) wastes away in its purchasing power with every passing day. Management, again, is refining methods of contracting the time lapse from project start to completion. Phased or overlapped design and construction—for many years a familiar procedure in the pressured fields of industrial and urban commercial construction—is gaining more attention (and some new buzz words, like "fast track") among other building types. Management methods for extending the scope and effectiveness of condensed schedules are being tested. The hazards and penalties of haste for its own sake are many and manifest; so, again, professionalism on the part of all team members—including managers—is the guardian of quality.

Management itself is the skilled discipline of method and is not of and by itself **Sorting out professional lines** professional within the context of our opening paragraphs. Neither, truth to tell, is architecture—or engineering—or medicine—or law—when its practitioners become entrapped in business without free and responsible agency toward their clients. That criterion of agency we now apply to the roles of management as they shift in emphasis from one phase of a project to another. The phases are not sequential like phases of the moon, but are concurrent, with interweaving surges of attention, like colored strands within a braid of common purpose.

Return now to ideas suggested at the beginning, wherein the processes are postulated servant to the art, and professions are set forth as ennobling to the state of man. Extend and adjust those notions to accommodate the natural limitations of individual practitioners. Consider the differences between comprehensive services and universal genius.

Then the architect of any of today's larger, multi-client works has the image of one man only in the singleness of his commitment and responsibility and in the consistent vocabulary of the building design. In actual performance of the work, the architect is a *firm of organized and directed skills.*

Similarly, the manager of one phase or another is a collation of skills and special knowledge; *a firm of experts*—not a superbeing to be appointed as absolute dictator. He may, in fact, be an architect, or a consultant, or a contractor.

So, the conventional images evoked by the terms *architect, engineer, owner, contractor* and *manager* remain singular within the concept of fundamentally unchanging professional relationships, while in practice, each is many men and women who work for the common goal of services to clients—and to mankind, if you please.

When all these lines of image and endeavor are sorted out, we can discern three different management roles that bear upon the fundamentally unchanged genesis and sequential logic of any architectural commission. One has identity with client decisions in matters of project need, feasibility, program, real estate

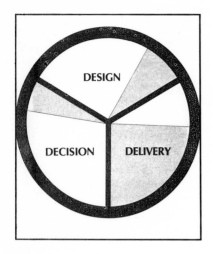

and finance. We call him (or his firm) *project manager or project administrator.* The other two, under the generic label of *construction management,* have to do with the *practique* of design and delivery of the project itself within the client's budget. Both require detailed and currect construction cost and method expertise, hence they are performed in any practical situation by a single firm acting as *construction manager.* It is important to keep in mind, however, that in the early phases of budget and design development, the input of construction management has to do with defining the cost-quality relationships of the architectural and engineering design options. As such, it could be more precisely labeled *construction consultation.* The second phase of construction management (which usually overlaps the first in time but not in function) is a control method for schedule and contract management—in short, *construction management* in its simplest connotations.

There are two good reasons for the triple separation described. The first is that each relates to a clear and separate focus in the role of professional agency toward the client. The second is that they all relate to the logic of the three-spoked wheel of Decision, Design and Delivery reproduced here from the article, "Proposal: a new and comprehensive system for design and delivery of buildings," by Robert F. Hastings in the November, 1968, issue of *Architectural Record.*

New labels for sustained ideas

The three segments of the 3-D wheel define the classic phases of attention that have always pertained to the generation of buildings: the decisions to build and to what purpose, scope and size; the design of the building; and the delivery of the building. Today, more than ever, those phases overlap, and the skills of delivery are germane—especially in large projects—to both the decision and design phases for reasons already outlined.

It is this condition of inter-permeation that brings us to grips now with the vital role of agency. The production skills of good contractors have long been—and continue to be—a reservoir of knowledge about technique and cost without which buildings simply cannot be built. Further, the costs to which each contractor commits himself have been—and continue to be—the real and final costs of each contractual component. Therefore, the successful contractor, as responsible entrepreneur, has conventionally had the ultimate responsibility for delivery of the building at a quoted price. For that he has been rightfully well-paid.

But two things have happened. First, the successful and responsible general contractor has withdrawn for good reason from both the competitive bidding of large work and the maintenance of diverse trade skills in his own work force. Second, the very skills and knowledge that have been his stock in trade are now needed to an increasing degree in the decision and design phases of building generation. But to purvey those skills in those phases, he must assume a role of professional agency toward the client just as the other professions do in those phases. He no longer works for a contractor's profit. He works for a professional fee.

Many contractors have found this transition difficult, but many have succeeded in it. In any case, the contractor's body of knowledge is neither mystic nor unique, and the capability for honest professional service in this field cannot be regarded as his exclusive domain. It is the professionalism of the service that is paramount, and staffing for its performance is key to its success.

So, may we not leave off anxiety and bickering and return to some admittedly arbitrary definitions of these professional services. Then, at least, we can all argue in one language.

What is a *project manager* or (some prefer) *project administrator?* He is the client's voice, agent and purse string. He rings the starting bell when a project exists as serious intent. He makes or expedites the owner's decisions at key points as the project develops. He may be one man or a department on staff of a sophisticated client. He may be, in fact, a special kind of architect. He is the rim and the spokes of our project wheel. He may or may not have detailed, technical construction expertise among his own resources. If he has, he should ideally use that knowledge only for communication with and critique of building design and delivery processes. If he is tempted to use it for direct input or control of those processes, he should recognize that a fundamental shift in his role is implicated and that there is a possible conflict of interest in that change. For example, as project administrator, he may be called upon for an ownership decision regarding a change that he himself has proposed while acting in the role of construction manager. The conflict is admittedly more philosophical than dangerous in most cases, but should be recognized.

What is a *construction manager?* "He" is a *firm* that applies knowledge of construction techniques, conditions and costs to the three phases of decision, design and delivery of a project. First, as *construction consultant* he clarifies the time and cost consequences of decision and design options as they occur. Second, as *construction manager* he enters, still as a professional, into construction scheduling, pre-purchasing of critical materials, advising on the method of obtaining contractors and awarding contracts, and coordination and direction of all construction activities, including those of the producers of systems and subsystems.

Some will recognize the last few phrases as echoing a definition developed during a December 1970 workshop of DHEW/FECA in which representatives of every sector of construction, public and private, participated. Further details of definition will be derived from similar researches of GSA.

This concern of public agencies with thoughtful analysis of current crises in construction will undoubtedly determine ultimate language usages in this field—at least insofar as *project management* and *construction management* are concerned. It is not only their giant purchasing power that prevails in this matter. It is also their clear acknowledgement of the primary role of professional agency in the management of public works and publicly supported construction that is being stated in terms of common usage—however limited in inherent clarity—that will ultimately gain general connotation for these terms.

Now it is time to call another spade a spade. The reason for this proper searching of the soul in public method is the virtual breakdown in effectiveness of the status quo. The laudable intent of legislation requiring acceptance of the low bid out of a public invitation simply has not been realized. Nor has the similar intent of legislation calling for multiple sub-section contracts. All of this is subject for more discussion, but the simple fact is: *someone* has to be responsible for *quality*, and the low-bid, multi-contract method simply has not worked as a guardian of quality—nor even of cost, when all changes are counted. So we now call for *professional* management to do two things: First, to enlist competent skills that have been by-passed under the non-qualified, low-bidder system; second, to apply those skills early enough to sustain quality and value within the budget during design development—rather than to accept those post-bid cuts that never seem to return the contractor's original profit mark-up to the budget pot.

The visible and historic professional is the architect. But he is many people, nowadays, and he must garner all the skills of many people to his purpose. If that be a team—let's make the most of it.

Budget control of the phased construction project

Following is an extract from a chapter on construction project anatomy in the book, "Professional Construction Management and Project Administration." This extract is based on conversations with Philip J. Meathe, Jr., president of Smith, Hinchman and Grylls, and Harry A. Golemon, senior partner of Golemon and Rolfe.

The ability to save time by phased design and construction commits the client to early purchase and construction starts of certain systems well before the bids are in on later systems. If he is committed to a fixed maximum budget—as he usually is—he may well ask what recourse or assurances he has if at, say, the half-way point in construction he finds the bids are coming in substantially over estimates, and he cannot fund the overrun. At least under conventional methods he can abandon the project—or re-design it—before construction starts, and he knows what his completed costs are going to be. That is, he has bid prices.

The answer resides in two important qualities of the construction management of phased construction, as described by Philip J. Meathe, Jr., president of Smith, Hinchman and Grylls. First is the early and continuously refined accuracy of what has been called the "conceptual" estimating process (as opposed to "take-off" estimating). The client's, architect's, engineer's and construction manager's own cost data, contractors' and manufacturers' price information and other resources of the industry make it possible to set reasonable "high-and-low" limits on probable systems costs at the end of the schematic design phase. Second, the isolation of those costs, system by system, makes it possible to spread design flexibility throughout components of the entire project rather than forcing a massive paring job on quality after all bidding documents are completed and bids have come in over the budget.

So, the control point for the client's "go" or "no go" decision on the project shifts from the over-all post-bid point to the end of the schematic phase. It is based on a summation of "high" estimates for some 30 or 40 itemized systems and subsystems. It further makes the assumption that subsequent cost developments, including the individually bid prices on systems, will average out well within the overall "high" limit plus a conventional contingency reserve.

If bids on any one system come in substantially higher than the "high" limit on that system—and thereby threaten the average—the owner, project administrator, architect, engineer and construction manager agree on one of three options (or a combination of all three):

a) re-design the system,

b) spread the overrun among probable margins left within other systems so far uncommitted,

c) dip into contingency reserves to make up the difference.

At that point, assuming previously bid systems have averaged well within their individual high-low ranges, there is also a cushion of reserve represented by summation of the differences or gaps between accepted bids and estimated "highs" on those systems. That gap is not listed among the three options above, because it exists mainly as an indicator of safety or freedom from re-design; and at any given point in the multiple bidding procedure, the gap may be either positive or negative within some acceptable margin dictated by judgment, experience and job conditions.

An example of how the method works is tabulated below in simplified terms of five systems. Note that, since the method depends on management control of averages, the system estimates are in terms of costs per square foot of the whole project. The plus or minus tabulation of the gap is, of course, a convention to express the cumulative gap as positive for overrun and negative for under-the-wire. The substantial difference between the ten-cent overrun in system C and the $1.25 overrun in system E calls for the application of different options and criteria in each case. The overrun of system E is big enough to "threaten the average" and calls for serious evaluation and direct action as described for alternatives *a, b* and *c* above.

System	Estimate Low	Estimate High	Lowest Bid	Gap	Cumulative Gap	Cumulative per cent of Job
A	1.00	1.25	1.05	−0.20		5
B	1.50	1.75	1.50	−0.25	−0.45	12
C	2.00	2.50	2.60	+0.10	−0.35	20
D	3.25	4.00	3.80	−0.20	−0.55	38
E	2.25	2.75	4.00	+1.25	+0.70	50
	10.00	12.25	12.95			

There are three important points involved here: 1) If the construction manager, acting as professional agent, has induced the client to make a financial commitment on the basis of estimates at the schematic phase, then he must do better than "explain" aberrations. He is now equipped with knowledge that enables him to make responsible correction of the overrun. 2) His own contract should spell out the limits of his liability in this area. 3) When the cumulative gap is still under the wire, he must do better than congratulate himself. He must advise the owner (or project administrator) of the implications of that underrun in terms of project finance. A few cents per square foot on a million square feet can mean a substantial sum in any money market, and the owner is entitled to take advantage of the earliest possible knowledge of any reduction.

One of the important adjuncts to these considerations is the inevitably increasing role of the owner (project administrator) in the whole building process. He becomes more intimately involved, not only in matters of budget and finance, but also in the design as it unfolds, system by system. He is enabled to see the design consequences of his decisions in time for those decisions to have a balanced overall effect on the quality of his project. In fact, this method will not work well at all unless the owner does maintain continuous participation in what has been called a "united team action program," UTAP.

Two simplistic questions may arise: 1) What do the new methods do to client-architect relationships? 2) How does the modest-sized architectural firm fit into the new pattern? The answers are, again: 1) There are no "new" client-architect relationships—unless more intimate involvement of the client in his own building can be called such. 2) There are no criteria of firm size involved. There are only the criteria of awareness of the problem and professional respect for the complexity of consultation services. They may be enlisted (but not entirely performed) by one man—theoretically. But in a real world, one can set criteria for at least three men involved in evaluation of any management services commissioned in this field. They are: 1) a designer, 2) a field expert, and 3) a manager. Without at least acknowledgment of the need for the expertise of those roles, the small office is not equipped to enter into this arena.

Pursuit of the guaranteed max

A variation of the system-by-system design-and-bid approach previously outlined is described by Harry A. Golemon, senior partner of Golemon and Rolfe Architects, Houston, as serving both to condense the over-all project time and to permit a firmly bid cost commitment for the whole project prior to the beginning of construction. The method again involves overlapping, but with the difference that AE processes and construction processes are inter-phased on both sides of a single bidding interval that is moved up much earlier into the design development phase. It still takes advantage of the logic of systems sequence. The procedure is to prepare sets of a modified kind of bidding document comprising complete specifications system by system but only partially detailed drawings equivalent to preliminary drawings plus certain key details. These so-called "drawn bid documents" contain only sufficient detail to begin the bidding process. Hence, the method calls for a schedule of pre-bid conferences among designers and interested contractors so that the points that are important for the contractors to consider can be carried forward from the preliminaries into the "drawn bid document" phase.

All systems then are bid at one time, either by a single general contractor or any variation of the multiple contract process. The method permits the overall design process to remain open so that any necessary adjustment of design to meet the budget can be applied freely to all systems in the project. The owner then has an assured (if not guaranteed) maximum cost bid before construction starts.

Many clients are eager for and sometimes insistent upon a guaranteed maximum cost quite early in the design development of their projects. This has worked fairly well in the past for office buildings and industrial structures where systems are relatively simple and cost histories are readily available. When the idea of the guaranteed maximum is carried into more complex buidings such as hospitals, laboratories and some educational buildings, the advantages of the guarantee as well as the certainty of the amount become illusory. Any guarantee of price calls for an added amount covering the margin of risk, and the amount grows larger with the risk.

There is a double-loading on the guarantee. First, the contingency element must be larger when the information available to the bidder is limited as it is in early design phases and may be in simplified versions of bid documents. Second, the price of the guarantee increases as competition shrinks. For these reasons, the "drawn bid documents" together with the pre-bid conferences must give participating contractors confidence in the conditions of the work, and the process must be held open to all available competition.

Drawn bid documents are not construction documents. The latter (i.e., conventional working drawings) are prepared after the bidding process by filling in the voids of detail not required for the bidding of the systems. The working drawings are prepared sequentially, so that, for example, the construction of foundations can proceed while working drawings for the later phases of the project are being completed.

To get maximum benefit from the method in terms of shortened project time span, it is important to develop the bidding documents on certain systems that are first in the construction sequence (foundation and structure, for example) to a more advanced degree, perhaps even to working drawings, so that the contractor can begin his work as soon as possible after acceptance of bids. It turns out that working drawings for those early systems tend to be the simpler ones of the sequence, so the pre-bid design time is not seriously extended by their detail.

There are two conditions of the design and construction process that must prevail if this method is to operate well. First, contractors must be prepared with both the skills and the willingness to evaluate the condensed form of drawn bidding documents, and they must commit themselves firmly to the price of the

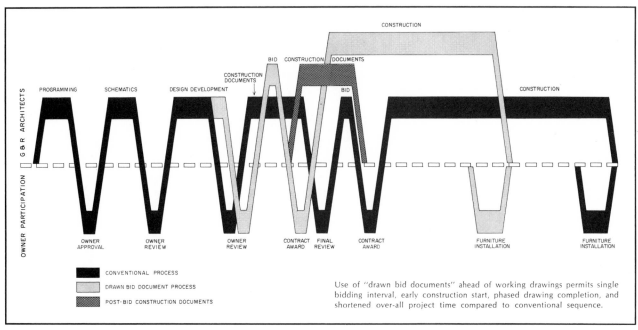

CONSTRUCTION

BID CONSTRUCTION DOCUMENTS

CONSTRUCTION DOCUMENTS

PROGRAMMING   SCHEMATICS   DESIGN DEVELOPMENT   CONSTRUCTION DOCUMENTS   BID   CONSTRUCTION

G & R ARCHITECTS

OWNER PARTICIPATION

OWNER APPROVAL   OWNER REVIEW   OWNER REVIEW   CONTRACT AWARD   FINAL REVIEW   CONTRACT AWARD   FURNITURE INSTALLATION   FURNITURE INSTALLATION

█ CONVENTIONAL PROCESS

▒ DRAWN BID DOCUMENT PROCESS

▓ POST-BID CONSTRUCTION DOCUMENTS

Use of "drawn bid documents" ahead of working drawings permits single bidding interval, early construction start, phased drawing completion, and shortened over-all project time compared to conventional sequence.

Use of "drawn bid documents" ahead of working drawings permits single bidding interval, early construction start, phased drawing completion, and shortened over-all project time compared to conventional sequence.

bid at that point. At the same time, the architect-engineer must have access to a sophisticated cost control system that enters into the process at the very beginning of project definition, so that he can begin to zero in on final costs as soon as the scope of the project is defined and the general order of spaces and materials is established. If the early cost projections relate to the systems and to a convention of specification classification that is widely understood, this provides a format that translates readily into succeeding phases of the process. It is suggested that the 16 categories of the Construction Specifications Institute might be considered for this format.

By involving the contractor not only in the pre-bid conference but also in the actual preparation of working drawings after bids are in on the "drawn bid documents," many problems in field interpretation are avoided. Mr. Golemon points out further that the conventional working drawing that is prepared as a bidding document sometimes reflects the architect-engineer's notion of how construction is done rather than the contractor's more immediate familiarity with the construction process and his individual modes of operation. A judicious increase in participation by contractors during preparation of both the condensed bidding documents and post-bid working drawings helps to avoid recycling of shop drawings, according to Golemon. Another advantage of the method is the fact that it can be applied by an architectural office of any size to a broad range of project size and to either competitively bid or negotiated contracts.

The time value of money affects design.—Richard Steyert

The architect today works in a world where some clients demand the utmost quality at lowest cost while others are willing to cut all possible quality corners to get maximum return on investment. Economic pressures endlessly constrain

Architectural economics: The concept of total cost

the design process, so that the highest quality design within those constraints demands that the architect be as conversant with the skills of what might be called "architectural economics" as he is with the fundamentals of design. He must be able to deal intelligently with return on investment in order to protect his clients' interests and his own professional role.

The economic success of a project is generally determined in the first few weeks of preliminary design. After that, conceptual changes increase cost by causing delay.

It is not always realized that about 90 per cent of design man-hours are spent on work that can affect cost about 7 per cent plus or minus, while about 10 per cent of design hours are spent on preliminary design decisions which can affect costs 30 per cent plus or minus. Sophisticated computer programs can be used to save pennies by reducing the number of bolts used with the structural steel, while outdated rules of thumb on building economy establish overall building form.

"Architectural economics," as defined here, seeks to bring analytic method into the cost-critical, early-design process. One can now do a number of alternate architectural layouts for a building or development site, input these alternatives into a computer, and receive an accurate, precise analysis of comparative economic feasibility. But the architect need not always have a computer at his disposal. Even simple calculations of the kind to be described can give new dimensions to design decisions.

Above all, it should be emphasized that quantitative analysis of this character is not meant to replace intuition and experience. It is meant to combine with the intuition and experience of the architect and developer and provide a proving ground for their ideas and concepts. Often analysis gives new insights which generate new springboards for design.

The developer and total cost   The developer for a project may be a speculative investor or may be a city trying to provide low-income housing. The speculator is interested in maximum return on his investment, whereas the city is interested in providing housing within well-defined cost guidelines. Both the speculator and the city are interested in all owning and operating aspects of cost, not just in construction cost.

The architect must realize that construction cost is only a part of total cost. Often, a savings in construction cost may, in fact, lead to an increase in total cost. The architect who keeps total cost in mind when making design decisions is a step ahead in satisfying his client.

Although many people are familiar with the statement the *Total Cost* is the sum of *Capital Cost* and *Future Cost,* the implications of exact definition of the components of those costs are by no means common knowledge—and they are important. The elements of capital cost are land cost, construction cost, design fees, and carrying charges. Future cost, in turn, contains operation cost, real estate taxes, and financing. These definitions are, in fact, simple enough, but a word of caution: calculating total cost is not quite as simple as it seems. We need first to develop the concept of the *Time Value of Money*.

The time value of money   The idea behind the time value of money is simply recognition of the fact that money invested earns money. If you put $1000 into a savings bank at 5.0 per cent interest, in fourteen years you will have $2000 in the bank. That is to say, the *Future Worth* of the *Present Amount* of $1000 at 5.0 per cent in fourteen years is $2000. Conversely, the *Present Worth* (sometimes called *Discounted*

Value) in 1970 of a *Future Amount* of $2000 in 1984 at 5.0 per cent is $1000. If a housewife were offered $1000 next week or $1000 fourteen years from now, she wouldn't need to consult an economist to decide which to take. But if she were offered $1000 next week or $2000 fourteen years from now, she might not so readily realize that the two offers are equivalent.

There is nothing sacred about 5 per cent. Different investors have different interest rates for their time value of money. The housewife's expectation may be 5 per cent in a savings account. A developer may expect 10 per cent since he has many investment opportunities at this level and would refuse a project earning less.

The formulas relating present worth and future worth are easily derived and can be found in texts on investment practice. Time value of money tables have been formed from these formulas. An excerpt from such a table is shown here.

Let us now consider a simple architectural problem involving the time value of money. An architect wishes to choose between a roofing product costing $6000 with no maintenance and one of lower quality costing $5000 with an expected $1000 maintenance charge after ten years and another $1000 after twenty years. The salesman for the higher quality product points out his costs only $6000, versus a total cost of $7000 for his competitor's product. But, he is wrong. He has not considered the time value of money. You can't add oranges and apples and you can't add present amounts and future amounts. The future amounts must first be converted to their present worth before the addition can be performed. Assume the work is being done for a developer whose time value of money is 10 per cent. Then using the time value of money table, the present worth of the first $1000 payment after ten years is $1000 × 0.3855 = $385.50. The present worth of the second payment after twenty years is $1000 × 0.1486 =$148.60. Then the total cost at present worth of the salesman's roofing is $6000, versus a total cost at present worth of his competitor's product of $5000 + $385.50 + $148.60 = $5534.10. The architect will save his client $465.90 by choosing the competitor's product.

The logic behind the above calculation is that if the developer were to invest $534.10 at 10 per cent interest, he could withdraw $1000 after ten years and $1000 more after twenty years to pay for the maintenance. In actual fact, the investor will be unable to find a bank which will pay 10 per cent on his invest-ment, but he will be able to earn 10 per cent in his own business.

These principles of the time value of money make possible the calculation of total cost. With these T.V.M. formulas, we can transpose future costs to present worth of future cost. Then, both future costs and capital costs will be at present worth. As such, they can be added to obtain total cost. We are now in a position to quantitatively understand the cost implications of design decisions consider-ing both capital and future costs.

In the bar graphs shown, p. 170, are indicated costs for a typical twenty-story, one-hundred-sixty-unit Manhattan luxury apartment. The first bar shows where the construction cost dollar goes. The second gets these costs into better per-spective by considering construction cost as a part of capital cost. In the third bar, the present worth of future cost has been added to capital cost to obtain total cost. The first bar presents the view of the contractor, but the third bar is the view of the client and of architectural economics. It should be the view of the architect.

A simple set of graphs of this form keeps cost in proper perspective. Changes in design which involve increased cost don't look quite so big when viewed as a part of total cost rather than as a part of construction cost. A 10 per cent in-

No. of Years	T.V.M. at 5.0%	
	Present Worth of Future Amount	Future Worth of Present Amount
5	0.7835	1.276
10	0.6139	1.629
15	0.4810	2.079
20	0.3769	2.653
25	0.2953	3.386
30	0.2313	4.322

No. of Years	T.V.M. at 10.0%	
	Present Worth of Future Amount	Future Worth of Present Amount
5	0.6209	1.611
10	0.3855	2.594
15	0.2394	4.177
20	0.1486	6.727
25	0.0923	10.835
30	0.0573	17.449

Note: More complete tables can be found in texts on investment practice such as *Engineering Economy*, by E. Paul De Garmo

Calculation of total cost

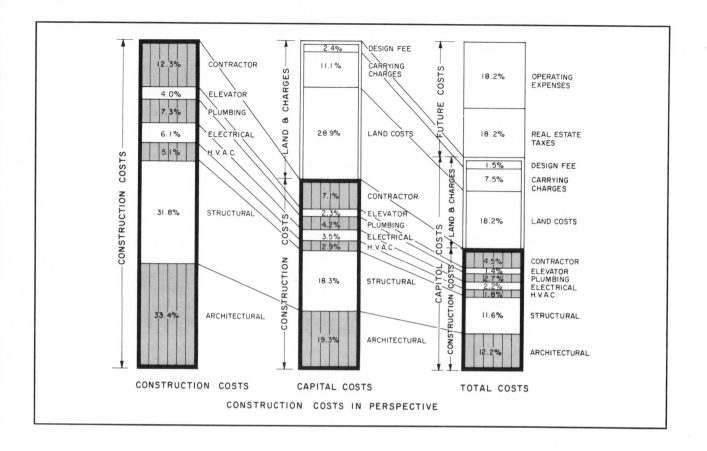

12.3% CONTRACTOR
4.0% ELEVATOR
7.3% PLUMBING
6.1% ELECTRICAL
5.1% H.V.A.C.
31.8% STRUCTURAL
33.4% ARCHITECTURAL

CONSTRUCTION COSTS

2.4% DESIGN FEE
11.1% CARRYING CHARGES
28.9% LAND COSTS
7.1% CONTRACTOR
2.3% ELEVATOR
4.2% PLUMBING
3.5% ELECTRICAL
2.9% H.V.A.C.
18.3% STRUCTURAL
19.3% ARCHITECTURAL

CAPITAL COSTS

18.2% OPERATING EXPENSES
18.2% REAL ESTATE TAXES
1.5% DESIGN FEE
7.5% CARRYING CHARGES
18.2% LAND COSTS
4.5% CONTRACTOR
.4% ELEVATOR
2.7% PLUMBING
2.2% ELECTRICAL
1.8% H.V.A.C.
11.6% STRUCTURAL
12.2% ARCHITECTURAL

TOTAL COSTS

CONSTRUCTION COSTS IN PERSPECTIVE

crease in structural cost sounds like a large increment to an owner. But structural costs are only 31.8 per cent of construction cost, (see graph), so this represents a $10 \times .318 = 3.18$ per cent increase in construction cost. And, structural costs are only 11.6 per cent of total cost, so that this is a $10 \times .116 = 1.16$ per cent increase in total cost. This increase in cost is more palatable when put in proper perspective. Whether or not the increase is justifiable is another question. The increase may be a small price to pay if the quality can generate higher rent.

Relating total cost to rent   Proper perspective of total cost can also indicate quantitatively the effect of changes in construction cost on rent. If an architect considers a design change which increases structural costs 10 per cent, he knows this will increase construction cost 3.18 per cent and total cost 1.16 per cent. But how much must rent be raised to cover the increased structural costs so that the owner maintains the same per cent return on his investment? Might in fact the improved design quality lead to a sufficient increase in rent to lead to increased profit?

It can be demonstrated mathematically that a 1.0 per cent increase in total cost will necessitate a 1.0 per cent increase in rent if the builder is to maintain the same per cent return on his investment. Hence, a 10 per cent increase in structural cost results in a 1.16 per cent increase in total cost and thus necessitates a 1.16 per cent increase in rent. The impact of changes in construction cost on rent now comes into perspective. The same method applies to office buildings, hotels, or low income housing.

We have seen that the way to obtain the increment in rent due to a 10 per cent increase in structural cost is to take 10 per cent of the figure attributed to structural cost in the total cost bar graph. An increase in land cost or operating cost would be treated analogously. Thus, the figure in the total cost bar graph represents a *Rent Amplification Factor* which, when multiplied times an increase in cost for the corresponding cost element, gives the required percentage increase in rent.

For example, consider the total cost of a high quality exterior wall with improved thermal insulation relative to a lower quality product. With the higher quality wall there is a 5 per cent drop in H.V.A.C. cost, a 4 per cent drop in building operating cost, and a 5 per cent increase in architectural construction cost. Then the effect on rent is as follows:

Cost Element	Change in Element	R.A.F.	Change in Rent
H.V.A.C.	$-.05 \times$	1.8% =	$-.09\%$
Operating Cost	$-.04 \times$	18.2% =	$-.73\%$
Architectural	$+.05 \times$	12.2% =	$+.61\%$
Total Change in Rent			$-.21\%$

Consider our twenty-story, 160-unit luxury apartment building. The architect has worked out a floor layout with 140 bathrooms back-to-back on 70 stacks and 20 baths on single stacks. He knows the single stacks are more expensive, but they just couldn't be avoided. In fact, forty additional apartment units would have a much more satisfactory layout if the architect didn't feel constrained by the maxim that wet walls should be back-to-back. Everyone, including the owner, knows singly-loaded stacks are more expensive, and this is enough to discourage a design change.

Baths on singly-loaded stacks cost $325 more per apartment unit than those on double stacks. The total cost of the building is $55 per square foot, and the average unit is 1100 square feet. Thus, the total cost per average unit is 1100 × $55 = $60,500. If we convert forty additional units to singly-loaded stacks, we increase the total cost of those units by $325/$60,500 = 0.54 per cent. We know that rent increases the same per cent as total cost if the owner is to maintain the same per cent return on his investment, so there must be a rent increase of 0.54 per cent. If rent is $450/unit/month, rent increases $450 × .0054 =$2.42/unit/month on the forty units converted to single stacks. Clearly a significantly improved floor plan can attract more than a $2.42/unit/month increase in rent.

This example demonstrates the difference between the qualitative and quantitative approaches. We know from the outset that construction costs would increase. But knowing the direction of change is not enough. One must know how much change. And one must know the interaction of that change in construction cost with other factors of cost. With such quantitative knowledge an intelligent decision can be made.

The estimate is not an end point. The square-foot vs. the "systems" estimate. The percentage fee: a moral issue.—Bradford Perkins

Cost knowledge: tool for budget, program and design

An experienced New England firm retained a professional cost consultant to make a single estimate at the end of design development. At that time, the project was still within the budget. However—during the period between design development and bids—the bidding climate changed, several seemingly minor design changes were made, a minority training program was added, and a number of other decisions with cost implications were modified. The resultant bids were 20 per cent over the budget.

Obviously, part of the error in this case was failure to consider the cost ramifications of the changes. This part of the error, however, was due to less visible underlying problems—the common view of estimates as an end product.

The construction cost estimate has been a valuable tool for many cost management programs. It is, nevertheless, only a tool. By itself, it is often an inadequate basis for meaningful cost control.

In today's complex and inflationary construction industry, most architects and engineers should be seeking something more from their in-house or consultant cost managers. Although every project will have different requirements, a typical, complete construction cost management program would include:

1. Evaluating the economic feasibility of project goals.
2. Establishing economical project parameters.
3. Establishing realistic budgets.
4. Evaluating alternative design approaches.
5. Making periodic assessments of total project cost.
6. Helping develop the most economical contract award strategy.
7. Evaluating change orders.

Clearly, such a program is something far more than a series of estimates. Most of the potential cost savings on the average project must be achieved in the earliest phases of planning and design. Estimates, however, are only one of the tools necessary to achieve them. Even the remainder of the potential savings requires something in addition to a detailed and accurate assessment of the total project cost. Therefore, it is worth examining in some detail how an architectural firm should employ its own or outside cost expertise to achieve an effective cost management program.

All too often projects are not evaluated for cost feasibility until the end of schematic design. Wherever there is any reason for doubt, it is worth everyone's while to have a realistic assessment of the probable net costs or revenues of a new project.

In some cases this assessment is not made because no one wants to risk killing the project before it has developed some momentum. At one recent conference, a group which hopes to sponsor a new race track commented that the last chart in the architect's presentation (the one showing the probable cost) was all they needed to see. The project the group had contemplated could not be justified on the basis of cost. Not to have calculated that unpleasant truth at this time would have resulted in a nice programming fee for the architect, but it would have been a misuse of the architect's efforts and the owner's money.

A good feasibility analysis will not halt most projects. The race track in question is going ahead on a more realistic basis. The feasibility study formed the basis for reevaluating the project in terms of its program, potential revenue, operating costs and financing arrangements.

In order to make such a study useful to most owners, the costs must be presented in a manner that facilitates decision making. In other words, the cost of each optional item should be noted. In the case of the race track, such items as the stable cost per horse, the cost of enclosing and air conditioning the entire viewing area, the variable cost per seat, probable annual maintenance costs and many other factors were all important in the development of the final program.

This information is most useful when it is structured in a manner that presents both a realistic picture of the initial approach and a means of developing the feasibility of alternative approaches.

Most projects are feasible, once they are launched, but often they are not programed in context with a rigid set of economical project parameters. It is at this point that the major portion of the potential savings is won or lost.

Someone should question the bid and completion dates as to whether they are so unrealistically tight that they will cause bid premiums, fail to take advantage of a slack period in the local construction industry, or are not timed to avoid adverse local weather conditions. Someone should also be able to advise on other areas such as the cost implications of materials options, the potential savings of alternative net-to-gross ratios, and the cost of optional program elements such as air conditioning.

This advice should coincide with a careful budgeting period. Systems budgeting is an important refinement of traditional budgeting techniques. Instead of overall square-foot cost, the architects and engineers should have cost goals for each of the major systems—HVAC, exterior wall, floor, etc.—so that judgments can be made with minimum constraint on design objectives.

The most important advantages of the systems technique are seen during schematic design, but the advantages of realistic budgets are felt throughout the project. This point has been made in some detail in previous sections.

Cost knowledge relates to budget, scope and design development

Throughout programing and budgeting, the cost expert can play an important role by directing the project's development toward realistic approaches. During schematics, moreover, the in-house or outside cost manager can support the architect's creative role by demonstrating cost consequences of various design approaches.

Increasingly today, project managers are sitting with their cost experts to establish the cost limits of alternative design approaches. As one project manager noted recently, "The most valuable part of the cost management program was being able to ask 'What wall systems can I get for $3.00 per square foot, what additional ones can I get if I have $3.50 per square foot to spend, and what ones do I lose if I have only $2.75?'" If this systems approach is established early, the designer is able to decide on the systems in context with the project budget.

Systems evaluations are also valuable techniques in the later phases of design. Detailed cost knowledge should be brought to bear on the increasingly detailed alternatives being evaluated. For example, in the later stages of design, and in contract documents, the relative costs of alternative details, structural systems, and other final design decisions require a more detailed evaluation than that provided by square-foot systems cost estimates.

The role of the cost expert at this point usually involves detailed quantity take-offs and pricing of real alternatives, since the exact cost options are increasingly important as the design is refined. If, in advanced design phases, it still becomes necessary to find means of reducing overall project costs, the cost manager's role in this area is to advise the designer of less-costly alternatives to various parts of the design. In extreme situations, this may involve drastic materials substitutions or even compromise of the mechanical or space programs of the building.

Value engineering: new name for doing it right the first time

In recent years, a newly-labeled technique called *value engineering* has been applied in the cost management process in order to minimize the negative effects of more simplistic paring operations associated with many cost-reduction programs. The goal of value engineering is not just to reduce cost; it aims at achieving unimpaired program results for minimum cost. Thus, a system that has been successfully value-engineered will still satisfy the same performance criteria as other more costly alternatives. In its simplest application, this technique has been used to check for over-design of structural members or unnecessarily complex, hidden details. In more sophisticated applications, it involves refinements in project specifications to eliminate costly contradictions and restrictions, detailed evaluations of mechanical systems, and careful refinements of the internal composition of major details.

The five essential steps to genuine cost control

All of these techniques require the ability to take off quantities and apply prices —the basic procedure of the cost estimator. The major use of these techniques is, of course, in the development of periodic assessments of probable total project cost. None of the assertions made in the preceding paragraphs should minimize the absolute importance of these assessments or estimates.

The basic guidelines for estimating as a tool for effective cost control include developing and organizing the level of detail necessary for decision-making, clearly noting the local market conditions which will affect the final contract price, and timing the estimates to reflect significant changes in the nature or amount of information available for the estimate.

No two projects will have identical estimating requirements, but the major parts of the average full estimating program are the following:

1. A budget estimate based on the program and a study of local construction market conditions. This estimate establishes the systems cost goals and also identifies the potential strengths and problems of the local construction environment.

2. A second estimate is based on schematic drawings to check the general feasibility of the systems selected.

3. An estimate is made as soon as the design has been developed sufficiently to permit a detailed quantity take-off. This estimate should give the owner and architect their first detailed look at the probable cost system by system.

4. A fourth estimate should be made as soon as the mechanical and electrical designs are developed sufficiently to permit detailed take-off. This estimate should be accompanied by an updated market study which can be used for planning contract award strategy.

5. The fourth estimate should be updated in a manner which will permit the owner, architect and cost manager to make a detailed evaluation of the contract price.

Market studies used for planning contract award strategy should identify the potential bidders and their level of interest, problems which can affect bidder interest, pending labor negotiations and the many other factors which can affect the timing and success of the contract award period. Cost advice on such areas as negotiated contracts, construction management and the other variations of traditional contracting procedures can be invaluable.

Cost knowledge is equally essential during the evaluation of the final contract price. Many bids, for example, can be negotiated downward if the negotiations are begun from a position of real knowledge.

The same strength in knowledge is true for change orders. Only someone who can make a detailed evaluation of the actual time and cost ramifications of an approved change can successfully negotiate a change order.

All of the above elements, from feasibility studies to change order analysis, are essential parts of a full construction cost management program. In addition, all of these services clearly provide a more meaningful level of control and a far greater potential for significant savings than the single estimate.

The percentage fee: a costly moral issue

On a certain large job, a midwestern architect cogently questioned his client on the wisdom of insisting on the percentage of construction cost method of compensation. As he pointed out, "If I do a good job and bring the job in under the budget, my fee will be reduced and the money will be used to pay the increased fee of a firm which overruns its construction budget." Unfortunately, that is exactly how it worked. The preliminary estimates revealed that his project, because of its design, could be built for at least five per cent less than the budget. The subsequent loss in fees represented most of the architect's projected profit. As a result, the design team had a strong incentive to use up the entire budget.

Most design professionals will ignore this incentive if they know how it exists. Nevertheless, the percentage of construction cost still nurtures the assumption that every penny of the budget should be spent.

Both the incentive to spend the full budget and the assumption that this is what is appropriate are wrong for most projects. As a first step toward correcting this long-standing problem, the architectural and engineering professions must make a concerted effort to divorce themselves from the concept that their compensation is in some way directly related to project construction costs.

The percentage of construction cost is the most common method of compensation and also the major problem. It has survived as the path of least resistance, but it has almost no virtues. Among its major flaws are the facts that:

1. It is arbitrary; fee practices in neighboring regions often vary by more than 50 per cent for identical projects; and the direct costs of architects in the same region can vary by more than 50 per cent for projects with identical fees.

2. It sometimes provides the same compensation for an exceptional degree of service as it does for a minimum program.

3. And worst of all, it impedes the profession's commitment to genuine cost responsibility.

This last point is the most costly for architects and engineers both in terms of reputation and dollars. In addition, experienced design professionals should be well aware of the vagaries of the U.S. construction industry today. With this in mind, it is hard to understand why anyone would willingly peg his own compensation to something over which he has so little real control.

The only solution is for architects and engineers to discourage the use of all of these methods as a commitment to a professional approach to construction cost control. The professional fee plus expenses, lump sum, multiplier and several of the other methods outlined in the AIA's publication, *Methods of Compensation for Architectural Services,* are all preferable.

The cost index: Working tool or trap?

For the pre-design projection of specific building project costs, the effects of building type and the local effects of labor rates, materials costs and availability, building codes and labor productivity all inject factors of modification into the judicious use of most published cost indexes. The New York consulting firm of McKee-Berger-Mansueto, Inc. sought to pinpoint some of these effects, and the following report on a two-city demonstration of their study was written in 1969 by Lawrence Jaquith, then staff economist for the firm.

When an architect makes a cost estimate on a current project, he often tries, using various multipliers, to relate his figures to a similar project he has designed in the past. He will take itemized costs from a former job and try to adjust them from one city to another and/or from the past to the present or to some future time. He often uses cost indices to accomplish this. Considering the frequency of inaccurate results, it must be asked whether an index is appropriate at all to the estimating process—and if so, when? Is it appropriate during all stages of design, or when a design is complete but the project is delayed? If an index is partially effective, what additional information is necessary to project a cost accurately?

Some of the problems with commonly-used indices are their lack of sensitivity in accounting for different building types and/or different methods of construction, and the limited number of cities and towns covered. The first objection applies to those indices where weighted price ratios of wages and materials are compiled. The second refers to the "summary of contract costs" index, which is usually limited to a few cities or a few building types because it is compiled mostly by contractors who, no matter how large, tend to have limited experience in certain areas and building types.

Detailed index prepared for conceptual-phase estimates

For its own purposes, our firm has developed an index which covers some fifty different building types for 200 cities in the U.S. Its use, while alleviating some of the difficulties mentioned above, nevertheless has underscored the restraint which must be employed in using any index to translate costs from one place or time to another.

A carefully compiled and judiciously handled index is quite helpful during the early stages of design when most features are still conceptual. Since the bid date is a long way off, and little design information has been developed, a figure developed through prudent use of a good index is about the only means available for preliminary cost estimation.

As the bid date approaches, however, and as the design features are elaborated, an index can serve only as a starting place in cost evaluation. The best estimates, of course, are prepared using known local unit costs. But accumulation of detailed local cost information is a difficult, costly and time-consuming task. It can be wasteful if applied when a design is in a phase of development and change. During that phase, the index is useful to update or translate historical costs, but the demands upon its sensitivity increase beyond prudent limits as the design reaches the pre-bid phase where accuracy falters in the pinpoint specifics of a given project. At that time greater accuracy is essential to selection of alternates if the budget so requires.

Local productivity and market can greatly modify index

Most published indexes available to architects do not give adequate attention to two important evaluating factors: 1) productivity of labor and 2) local market conditions. These may, in some cities, have such effect as to greatly modify or even reverse the relative values which may be derived from popular indexes.

A recent comparison, made by our firm, of cost differences between two Mid-

What items are being delayed? For how long? Are these delays regular or infrequent? Are there any anticipated delays not now being experienced? How are these delays affecting costs? What percentage of the project cost will be affected by current or anticipated delays?

2. *Adequacy of fabrication facilities*

How many facilities are available in the area? Are they adequate for the amount of work at present or for that anticipated? Have delays or poor workmanship resulted? Has this been regular or infrequent? How has this affected cost? What percentage of the project cost is involved?

3. *Shortage of labor*

In what trades are there shortages? Indicate the number of men in each area by trade. How severe is the present shortage? Is it temporary or permanent? In what trades will men be needed? How has this affected the quality of work? How has this affected cost? What percentage of the project is involved? How has this affected project duration and scheduling? Are there any anticipated shortages that do not exist at present? If tradesmen are coming from other areas, what areas are they coming from? What trades?

4. *Overtime and premium pay*

What trades are receiving overtime and premium pay (including travel pay)? In terms of number of hours, what is the average weekly overtime by trade? What is the average premium pay in terms of dollars per hour by trade? Is it a temporary or permanent condition? How is this affecting cost? What percentage of the job cost is affected by this condition?

5. *Construction volume*

Information should be obtained from building permits, the Department of Commerce (Construction Statistics), Building News Service, Hill-Burton Register, etc. What is the present and anticipated volume of construction by building type? What is the percentage increase? (*Note:* Item Number 5 is important as related to items 1–4 and item 6.)

6. *Competition*

How many contractors bid on similar work in each locale? What is the average number? This information should be grouped in terms of different size projects. What do the contractors anticipate as a work load for themselves next year?

7. *Seasonal factors*

Are there any seasonal differences that would account for a cost differential?

8. *Work jurisdiction and other problems*

Are there work rules that add to the cost of a job in one area more than in other? (Note: this may be accounted for in productivity.)

9. *Building codes*

Are there building codes that add to the cost of a job in one area more than in the other?

These questions should be answered as specifically as possible to produce an accurate index adjustment. After speaking to numerous contractors in both areas, and evaluating their reports of market conditions, a project surcharge of 4.75 per cent was added to City Y. Adding this element to the indexing equation yields a new index number for City Y—when City X = 100, City Y ≐ 111, i.e. any given project will cost 11 per cent more to construct in City Y than in City X.

To review the breakdown of comparison calculations for the two cities:

a) Labor and material cost differences:

City Y = 101.27; City X = 100

b) Application of productivity factors:
City Y = 105.7; City X = 100
c) Market condition surcharges:
City Y = 4.75; City X = 0
$105.7 \times 1.0475 = 111.0$

Consideration of these two factors has, therefore, altered the original index number by 9.6 per cent; a substantial amount when one is dealing with projects worth millions of dollars.

Studies may help pinpoint complex value judgments

At the present time, there is no easy method of quantifying either productivity or market conditions as factors for inclusion in a general indexing equation. Both require careful and extensive research. Currently there are many studies under way for measuring productivity in cities throughout the U.S. Market conditions are more difficult to pin down since they are short term in nature. However, the study discussed above illustrates the importance of both productivity and market conditions in project cost determination and, therefore, the need for their inclusion to produce a more sensitive and workable index for the architect's use.

Guidelines for early planning estimates

The relationship of building complexity to construction cost, while obviously positive, has been one of the most difficult functions to quantify in terms of both budget estimates for clients and fee structures for architects.

A 1970 study of estimated building costs for the City University of New York sought to develop guidelines based on data gained in prior planning estimates involving some $316 million in construction for six other metropolitan New York colleges. While the whole study would be more particular than useful, one section of it, a checklist of trade-related elements arranged in order of complexity, reprinted below, may be a useful outline for others whose costing resources can adapt the method for other building types and locations.

By relating each project to the listed elements and a set of current square-foot costs, it is possible to increase greatly the sensitivity of advance estimates. Further, this approach offers an itemized scrutiny of design options related to cost control as well as a realistic basis for fee negotiation.

Prior to using the checklist, the estimator needs certain documents and information in hand: the owner's program regarding quality and substance of his needs; the architectural program of net and gross space allocation; advance drawings showing general configuration and physical scope of the project; qualitative information about foundation problems, structural and mechanical systems, basic materials and finishes and any site or schedule problems that may affect costs.

The procedure is successively to refine an approximate overall estimate based on rational square-foot costs through discussion and detailed evaluation of the trade-related items below. Confirmation of the "complexity-related" approach developed in an analysis of university buildings by type which showed that each of seven types was represented at all three levels of complexity with surprisingly uniform brackets of square-foot costs: "simple" in the low $30's; "average" in the upper $30's; "above normal" between $40 and $50. The logical overlap of an "above normal" gym with a "simple" lab further confirms the complexity of the approach.

The following table shows the range of trade-related values applied in the New York project:

	Simple	Average	Above normal
Structural*	$ 4.50	$ 6.00	$ 7.00
Architectural treatment*	15.00	19.00	22.00
Plumbing	1.00	1.50	2.00
Plumbing w/labs	3.50	4.50	6.00
HVAC	5.75	7.00	8.50
Electrical	5.75	3.50	4.50

*In New York State, these items comprise "general construction," one of four basic contracts. See scope of each in checklist below.

Note that a mixture of complexity categories occurs in almost all projects. Further, users are reminded that these figures are for a particular time and place and must be adjusted for any other use. Also, the following list is adaptable and is shown to demonstrate a method, not to limit applicable cost considerations.

STRUCTURAL

Simple

Unclassified earth excavation, minimal elevation deviations.

Stockpiling of excavated material on site.

Balanced cut and fill.

Uniform spread footings.

Continuous wall footings, nonstepped.

Concrete block or poured concrete foundation walls.

Concrete slab on grade.

Minimal interior foundation wall requirements.

Simple bay size layout.

Masonry load-bearing walls.

Exposed steel frame, spray-on or masonry fire-protected. Bar joist framing with poured concrete plank decking.

Generally simple shaped building, easily framed.

Average

(25 to 45 per cent higher in cost than "simple" construction)

Unclassified earth excavation, some variance of grade elevations.

Stockpiling of excavated materials on site.

Balanced cut and fill.

Spread footings generally uniform dimensions with some oddities.

Continuous wall footings, with stepped requirements.

Poured concrete foundation walls.

Concrete slab on grade.

Some interior foundation wall requirements.

Usually uniform bay size layouts for structural system, including variances for special conditions.

Reinforced concrete frame and arches.

Structural steel frame, masonry or spray-on fire protection.

Simple-use precast concrete or architectural cast concrete members for structural purposes.

Generally more complicated building shape with breaks, corners, cantilever requirements requiring an experienced contractor.

Above normal

(Over 45 per cent higher in cost than "simple" construction)

Classified earth excavation such as hardpan, clay, boulders, rocks, etc.

Great variations in grade.

Dewatering problems.

Required bracing, shoring, etc.

Unbalanced cut and fill resulting in need of borrowed material.

Foundation complications requiring spread footings of varying sizes and shapes; special foundations, such as piles.

Grade beam requirements more often than typical, continuous wall footings and foundation walls.

Structural slab not on grade.

Interior requirements for foundation walls and footings.

Varying bay sizes.

Complicated reinforcing concrete frame and slab; structural steel frame encased in concrete fireproofing.

Involved precast concrete or architectural concrete details.

Generally complicated shaped structure requiring unique structural design solutions or considerations requiring high-caliber contractor.

Design for future expansion.

ARCHITECTURAL TREATMENT

Simple

Simple shaped building with minimal architectural features.

Exterior brick or block with stock window shapes, some stone work or precast trim, low ratio of windows.

Unplastered block or drywall partitions in most areas.

Resilient tile floors, V.A.T., predominantly used.

Painted exposed ceilings in most areas.

Hung ceilings in corridors and offices.

Flat roofs with parapets.

Simple waterproofing requirements.

Vitreous spray or cement enamel in lieu of ceramic tile, minimal use of vitreous materials except for floors in wet areas.

Simple program requirements.

Low ratio of interior work.

Hollow metal doors and bucks at normal heights.

Simple stair exiting, and fire protection requirements.

Minimum provision for future flexibility.

Minimum circulation space, double loaded corridors.

Average

(20 to 40 per cent higher in cost than "simple" treatment)

More complex shaped building expressing architectural features.

Exterior glass brick, architectural concrete, larger ratio of windows, special size windows, moderate use of stone work.

Unplastered block partitions utilizing expressive bonds. Use of more expensive interior finishes, especially in public areas.

Resilient tile floors, V.A.T., predominantly used, some use of carpeting or other more costly finishes.

Greater requirement for hung ceilings, simple suspension system and economic use of acoustical tile.

Flat roofs with some setbacks on different levels.

More complex waterproofing requirements.

Greater use of vitreous materials on walls and floors in wet areas.

More complex program requirements, modular design.

Greater density of interior work.

Solid wood doors and metal bucks;

heights may vary according to need and location.

Greater fire protection and exiting requirements.

Modest provisions for flexibility.

More circulation space requirements.

Greater need for mechanical equipment space.

Modest use of varied materials for interior finishes.

Above normal

(Over 40 per cent higher in cost than "simple" treatment)

Complex shaped building requiring architectural treatments such as plazas, stilt designs, overhangs, setbacks, multilevels, etc.

Exterior walls expressing and accentuating architectural esthetics predominantly utilizing stonework, precast or architectural concrete units, special window shapes and details, high ratio of glass work, greater use of metal alloys for trim and decorative purposes.

Plastered interior partitions, greater use of vinyl wall coverings, and glazed ceramic or vitreous finishes on walls.

Greater use of vinyl tile floors and architecturally expressive finishes.

Greater use of hung ceilings in most areas.

Multi-level roofs, setbacks, penthouses, promenade decks, etc.

Costly damp-and-waterproofing requirements.

Ceramic tile or glazed block used on floors and walls in wet areas.

Complex program requirements for multi-purpose occupancy.

High density requirements for interior work; single-loaded corridors.

Expensive vertical and horizontal transportation equipment.

Large degree of flexibility inherent in layout and design to accommodate future changes and requirements for mechanical and electrical trades.

PLUMBING

Simple

Gravity type sanitary and storm system using extra heavy cast iron pipe and fittings.

Domestic hot and return water systems utilizing submerged tankless coils in boiler.

Gas distribution for gas unit heaters, rooftop cooling and heating units and boiler.

Austere fixtures.

Economical toilet layouts, i.e., typical in-line facilities.

Fire standpipe system, if required. insulation for mains, risers, water lines and horizontal storm drains in finished areas.

Average

(Includes "simple" category plus the following items resulting in more than 40 per cent higher cost than for simple systems.)

Sump and ejector pump systems.

Hot water generator.

Domestic water pressure system.

Emergency generator—gas connections.

Standard fixtures.

Kitchen work.

Tempered water for showers.

Above normal

(Includes "simple" and "average" categories, plus the following, which will add 90 per cent or more to "simple" costs.)

Galvanized steel or wrought iron above grade for sanitary and storm systems.

Foundation drainage if required.

Preheater for domestic hot water.

Water treatment if required.

Gas piping for laboratories.

Acid-neutralizing system for labs.

Exotic gas systems for labs.

Emergency showers and eye wash.

De-ionized and distilled water systems for labs.

Heavy kitchen work—i.e., slurry systems with extractors and pulpers.

Air compressors, vacuum pumps, distillers.

Fire pump and jockey pump.

Insulation of all domestic water piping and all horizontal storm piping.

Luxury fixtures.

HVAC

Simple

Low pressure, one pipe steam system. Two pipe circulating hot water system.

Ventilation only, of interior areas (toilets).

Self-contained, low pressure heating and air conditioning systems, all air.

Forced air heat only.

Self-contained boiler rooms.

Insulation of piping and supply duct work.

Electric automatic temperature control system.

Average

(Includes "simple" category plus the following which will add 20 to 40 per cent to cost.)

Central station heating and air conditioning (single zone).

Multi-zone heating and air conditioning systems with reheat coils.

Fan coil perimeter system, two or four pipe.

Unit ventilator system, two or four pipe.

Kitchen and "simple" laboratory exhaust.

Mechanical equipment rooms, including converters, chillers.

Acoustic lining.

Automatic sprinkler system (fire prevention).

Pneumatic controls, electric-electronic controls.

Above normal

(Can include "simple" and "average" categories, plus the following which will tend to increase costs more than 40 per cent above costs for "simple" systems.)

Dual duct system with mixing boxes, or terminal reheats.

Induction system.

Fume hood exhaust.

Dust collection system.

Thermal wheel heat exchange.

Run-around heat reclamation.

High pressure steam, with PRV stations.

Radiant ceilings and floors.

Air-light distribution systems.

Heat pumps.

Glycol and/or brine systems.

Steam humidification.

Snow removal systems.

Water treatment systems.

Boiler feed system.

CO_2 fire prevention system.

Remote power plant installation.

Central station, computerized monitoring for automatic temperature controls.

Sound attenuation systems.

Design requirements for future expansion.

Design for a high degree of flexibility.

ELECTRICAL

Simple

One main distribution panel (wall mounted) serving simple 120/208V.

Feeders: runs feeding one or more panels at a time.

Lighting fixtures: fluorescent fixtures mainly in continuous rows. Few incandescent fixtures.

Branch circuit work: use of one light switch per average room, receptacles used sparingly.

Motor work: individually mounted starters furnished by others.

Fire alarm system: master control board with stations and gongs at stairs and exits. Non-coded, non-zoned.

Sound system: master amplifiers with microphone and page common to all speakers.

Clock: inexpensive clock with cord plugged into outlet on wall.

Emergency lighting: wall-mounted battery units with headlamps.

Average

(Items resulting in 20 to 50 percent higher cost than "simple" systems.)

Service and panels: one main distribution board (free standing) serving light and power panels. Simple 120/208V service.

Feeders: runs feeding one or more panels at a time.

Lighting fixtures: fluorescent fixtures mainly in continuous rows. Few incandescent fixtures. specialty lighting where necessary plus some architectural lighting for esthetic purposes.

Branch circuit work. Two or more light switches for each major room controlling different rows of fixtures. Use of three-way switching. More generous employment of receptacles—both duplex and special.

Motor work: motor control center furnished by electrical contractor.

Fire alarm system: master control board with stations and gongs at stairs and exits plus zoning and coding of fire signal. Use of some heat and smoke detectors.

Sound system: master amplifiers with microphone and page common to all speakers.

Clock and program system: master control cabinet plus devices in major rooms and halls.

Television system: antennas, amplifier and receiving outlets throughout building.

Emergency lighting system: use of emergency generator and automatic transfer switch feeding one emergency panel.

Laboratory work: wiremold raceway with receptacles on laboratory walls.

Above normal

(Items resulting in more than 50 per cent higher cost than "simple" systems.)

Service and panels. 480/277V service into building, one or more free standing main distribution boards, 480/120-208V transformers, sub-distribution panels, light and power panels.

Feeders: multiple sets of feeders between main distribution boards, and from main distribution boards to sub-distribution panels. Single feeder runs from sub-distribution panels to light and power panels. Possible use of bus duct for main feeders.

Lighting fixtures: fluorescent fixtures mainly in continuous rows. Few incandescent fixtures. Specialty lighting where necessary plus some architectural lighting for esthetic purposes. Dimming effects and luminous ceiling areas. High intensity lighting for special areas.

Branch circuit work: two or more light switches per major room controlling different rows of fixtures. Use of three-way switching. More generous employment of receptacles—both duplex and special.

Motor work: motor control centers plus intricate interlocking and control devices, fan shutdown coupled with fire alarm system.

Fire alarm system: coded and supervised fire alarm system plus complete smoke detection, heat detection and sprinkler alarm systems. Fan shutdown facilities coupled to motor control centers.

Sound system: master system plus subsystems in other facilities inter-connected for selective paging.

Clock and program system: master control cabinet plus devices in major rooms and halls.

Television system: antennas, amplifiers and receiving outlets throughout building plus program originating and sending facilities. Possible television studio.

Emergency lighting system: emergency generator plus complete system of feeders and panels to all areas.

Public telephone system: complete system of feeder conduits, terminal cabinets and outlets.

Stage lighting and dimming: theatrical stage lighting with complete dimming facilities.

Intercom telephone system: automatic exchange plus handsets.

Laboratory work: special lab panels with contactors, wiremold raceway with multivoltage receptacles lab bench wiring, explosion proof areas.

Surveillance and security system: All exterior and stair doors, plus door to special rooms, wired to central security console. Possible closed circuit television hookup included.

Design for future expansion.

Design characteristics reflecting high degree of flexibility.

Some common errors in cost control programs

"If you were to outline for architects the basic guidelines of an effective cost control program, you would insult the architects' intelligence." This statement (by an industry expert) is true, by and large, but under today's increasingly complex operating conditions even the profession's more sophisticated firms are prone to misapply or ignore simple rules of cost control that can only be called basic guidelines.

The three case histories that follow illustrate some common mistakes and the lessons that should be learned from them. While these cases are based on actual experiences of architectural firms, they are not intended to imply that the profession is not concerned with building costs. But the growing complexity of design and construction processes—as well as additional problems of inflation—have made it far harder to avoid fundamental errors. Hence, the following case histories are not an indictment, but they do illustrate how faulty approaches to cost problems can be damaging to the reputation of the profession and to the purchasing capability of its clients.

■ **Case One:** A private hospital board submitted a program for a new hospital and an inflexible budget of $11 million to its architect. After a brief examination, the architect accepted the program and budget as reasonable.

After design development, a detailed review of the project and its potential cost showed that the project would cost $16 million. Independent consultants agreed there was virtually no "fat" in response of the design to the program. The simple fact was that the project, as programed, could never have been built for $11 million.

Many of the country's most unhappy owners have been outraged by the results of similar over-optimism on the part of their architects and themselves. All project programs and budgets should be given critical analysis at the beginning of the project—not at the end of design development or after bids have been opened.

Few owners have highly flexible construction purchasing ability that can respond to post-design increases. Public bodies, in particular, are being squeezed by severe financing problems, and a rate of inflation augmented by padded bidding so that it often exceeds that for private work. Therefore, unless there is a clearly-stated understanding between the architect and the owner that the project budget may have to be revised at the bidding phase, the budget should be assumed to be fixed.

The architect must make a careful review and analysis of the program and budget whether the budget be fixed or not. This is important for buildings, such as hospitals, which are rigidly constrained by building codes and the interdependency of the program elements. A large cost estimating mistake is hard to correct later in such a project.

A good review process takes into account more than updated square-foot costs of similar projects. It considers other influences on bids such as how busy local contractors and labor are likely to be at the time of bids, the size of the project, and the amount of interest contractors are likely to show. Large public projects, for example, are currently having a difficult time finding responsive bidders. Contractors are understandably wary of projects that run beyond the life of local labor contracts and are subject to the slow payments and extra administrative costs for which public projects are notorious.

Opened bids on a community college near New York City illustrate what can happen. The project was originally budgeted at $12 million, and the architect convinced the client that the building called for in the program would probably cost as much as $16 million. This estimate did not take into account the lack of interest that contractors were showing for such projects, and the bids came in at $30 million.

This type of overrun is usually impossible to predict, but the owner and architect should be aware of situations in which it is likely to occur. Moreover, they should take steps to avoid such situations.

This architect did take one important step. He told the owner that the budget was unrealistic. Some architects are hesitant to do this. They fear that if they tell the client the project cannot be built for the budget, the client will find another architect who will say that it can.

Ethical considerations should prevent the architect from keeping silent; and practical considerations make a straightforward approach imperative. The architect faced with an unrealistic budget should take action to convince his client that increased funding is necessary. If the architect's persuasive powers and the weight of his own cost data are not enough, he should obtain additional support from a consultant. If the owner still is not convinced, the architect must develop a design approach that is compatible with a restrictive budget. Under no circumstances is it wise to ignore this problem, for the consequences later in the project are costly for both the architect and the owner. None of the post-design solutions—of which there are only three—are very palatable to either the architect or his client.

The first solution is to try redesign. Unfortunately, if the budget is tight or the program is rigid, the first sacrifices are usually the materials, details and special areas which are so important to the esthetic and environmental quality of the project.

The second solution is to find construction techniques that can reduce bid levels. These include phasing construction and letting many small, rather than several large, contracts. This solution has been used with considerable success but it is always a gamble. Moreover, the extra construction administration costs and headaches for both owner and architect may be prohibitive.

Another solution is to cut the program and that is a last resort on almost all projects.

■ **Case Two:** An architect was commissioned to design an $8-million school in a town far from his office. An independent estimate of his design solution revealed that the probable bids would be over $13 million. His mistake: he did not understand the construction "habits" and requirements of the area in which the school was to be built.

Understanding the construction process is vital for effective cost control. Typical of the design decisions that showed construction naiveté in this case was the architect-specified special window system. These windows had to be shipped from the architect's home area to the project site, and were difficult to install.

Every architect knows that special items cost more money, but understanding the reason why is equally important. On major items, such as foreign-made electrical or mechanical systems, a contractor will prepare a higher bid which includes a contingency allowance for installation problems, labor objections and similar unknowns. On smaller items the contractor's justification is based primarily on the possibility of installation problems.

This happened with the window system in this case. The contractor was correct to include a contingency amount, for he found that the window system was hard to integrate with the wall system and that there were delays in delivery and installation. Specification of equipment and materials that local contractors know and understand will often minimize such problems.

Esthetic and environmental considerations will make some expensive items justifiable. Nevertheless, the architect should be aware of the potential construction problems caused by all such design decisions.

Once the architect is aware of these potential problems, it is possible to attempt value engineering. Value engineering is a design effort to achieve the same result for less cost. On a recent project, the architect found that a seemingly insignificant simplification of one detail, which was repeated throughout the project's interior, reduced the millwork bid by half. The detail was redrawn to minimize the work required of the carpenters.

In the case of the school project under discussion, the most serious error was a failure to understand the local construction requirements. The project's precast concrete requirements, for example, were beyond the capacity of the local construction industry.

This particular example may seem atypical, but it is actually illustrative of a type of error that many architects make. Architects in an area with many skilled carpenters will design a complicated poured-in-place concrete structure for an area where the necessary skilled labor is not available; designers in colder climates overdesign for weather conditions in more temperate areas; and many other design professionals have shown similar disregard for the limitations and opportunities that exist in every locality.

Failure to adhere to these guidelines results in costly redesign, unhappy clients, a problem-plagued construction phase and all the other well-known headaches which accompany over-budget projects.

■ **Case Three:** A New York City community college was bid one year as a single package for each of the four major trades. The resulting bids totaled $103 million. This total was far more than the final estimate of $55 million. These bids, which represented a square-foot cost of almost $100, were clearly unreasonable, and they were rejected. New bidding packages were split into five phases which then came in at or near the original $55-million estimate level.

This case is not an illustration of a major mistake. It has been included to show the value of intelligent contract-award planning.

Spiraling labor costs have received virtually all of the blame for the construction industry's chronic inflation, but, as this case shows, there are other significant forces behind high bids. The most important of these other forces are the contractors. Contractors in today's construction market often push bids far above reasonable levels. This is due in part to the over-burdened, non-competitive nature of much of the industry, and in part to the poor contract-award planning of the owner and architect.

Contracts can be planned to minimize costs. In an over-burdened construction market, careful planning of this single area can often lead to larger savings than careful selection of materials or careful design of the project's systems and details.

A well-planned contract is usually the result of at least three major actions on the part of the owner and architect—the establishment of an appropriate project schedule, the development of a project package which is attractive to a competitive group of contractors, and the selection of a qualified contractor.

Project scheduling is particularly important when unstable costs are escalating at a rate which can exceed one per cent per month in many areas. Careful scheduling, through the use of the Critical Path Method or other techniques, allows the owner and architect to compare the feasibility of expediting procedures, such as phasing or crashing, to avoid part of the inflationary spiral, with a more conventional construction schedule.

Other benefits of careful scheduling can lead to even more significant savings than those achieved by merely shortening the period to completion. Scheduling can permit owners and architects to put projects out to bid during lulls in construction activity, to avoid the higher bids associated with unrealistic completion dates and to begin construction during a month which is best for local contractors and construction techniques.

The architect of a project which could possibly run into bidding difficulty can evaluate whether any special approach to contract scheduling is warranted by getting answers to some simple questions: Will the contract run beyond local labor union contracts? Are there large unpredictable cost areas, such as unknown subsoil conditions, included in a lump sum contract? Is the contract too big for all but a few already busy contractors? These and many other contract provisions, such as slow payment procedures or excessive inspection conditions, can lead to unnecessarily high bids.

Three examples of changes that might be recommended are: for unusual subsoil conditions, a separate cost-plus contract; where there is a shortage of interested large contractors, dividing the contract to interest smaller firms; and phasing a long construction period to match bidding periods to local labor contracts. The latter two approaches were the ones chosen for the project in Case Three.

None of these actions is guaranteed to provide solutions, and, if not handled carefully, all can have negative repercussions. For example, separate contracts usually mean more management problems, and a single lump sum bid can at times be lower than a phased or split-contract approach. Nevertheless, when carefully planned and implemented, many of the special contract-award approaches discussed above can often result in significant reductions in construction costs.

All of the above recommendations are, of course, of little value if the project is built by an incompetent contractor. Wherever possible, the architect should help the owner encourage qualified contractors to bid, and disqualify those who are not fully capable. A good pre-qualification procedure evaluates each builder's workload, experience with buildings similar to the project, ability to undertake work of the project's size and reasons for failing (if ever) to complete a previous project.

Ability to handle the project is probably the most important of the above considerations, for contractor failure is a growing problem for both owners and architects. In 1967, for example, over nineteen per cent of the nation's business failures were bankrupt contractors. The cost of contractor failure for all parties is well known.

The contractor's experience with similar projects is also a very important consideration. Recently, a large financial institution hired a noted architect and a competent contractor to build a housing project on a cost-plus basis. The original budget was $8 million, but the contractor's estimate was $12 million. Inflation, an inefficient design, and several other factors accounted for part of this overrun. A significant portion of the increase, however, was due to the contractor's complete lack of experience with housing. Because of residential construction's many repetitive elements, builders specializing in this type of work have been able to develop many cost-cutting shortcuts. The owner's failure to choose a firm which knew these shortcuts was a major cost error.

Evaluating hidden cost factors

Exact quantity take-offs and careful unit pricing do not always insure an accurate construction cost estimate. Care in both areas is essential, but there are many other factors which have significant effects on the final cost of a construction contract.

Some of these factors—for example, the accuracy of the contractors' own estimators—defy prediction. Others, however, can be analyzed and, to some extent, quantified. Therefore, qualitative and quantitative analyses of local construction markets are becoming increasingly important elements of cost management programs.

These analyses do not have a standard format because each project differs from all others, but some general areas covered are: 1) local geographical, sociological and economic factors; 2) contractors' interest in and capabilities for the job; 3) labor availability and cost; 4) availability of materials; 5) owner and designer factors.

The first set of factors, including data on population density, proximity to urban centers and accessibility via major traffic routes, can readily indicate potential problems. The construction industry's capabilities in smaller towns can be strained by the requirements of a large project, so the estimator should take note of the work experience and size of local contractors' firms and labor pools.

The character of a town can also have other potential effects on costs. In one town outside New York, for example, the construction industry depends heavily on one owner for work. Therefore, local work has to be suited to this employer's construction program. In another area, organized crime may determine the number and interest of bidders.

Generally published market information rarely provides the detail necessary for either design decisions or final cost estimates, but it does indicate where further research is necessary. It is the research on local contractors, labor, material and owner-architect factors which can and should help shape the final plans.

Lack of interest raises costs

Contractor interest and capabilities are often the major additional cost considerations. A New York community college was bid at over $100 per square foot in 1969. In retrospect, this well-known disaster resulted, at least in part, from a shortage of contractors with both adequate bonding capacity and interest in the project. Only two firms were willing to bid on a city project that would last four years, and neither was willing to take it without premiums which approached 100 per cent.

Shortages of large, interested contractors have been common for several years in the major cities. However, similar situations appear on small projects in other areas.

A development of the reverse type is the "negative escalation" experienced on small projects in many regions. Smaller projects tend to dry up sooner because their owners are more sensitive to national economic slowdowns, inflat and financing problems. In many smaller cities, for example, owners have reported as many as eight bidders on projects under $5 million. As a result, some over-all project costs temporarily leveled off or declined in spite of the continuing increases in labor and material prices.

Multiple contracts help on large jobs

Interest is only one of the two important contractor considerations; the other is capability. In small cities and rural areas, local contractors may not be able to build a complex project efficiently. An inexperienced contractor facing a complex project usually adds a significant premium to his bid—if he bids at all. What usually happens is that large outside contractors have to be encouraged to bid since they have to expect problems working in a new area with a limited pool of skilled labor—large outside contractors add premiums also. It was in part this experience which at one time prompted Cornell University in upstate New York to let a large project in several small packages so that it could be handled by local contractors.

On a smaller scale, many contractors will add a premium for handling new materials. Fiberglass duct, for example, should be cheaper than metal in many cases, but the premiums being added by inexperienced contractors have made it more expensive than sheet metal on some projects.

Check list of key questions

Unfortunately, there is no central source for this information. However, by calling A.G.C. chapters, local contractors, and other industry sources, it is usually possible to obtain partial answers to the following key questions on this subject of contractor interest and capability:

How many contractors in one area work in a given category of construction?

How many bids does a project of a given size normally receive?

Is there so much directly competing work in the area that there is a reduction in the number of potential bidders?

Is the seasonal factor any more pronounced than is normal for the construction industry?

Are there ways of stimulating increased contractor interest?

What is the prevailing contractor attitude toward unusual design or site location?

Are local contractors familiar with unusual materials which might be employed on the project?

Is there likely to be any reduction in the number of bids or bid premiums resulting from minority hiring or training requirements?

Are local contractors finding construction loans unusually difficult to obtain?

Labor shortage may restrict design options

A major factor in contractor interest and capability is, of course, the local labor force. A cost estimator must know the local wage rates, be aware of shortages in critical trades, prevailing premiums necessary to obtain local labor or induce migration, trade jurisdictions, and any other factors which can have cost ramifications.

Shortages can be an important factor. In one case, an architect designing a project in upstate New York was informed of a shortage of carpenters. This helped him during schematic design as he realized that several design options, such as a poured-in-place concrete structure, were closed. In another case, all estimates and designs in the Lordstown, Ohio, region had to take account of a shortage in most trades due to the heavy demands of a new General Motors plant being built there.

Local work practices are also important. In many areas prefabricated components such as pre-hung doors are disassembled and then reassembled on site because of local union rules. In other areas, belligerent locals prevent use of any new labor-saving materials or techniques.

Training programs can add premiums

Currently, the most controversial labor factor is minority employment. Few building-trade locals, other than laborers, have significant minority membership. This has made it an explosive issue. In response to community pressure, an increasing number of public and private owners are inserting minority training and hiring clauses into their construction contracts.

Not only have the unions resisted, but the contractors have regarded such programs as an additional risk and an unknown cost. As a result, some contractors avoid projects covered by such clauses and others add premiums. Despite contractors' denials that they add premiums, detailed bid analyses indicate that most add as much as 10 to 20 per cent to their bids for large minority hiring and training programs.

Strikes are a similar risk and another unknown cost for the contractor to estimate. Therefore, it is important to check on the expiration date of existing contracts, the likelihood of strikes, the size of the increases likely to be negotiated in the next contract and related factors. The high bids on the community college mentioned earlier resulted in large part from the contractors' uncertainty about future labor settlements. In such extreme situations it has become necessary to split the project into smaller contracts to fit the schedule of major contract negotiations.

What to ask about labor

Information on these and other labor-related cost factors can be supplied by the local contractors and construction trade associations, minority group representatives and other related sources. These are important questions to ask:

Are the jurisdictions of unusual size?

Are there any jurisdictional disputes which might affect the project?

Are there significant variations in the labor supply due to seasonal factors?

Are there extreme shortages in any trades, and if so, will they cause premiums and/or delays in construction schedules?

What inducements are required to encourage migration to the area?

What is the impact of training programs; and what is the availability of minority workers?

What are the basic and fringe rates for each trade?

When do local contracts expire, what increases are scheduled in existing contracts, and what percentages are predicted for the next contract?

Is local labor cooperative or belligerent, and what is its level of interest in the project?

What to ask about materials

Materials are usually less of a problem than either contractors or labor, but on some projects material supply considerations are critical. Too often designs include materials that are either unavailable locally or unfamiliar to local contractors. In other cases too many projects are competing for the same material. Where any of these situations occur, it is worth devoting part of the market study effort to this subject. Some of the basic questions are the following:

Are any of the critical materials unusual or difficult to obtain?

How near—or how far—is the project site to the nearest major source of materials?

Are there other projects in the area that may compete directly for the same materials?

Are there complications—shipping limitations, delays, etc.—in supply due to unusual materials?

Which materials are on national rather than local price scales, and are any local materials unusually expensive or inexpensive?

What about job conditions

The last area, and most difficult to research for a full market study, is the owner-designer factor. There are a few good clients who actually attract additional bidders or an unusually large number of bidders for their projects.

Most owner-architect cost factors are negative, however. In 1970, New York's subcontractor association told the city that its members had to add up to 20 per cent to their bids on city projects to account for slow payments.

Certain architects are known to cause bid premiums, too. Consistently incomplete construction documents, disruptive actions during the construction phase and characteristically complex designs are some of the most common reasons.

Therefore, more market studies are including such questions as the following:

Do the owner's administrative or inspection procedures cause significant problems for the contractor?

Does the architect have a reputation for causing problems or providing inadequate construction documents?

Are there problems which the owner or architect can help mitigate?

If the market study reveals serious problems in any of the above areas, it is possible to save more money concentrating on overcoming adverse market conditions than by refining costly segments of the design. The difference between an efficient and inefficient design is often less than 15 per cent, while market conditions can add up to 100 per cent in premiums.

Adverse market conditions can usually be overcome. Split contracts, expedited payment procedures, careful selection of local materials, contractor orientation meetings, and careful timing of bids and other techniques are being used with increasing frequency to solve market problems. The first step, however, is to identify the problems.

Computerized cost estimating is ready now—almost

Architects are now devoting more time to planning for the introduction of currently feasible computer systems than (as in the recent past) to contemplating dream applications. Fewer articles are being written predicting that the draftsman will be replaced in five or ten years by cathode ray tubes, electric light pencils and automated drafting equipment. Instead, architects and their consultants are showing a growing interest in such areas as accounting, management information and control, specifications and scheduling and cost estimating systems where EDP solutions are more readily attainable. Today's rampant inflation in the construction industry has made the last of these system types particularly attractive. As a result, more and more firms are currently developing or expanding automated cost estimating systems.

There are a number of basic ways in which computers can be used in the estimating process:

1. *Take-off assistance*—where the computer is employed—via digitizer and keyboard—to translate lines, areas and building material counts to construction quantities.

2. *Pricing assistance*—where the computer stores a library of costs to apply against estimated quantities and performs all multiplications and totaling.

3. *Inventory systems*—where the computer is employed to organize an estimate into a variety of formats: i.e., by building element, contract trade, supply source, etc.

4. *Accounting assistance*—where the computer interfaces an essentially manual estimating effort with a computerized cost accounting system for use by contractors.

5. *Data file storage and indexing*—whereby historic cost information is kept current and available for many output requirements.

6. *Exploded detail generation*—wherein simplified building systems or composite building elements are measured and "exploded" via computer to a detailed bill-of-materials format.

7. *Unit cost synthesis*—wherein the computer analyzes a more or less detailed data file to determine composite building element costs; i.e., cost per square foot for a heating system, etc.

All of these systems and appropriate combinations of them are attempts to create a tool for the basic cost management needs of professionals and clients —establishing and evaluating budgets, evaluating alternative design decisions and providing a basis for predicting, evaluating and controlling the project's actual cost.

A secondary goal, of course, is to make such a system more rapid and accurate and less expensive than the currently available manual techniques.

Unfortunately, none of the extant approaches has been developed to a point where it fully satisfies either the primary or secondary objectives for more than a handful of users. Therefore, it is worthwhile to move beyond the dazzle of the concept and take a close look at the problems and potential of each of the major approaches to computerized estimating.

Historical bid and estimate data have been a traditional base for many firms' estimates. Recently, several firms have been automating this data base in order to speed information recall and manipulation.

Use of historical cost data needs sophisticated approaches

In the least sophisticated systems, the costs for an entire building are recalled and are updated via a published index.

The usefulness of this basic approach is often limited because of its lack of sensitivity to the differences among projects, especially in program scope and method of construction. To meet this problem, several firms have taken the historical-data approach one step further and have organized their data by systems or components rather than building types. In some cases, this has meant cost information can be recalled for such categories as elementary school classrooms, hospital bed wings, hospital operating suites and similar facility components.

In others, past project costs have been divided into the costs of the wall, floor, electrical, HVAC and other systems. Data are stored on the cost per linear or square foot for concrete block walls, poured-in-place concrete slabs, metal stud and dry wall, different HVAC components and the other basic building systems. If the data base is sufficiently large, information can be recalled and adjusted to form a cost cross-section for any project.

Retrieval concept is simple but the data base is huge

Conceptually, the historical data approach is quite simple—store historical data, recall that which is relevant to some outline description of the proposed project, modify it for inflation and geographical considerations, and one has a reasonably accurate estimate of the probable construction cost. Unfortunately, while the concept is simple, the implementation process is expensive and difficult.

The data base, for example, must be extremely large if it is to be at all comprehensive. The number of building types, building facility components or building systems which must be included is immense. One high school is obviously not a sufficient data base for all projects of this building type. Even a wealthy suburban high school's science wing is not fully comparable to the science area of a less-affluent rural district's facilities. And the possible variations in building systems are equally large. Therefore, even firms with specialized practices will require a large, carefully selected data base to provide the detail required for reasonably accurate estimates.

Format of the bid limits pricing detail

A problem closely related to size of the data base is the fact that few bids or detailed cost estimates are prepared in a format which permits development of the detail necessary for the data base. Costs are almost always prepared in terms of the entire facility rather than the important facility components or systems, unless these components are quoted as alternates.

Even if a good data base is obtained, however, there is at least one other major problem facing the systems analyst—the creation of accurate indexes to reflect locality and time differences.

Computer programs call for more sensitive price indexes

Basically, most indexes are not sensitive to differences among building types and methods of construction. An index which assumes that each building type uses the same relative amounts of the specific types of labor and material cannot be a true reflection of the differences in the cost movements of one facility type versus another. And an index which is not modified for unique price situations in trades and materials in an area overlooks a most vital consideration.

Although indexes have been designed for the estimating systems currently in operation, none is sufficiently comprehensive or flexible to meet more than a few estimating uses. However, indexing systems for each major building type keyed to a cost and productivity data base have been developed and are currently being integrated into a cost estimating system.

The ideal is known but needs a little work

An ideal cost estimating system for use by architects would contain these features:

1. Cost models of buildings, building systems or building elements of suf-

ficient number and diversity to embrace all the kinds of buildings the architect would encounter and all the major design alternatives available to him.

2. A file of individual product or material unit prices.

3. An indexing system which permits the cost models and the cost file to reflect accurately any desired construction market profile.

4. A versatile coding system or chart of accounts to permit estimate interfacing with CSI codes or contractor bid formats.

Unfortunately no such ideal estimating system has yet been developed although several approaches are in process. Chief difficulties lie in the immense range of detail required for an adequate data base and in the problem of universal indexing.

Several firms have developed approaches based on cost models of a number of building systems. Under one development, for example, the model for a particular wall system is made up of quantity and size of lumber, quantity of nails, hours of carpentry, etc., all developed as a function of the linear foot of a number of types of walls. The computer stores these quantities and a file of unit cost expressions for each. When the system measurements are input, the computer produces a priced bill of materials and a labor estimate for each system.

A less ambitious but more attainable model-based approach is that followed by at least one public agency system. In 1968 consultants developed a system to provide HUD with cost data to evaluate the price of turnkey housing proposals.

Instead of models for individual systems the consultants created models for thirty different Federally financed housing types. A base price for each of these building models was then established. The final step was to create an index based on fifteen trade wages and fifteen material prices. An indexing equation was developed for each of the building types, expressing its relation to each of the wage and price indicators. This "differential" indexing thus permits building costs to be indexed in a way which reflects true differences between building costs in different locations; steel vs. concrete, high-rise vs. one-family, etc.

The construction of similar models and indexes for other building types is a manageable task. However, like all shortcuts this approach has several limitations. The most important of these is that this approach will not provide a sensitive cost estimate for buildings which deviate significantly from the model. Since most buildings will deviate from all of any feasible number of models, this approach should only be employed for establishing and evaluating budgets.

There are several programs available which are computerized replacements for the quantity survey approach. These approaches require a detailed take-off of construction material quantities, whether by traditional manual methods or with the assistance of a digitizer and/or desk-top computer. The quantities input under this system are then related to a material and labor unit cost data file to produce a priced estimate. Such systems are more useful to a contractor than to an architect since they require a sophistication about unit costs which only a contractor is likely to have, and further, they require rather fully developed working drawings to produce the necessary quantities.

Quantity take-off input needs good price data

It seems certain that more efforts will be made to produce an estimating system of real value to architects. Just such a program may be developed by the A.I.A. or its chapters; it is currently under preliminary consideration.

Certain government agencies, national contractors and developers have sufficient project experience to support development of an extensive cost data file, and some have begun the development of an estimating system for their own use. These systems may be available and useful to the design professions, but there can be no guarantee of this, since the purposes for which they are being developed are not parallel to the architect's needs.

The National Bureau of Standards is currently investigating the feasibility of a massive computerized cost data file and estimating system for use by government agencies. As in other applications the chief difficulty seems to be in the collection of reliable data. As a means of generating these data, the Bureau of Standards is considering the possibility of sponsoring a major change in Federal contracting methods. It is thought that bids based on a detailed bill of quantities, as in British practice, would facilitate development of a comprehensive pricing code and require contractors to reveal their unit costs. These costs could then be tabulated, analyzed, indexed, etc. to provide a cost data file. This study is in its very early stages and such major questions as industry acceptability have not yet been answered.

Key to any solution: a unified pricing base

It is clear from the above that the major obstacle to a solution for the architect's estimating dilemma is the elusiveness of reliable unit costs. This, of course, is a problem not confined to computerized estimating applications. Manual estimating systems have traditionally relied on an intimate knowledge of local construction costs supplemented by a general survey of such costs contained in commercially published unit price books. None of the books claim to be comprehensive and they reflect a general area of prices rather than prices identified with a specific construction market. Because no single chart of accounts for construction costs has gained wide acceptance among contractors, there has been no uniformity in the way in which cost records are kept.

The electrical contractors are an exception. Having developed a uniform code of accounts some years ago, electrical contractors have been able to develop intelligent, useful computerized estimating techniques and several are now in operation.

Automated estimating will never produce an infallible estimate. As we pointed out in previous pages, no system can ever account for all the vagaries of the construction industry. This point emphasizes the need for human judgment. No estimate which fails to account for contractor interest, the strengths and weaknesses of the local construction market, and the many other variables which are so difficult to quantify, will be fully satisfactory. Because of these factors, machines will become increasingly useful tools, but they are a long way from replacing experienced human judgment as the final source of accurate cost decisions.

A computerized cost estimating system

A program for pre-bid estimating and design development checking takes a giant step toward a usable data bank.

The notion of computerized cost estimating has been an engaging one for many years. In the previous section *(Computerized cost estimating is ready now— almost)* Bradford Perkins pointed out that the greatest stumbling blocks have been the gigantic proportions of any useful data bank and the horrendous problem of keeping such a bank updated in the shifting sands of today's construction market. A series of commissions by public agencies to Amis Construction & Consulting Services, Inc. went far toward removing those stumbling blocks and providing effective computerized cost data for several building types.

Further, advances in economical means of tapping central stores of these data by relatively simple telephone-adapted equipment have made the data accessible to an increasing number of small- to medium-sized firms.

As of August, 1972, the data bank had been set up to provide estimates for six building types in eight cities in Eastern states. The building types were: libraries, firehouses, police stations, combination police and firehouses, office buildings and intermediate schools. Floor areas for which programs are set up range from five thousand to five hundred thousand square feet layered in all practical numbers of floors. The cities are: New York, Boston, Harrisburg, Philadelphia, Pittsburgh, Reading, Erie and Washington, D.C.; and provision is made for adaptation to any other location in the nation by introduction of key local factors of material and labor costs as input by the user.

In describing his firm's approach to organization of the basic data, Alex Wineberg, president of Amis, points out that the take-off method of cost estimating practiced by contractors in the bidding process, is neither accurate nor available as a practical, hand-operated method in earlier phases of the estimating process. And of course, such a method is not possible at all during the budgeting phase, when specifics of both design and materials are unavailable.

There is, however, a growing need for a rapid and rational method of establishing realistic budgets for construction of new facilities and a related need for a system for monitoring the cost consequences of design options during development so that facilities can be kept at highest feasible quality within the appropriation. The demand for cost control during design development introduces a requirement for significant systems detail in the cost data bank and for easy access to data for comparable alternates.

Estimating methods, based on extrapolated square-foot or other unit cost data from existing comparable buildings multiplied by the rough number of units required by the new project are not very precise. Yet budgets established in this way become binding on all parties. Further, such budgets do not contain sufficient actual or assumed component detail to establish the explicit intent at the very beginning; so important in further communications between owner and designer.

How the system works

The system developed by Amis is based on a computer program able to simulate cost elements of a complete facility based on input of minimum design criteria known at the early pre-design stages; i.e., building type, functional space allocations, geographical location and time of construction.

The heart of the system's computer program is a mathematical model capable of extending those minimum basic design criteria, through tested assumptions governing the remainder of the elements incorporated in such a project, to application of a cost data bank containing pertinent information as to cost of every material, equipment, labor production levels and rates necessary to perform every construction activity in the area and at the proposed time of construction start.

Criteria not defined by the user are realistically assumed by the computer program based on sound design data derived from a typical design cross section of a representative number of buildings in the given category analyzed for that purpose. The computer printout will identify all elements (either actual design or model-based assumptions) necessary to realize the project. The program computes their respective areas, volumes and material quantities and then retrieves from the cost data bank the pertinent materials and labor costs. It prepares a complete cost estimate sorted by indivdual activities within a trade, subcontract or system and modified by appropriate geographic and cost escalation indexes.

In the budget preparation stages, when limited criteria are available, the system of detailed assumptions will enable the user to obtain information for an advanced itemized scrutiny of cost and quality of each component. The cost of different types of space usage and construction components of a facility can be converted to a square- or cubic-foot cost figure that will accurately reflect the cost impact of each component.

Labor costs are stored in man-hours, so a total man-hour requirement by trade and activity can be obtained. This will provide a base for progress scheduling and labor availability analysis.

Since the cost data bank is created to service a broad spectrum of governmental, municipal and private sectors, actual cost information obtained from ongoing construction is fed into the computer continuously to update and refine the cost data bank.

As more actual criteria become available during the design development stages, the information is fed into the computer, and progressively refined cost estimates are obtained enabling the user to identify in great detail the cost of the project vs. design complexity and specific site or other abnormal conditions. If the actual design results in higher cost than anticipated in the budget, a review of given and assumed criteria can be made, alternate solutions explored and respective cost results obtained in a matter of minutes. Thus, the system provides a correct scale of cost consequences for various design approaches and enables emphasis to be placed on deeper conceptual and functional aspects of design.

The system will be sufficiently flexible to provide accurate cost figures to preliminary planners on the basis of square-foot costs for each of the many types of functional areas and at the same time provide accurate cost targets in terms of building systems such as hvac, foundations, structural, decorating, fixed equipment, etc. so that the type of project designed will be commensurate with the type of project desired by the user.

Communication with the computer is based on a conversational mode via remote computer terminal. After coded log-in procedure, the pertinent input questions and instructions as to the formulation of answers appear at the terminal. The user answers the question, thus providing the necessary pertinent data for operation of the model simulation and cost estimating. The results in the desired report format are printed at the terminal, in a matter of minutes, thus providing the user with a printed copy of the entire conversation for his records. Available formats include: complete cost estimates with quantity surveys, cost estimates grouped by sub-contracts, major system costs, costs per square or cubic foot for the entire facility. Computations determining the foundations, structure or other systems can be retrieved for more detailed scrutiny.

Introduction to CPM

A step-by-step primer of the basic elements of critical path network planning.

Defects in methods of job planning and schedule control used in the past have begun to emerge due to three burdensome characteristics of practice which have evolved and have become prevalent in recent years.

First, more tasks are being defined as "projects" wherein a definite goal is set up for attainment at some specific future point in time.

Second, greater size of projects and more technical complexity have required more technical specialists in narrower fields, more complex administration, more problems in communication. It is, in short, more involved to do business.

Finally, target dates are sometimes set by fiat, due to various pressures, so that time is severely limited, leaving the project manager hard constrained to make optimum use of men, money, material and machines.

The old methods of planning and scheduling (bar charts and Gantt charts) show only limited relationships of job phases, fail to adjust automatically for unexpected delays, lack specificity in spelling out trade-offs of men and machines (as in the progressive forming and pouring of concrete wall sections, for example), fail to predict accurately where to expedite, do not deal with details of planning. Lacking detailing, the manager cannot accurately know what is critical, and all activities tend to receive equal executive attention. The Critical Path Method (CPM) overcomes all of those limitations.

CPM is a formal and graphic means of determining the relationships between tasks associated with any project. Each task that is time consuming *and* definable is represented by an arrow with its origin at an initial (*i*) node representing completion of all necessary previous tasks and its head at another junction (*j*) node representing its own completion and end-to-end junction with subsequent tasks. The arrows form a closed network bridging the interval between two terminal nodes representing the beginning and end of a whole project.

The arrow diagram, then, represents the sequence and interrelated dependencies of all the operations that comprise the project. When a time lapse is assigned to each arrow, the longest end-to-end total or "main chain" of these operations forms the Critical Path through the network, and any delay in the performance of tasks along the Critical Path will directly delay completion of the project. The fact that only a small fraction (usually less than 15 per cent) of the operations of any project lies on the Critical Path means that proper control of these key operations produces better results in the duration and cost of the project.

At this point, we should clarify some definitions and provide one theorem. The theorem is: "Every critical job (with the exception of the first and last) has at least one critical immediate predecessor and at least one critical immediate successor. Every project has at least one critical path, and every critical job lies on one or more critical paths." The definitions are shown in the glossary.

Questions of precedence, concurrency, and succession must be asked about each activity to form the basis for setting up a project network. Although each activity is represented by an arrow, CPM is not a vector technique in that the length of the arrow is meaningless and has no effect other than a visual one on manipulations. We start at the beginning and connect the arrows, usually from left to right, to show the logical flow of work. As each activity is added to the diagram, we examine it in relation to the other jobs and ask:

1. What other activities must be completed *before* this activity can start? (Precedence)

2. What other activities can be done *while* this activity is being done? (Concurrency)

3. What activities cannot start *until* this job is done? (Succession)

The answers to these questions will form the basis for drawing the network

Key questions for network logic

GLOSSARY

Activity: Any definable, significant, and time-consuming task, operation, or function to be executed in a project.

Critical Path: That longest sequence of activities in a network which establishes the minimum length of time for accomplishment of the end-event of a project. The path from the first event through the end-event that consists entirely of critical activities.

Dummy: A logic rectifier that is not a definable activity and is of zero-duration, but appears as a dummy activity in the network to show logical sequence of parallel events while avoiding the illogic of having more than one arrow originate and terminate in the same pair of nodes. (See Figures 1 through 9.)

Float: Also known as slack. It is the amount of time that an activity can be delayed without affecting the project duration. Only non-critical paths can have float.

Network: Also called an arrow diagram. A project graph. A set of numbered nodes connected by arrows representing activities.

Node: Also known as event, verse or burst. Each activity has a node at the tail of the arrow, called the "*i*" or "initial" node and another node at the head of the arrow, called the "*j*" or "juncture" node. A point in time indicating beginning (*i*) or ending (*j*) of one or more activities.

Planning: The establishment of project activities, their logical interrelations and the sequence in which they are to be accomplished, exclusive of time.

Project: Any organized undertaking consisting of many activities required to attain a single goal.

Scheduling: The assigning of time intervals and dates to activities in development of a project time plan.

and identifying activities in an ordered sequence of relationships. This is network planning, a distinct phase of the operation that is followed by scheduling.

Constructing arrow diagrams

'Each arrow on a network is separately identified by its activity description and/or its *i-j* numbers. Thus, Figure 1 could be identified by an activity description, such as "Place Concrete Forms," or by the definition, "activity 10–12." Each arrow must have a separate and unique *i-j* sequence.

The nodes (bursts, burst-points or intersections) are points in time and cannot represent work as the arrows do. In CPM the nodes are usually sequentially numbered so that every *j* node has a higher number than its corresponding *i* node. In the examples illustrated here, nodes are numbered with skipped numbers. It is possible to number nodes sequentially and by units, but this limits flexibility. Not infrequently, in developing the network, one finds the need for inserting an additional activity or a dummy (see glossary and Figure 7 to 9). When such an addition is made, the availability of a number that can be sandwiched into the network can prevent a great deal of erasure or redrawing. A good rule-of-thumb for numbering is to divide the number of nodes in the network into 1,000. In other words, if there are 250 nodes, sequencing may be by fours. This rule will accommodate three-digit computer entries; i.e., up to 999. Where a computer will go to 9,999, the rule-of-thumb would be 10,000 divided by number of nodes.

Although CPM is essentially a manual technique, it is readily programed into either punch-card or magnetic storage computers. The computer identifies each activity by node numbers at beginning and end of each arrow. Three-digit entry means simply that these numbers can lie anywhere between 000 and 999. A computerized network gains significant advantages in accuracy and scope even where only 50 to 75 activities comprise a project. Larger projects gain proportionately, especially during network planning when repetitive runs with various sets of time and cost data are required.

Figures 2 through 9 show some network segments and their interpretations. They demonstrate restraints, constraints, dependencies, succession, concurrency and precedence. They illustrate why, if two or more activities are given the same *i* and *j* nodes, the mind of man might resolve the inconsistency but a computer, lacking unique forwarding instructions for each activity, would get "caught in a loop" and must be corrected by a *numbering* dummy. The *logic* dummy is shown as an actual restraint with no time or work value.

The network emerges as some sort of geometric shape determined by relationships between tasks which must converge at a final point in order to complete the project and tell us: (1) the expected project duration; (2) the tasks that are critical; (3) the point-in-time when tasks can begin and finish; (4) where tasks *must* begin and finish in time so as not to interfere with the over-all project duration; (5) where tasks (and which ones) must be expedited to reduce duration; and (6) the leeway (float) available for scheduling.

A network which demonstrates all the points made thus far is shown in Figures 10 and 12.

Temporal evaluation

The Critical Path Method uses just one time estimate for each job or activity. The philosophy here is that one time estimate is just as reliable and realistic as the statistical average of three time estimates, such as PERT uses. Since most estimates are in terms of man-hours or man-days, it is relatively simple to establish activity durations in any logical and consistent system of time units.

Figure 1. Basic element of a network diagram.

Figure 2. Q (activity 14–24) cannot begin until P (activity 8–14) is completed.

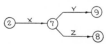

Figure 3. X (2–7) must be finished before either Y (7–9) or Z (7–8) starts.

Figure 4. E is restrained from starting until C and D are finished.

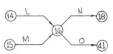

Figure 5. Both L and M restrain beginning either N or O.

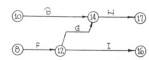

Figure 6. H cannot begin until B and G are complete. Neither G nor I can begin until F is completed. Thus, B and G restrain H; F restrains G and I.

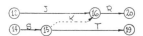

Figure 7. K (15–16) is a dashed arrow called a "logic dummy," which has no activity description or temporal value. It keeps the network's logical sequence intact. Here we are saying that J and S must be done before R can start. T is only dependent on S, not on J.

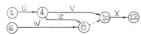

Figure 8. Activity 8–10 is a "numbering dummy." The computer can get caught in a "loop" (i.e., have identical instructions for two different activities) if more than one activity begins and ends in the same two nodes. Hence, although both V and Z could be activity 4–10, we "correct the loop" by placing 8–10 into a network. Thus, V and Z cannot start until U is complete; V, W and Z must precede X.

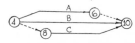

Figure 9. Numbering dummies again. Here, activities A, B and C are concurrent, beginning and ending at common points. The numbering dummies have corrected the loop. Note that the dummy can precede or follow the activity.

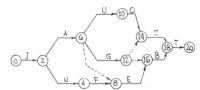

Figure 10. This network says that J is the initial task in our project and must precede both A and N, which may be done concurrently. F follows N. Both A and F restrain E. A, alone, restrains commencement of both U and G. Both E and G restrain B. U alone restrains O. Both G and O restrain C. T is dependent on C and B, and is the last task in our project. A segment of this network is shown in Figure 11 (right) to clarify the concept.

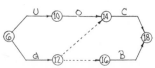

Figure 11. Can a node hang as node 12 is hanging? In order for G to restrain both C and B, why can't you make G a solid arrow from 6 to 14 and tie 14 to 16 with a dummy? Note the logic: if G restrained C directly and B by a dummy, B would also become dependent upon O. Our logic diagram does not intend this. The only restraint on B should be the activity G; however, both G and O restrain C. Thus, both activities 12–14 and 12–16 must be shown as logic dummies.

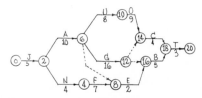

Figure 12. Figure 10 with time units assigned to each activity.

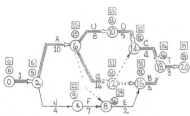

Figure 13. Assuming the time units assigned to Figure 10 are days (for ease of reading), note that the earliest start for activities A and N is on the fifth day. As one moves forward through the network and places the highest cumulative total days in a circle near each node, the earliest day for starting each succeeding task is established and the Critical Path of longest elapsed time is readily determined as J, A, U, O, C, T.

Note that a second critical path exists in this example along J, A, G, B. Since both paths arrive at node 18 in 36 days, the earliest one can start 3-day task is on the 37th day and the total for completion of the project is 39 days, it is not possible to start activity B until G is finished.

By definition, there is no "float" along either of the critical paths in this figure, and the earliest start is also the latest permissible if the target date 39 days is to be met. To determine the latest possible date to start each activity along the non-critical path, N, F, E, start at the terminal node 20 with 39 days and make a "backward pass" subtracting each task duration, putting the lowest result in a square near each node. The earliest and latest starting dates for each activity thus become visible.

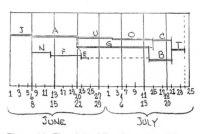

Figure 14. The dotted line from June 25 to July 14 is float on activity E if activities N and F are on early starts. That float can be shared with both N and F if needed.

TABLE 1.—ANALYSIS OF FIGURE 13

i	j	Activity	Duration	Early Start[1]	Early Finish[3]	Late Start[4]	Late Finish[2]	Float[5]	Critical Path
0	2	J	5	0	5	0	5	0	x
2	4	N	4	5	9	18	22	13	
2	6	A	10	5	15	5	15	0	x
4	8	F	7	9	16	22	29	13	
6	8	dummy	zero	15	15	29	29	14	
6	10	U	8	15	23	15	23	0	x
6	12	G	16	15	31	15	31	0	x
8	16	E	2	16	18	21	23	5	
10	14	O	9	23	32	23	32	0	x
12	14	dummy	zero	31	31	32	32	1	
12	16	dummy	zero	31	31	31	31	0	x
		C	4	32	36	32	36	0	x
16	18	B	5	31	36	31	36	0	x
18	20	T	3	36	39	36	39	0	x

[1]Early Starts are the "circle" entries at the tails of arrows, the *i*-nodes
[2]Late Finishes are the "square" entries at the heads of arrows, the *j*-nodes
[3]Early Finishes are the Early Starts plus Duration
[4]Late Starts are the Late Finishes minus Duration
[5]Float is the difference between Early Finish and Late Finish; thus, Float = LF-EF. Also, Late Start minus Early Start will yield Float. The computer reads Late Finish minus Early Start minus Duration for Float. This Float is called "Total Float"

Figure 12 shows the same network as in Figure 10 but with the addition of durations in the form of time units. It should be remembered that, as of this point, we are still in the network planning phase and we must establish time boundaries before we can establish any schedule; in other words, we are still dealing with work-logic.

Figure 13 and its caption show how temporal evaluations are made and how the network communicates job durations and so-called criticality of the longest continuous path through the network. Numbers under activities are durations; numbers in circles adjacent to nodes are cumulative times in a forward direction which represent the earliest time that each event can be completed. When we went through our forward pass additively (as described in the caption for Figure 13), the largest totals became the earliest finish times. Then we made a "backward pass," a subtractive computation, in which the lowest answer, entered in a square, represents the latest time for starting work at each node. With single-tailed nodes, we simply subtract from the preceding nodal value and enter our late time in a square near the node. Each node must have as many calculations as it has tails to be certain of its actual minimum value for the square. Thus, although values in squares along the critical path are by definition identical with those in the circles, the value in the square for node 6, for example, must be computed three times to find the appropriate late time entry; i.e., calculated from nodes 10, 12 and 8. Similarly, from nodes 4 and 6 to node 2, days 5 and 18 are possible late times and the lowest computation, 5, is entered. One final check should be noted: final evaluation of the backward pass must come to zero at the origin node of the network. If it does not, an error has been made.

In this process of the backward pass, we begin to see the concept of "float" emerge. For instance, activity N can begin on day 5 and end on day 9; since it can end as late as day 22 without affecting the project duration, and it is a 4-day job, it can start as late as 22 minus 4, or the 18th day. Thus, we have 13 days of float, or slack. We have the same float in activity F if we start on day 9 and proportionately less float up to day 22, when F *must* start, and so on.

Criteria for establishing the critical path are: (1) early and late times at the head of each arrow are equal; (2) late and early times at the tail of each arrow are equal; and (3) the difference between the early and late time at the head and tail of each activity is equal to that activity's duration.

Having completed the networks and made manual passes, we must next tabulate the information thus obtained to determine float. The tabulation will follow what is known as an *i*-major, *j*-minor sequence; all the *i* numbers will form sets of ascending values and the accompanying *j* numbers will ascend within the *i* sets. Also, we will include a definition of each activity, its duration, and start and finish times. Then we compute float. Table 1 is the tabular entry of Figure 13 data.

One scheduling use of a network is the employment of what is called calendar-dating. We can look at an example of this to see how it develops a ready-reference of criticality and float. In Figure 13 and Table 1, note how the critical activities run through the center and the float activities branch off. Using June 1, 1964 as a starting date, a calendar-dated chart is shown in Figure 14.

The essential rule in network preparation should normally assume reasonable resources in estimation. In all cases, estimating is the life's blood of network analysis. Sometimes project duration works out to be longer than can be tolerated. When this is the case, the network must be searched for those activities that can be shortened by the application of resources from float activities. The fact is that limited resources can, and frequently do, place restraints that will increase project duration. This and an inflexible imagination comprise the major limitations on the use of the Critical Path Method.

A critical path method example

Note: Despite some redundancy with the previous "Introduction to CPM," This report of an actual (early 1962) experience by E. R. McCamman, then a project director for Giffels & Rossetti, Inc. (a large Detroit firm since succeeded by Giffels Associates, Inc. concurrently with the separate formation of Rossetti Associates) serves to clarify application of some of the principles of CPM.

Critical path scheduling (familiarly CPM) is a method that makes it possible for architects to apply positive controls to the problems of construction sequences, schedules and costs.

First developed, in 1956, by E. I. duPont as a method for close coordination of the many inter-related construction activities on large projects, CPM has since been adopted by a number of architects, and their clients, because the method has obvious advantages over the older bar-graph type of scheduling. The critical path method makes possible complete analysis, in advance, of construction activities, of any degree of complexity, in whatever degree of detail that seems useful. With CPM, management decisions may be made prior to and during construction, on the basis of more reliable information than was formerly available. During all phases of construction, the exact status of activities will be readily apparent. All of this can lead to savings in time; and during construction, time is directly related to money.

A project involving the rebuilding and expansion of industrial plant office facilities will serve as a demonstration of the critical path method. In this example, the existing office abuts a manufacturing building in a highly congested industrial area. Since no new land is available, the existing office building must be demolished before the new building can be constructed in the cleared area.

As is usual in critical path scheduling, the method can be divided into three phases for this project: planning, scheduling and cost study. In the initial phase—that of planning—the activities that must occur in the construction of a project are defined and the order in which these activities must take place determined. In this phase, the project is subdivided into activities or jobs. In the scheduling phase, project time tables are produced based on the planning phase and costs. In general, the greater the degree of subdivision, the more efficient will be the results obtained from the critical path method of scheduling.

For simplicity, the office building project used as an illustration has been subdivided into only twelve activities: demolition, construction of new foundations, installation of underground services, structural steel erection, exterior wall construction, roof and roofing installation, first floor slab construction, second floor slab construction, start of mechanical and electrical services installation, finish of mechanical and electrical, interior partition construction, and painting and finishing.

The arrow diagram is the key to the planning phase. Each of the twelve activities is represented by an arrow in a diagram, as shown in Figure 1 (next page). When completed, the arrow diagram will show the logical flow of work in the project. The time flow of job arrows is from tail to head, with the head representing completion of the job. The length of the arrow has no significance.

Before each arrow is added to the diagram, the relationship of the activity the arrow represents to the overall project is examined by means of the following questions: (1) what jobs must be finished before this job can begin; (2) what jobs can be accomplished concurrently with this job; and (3) what jobs cannot begin until this job is finished.

In the present example shown in Figure 1, before any new work can be performed, the site must be cleared of the existing building. Therefore, demolition is the initial job arrow in the diagram. After the site has been cleared, two other jobs can proceed concurrently: construction of new foundations and installation of underground services. The simultaneity of these two jobs is indicated by job arrows drawn from the head of the demolition job arrow. The process is continued until all of the jobs have been placed in the diagram. The dashed arrows (dummies) are not used to indicate jobs, but rather restraint on jobs that follow. For example, the first floor slab construction cannot begin until both steel erection and underground services are complete.

In the arrow diagram, Figure 1, event numbers have been added at the junctures of the heads and tails of the job arrows. These event numbers provide computer orientation, if this is required. The numbers also make it possible to identify jobs numerically; e.g. demolition is Job 1–2.

Since all subsequent phases of the method are based on this arrow diagram, this initial phase should be prepared by personnel who are thoroughly familiar with construction operations. The next phase, scheduling, determines the timetable for the project. The schedules tell when each job must be done, when deliveries must take place, when the project will be completed, which jobs are critical, how a delay in one job will affect subsequent jobs.

The first step in scheduling is the determination of the normal time duration for each of the activities. This step is accomplished by analysis of the work and the labor force available. Since the effectiveness of the critical path method is dependent on the reliability of the time estimates used, careful analysis should be made of each job. In the example, the time element is a day. However, any time element may be used provided the element is consistent throughout the network.

After the normal time durations of jobs have been determined, they may be shown, as in Figure 2, approximately at mid-points of arrows. Then the earliest event times can be computed and indicated on the arrow diagram. The earliest event time is the earliest time at which a given event can occur, or in other words, the earliest time when the longest job train leading up to that event can be completed. The earliest event times, shown in Figure 2 as the numbers in squares, are computed by working from the start to the finish of the arrow diagram. For example, the earliest event time for event number 5, considering that the project started at zero time, would be the sum of job train 1–2, 2–3, 3–4 and 4–5, and is equal to 8 + 14 + 5 + 0, or 27 days.

If the project can be completed in 65 days, as shown in Figure 2, presumably that is also the latest time it *should* be completed. Allowing any further delay would be wasteful of time and money. Therefore the latest event time for the end event is also 65 days. Working backward through the arrow diagram, the latest event times are computed. The latest event times, shown in Figure 2 as the numbers in circles, are the latest times at which given events can occur if subsequent jobs are not to be delayed.

At this point, the network can be tabulated, as shown in Figure 3, and the earliest and latest job start and finish times and the float can be determined. The earliest job start times are equal to the earliest start event times. The earliest job finish times are equal to the earliest start event times plus the job durations. The latest job start times are equal to the latest finish event times minus the job durations. The latest job finish times are equal to the latest finish event times.

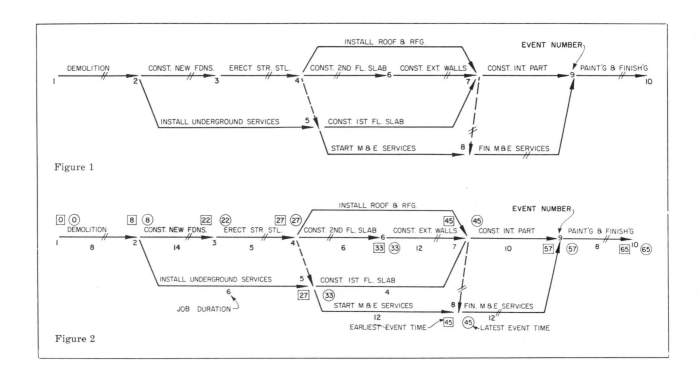

Figure 1

Figure 2

I	J	Description	Duration	Earliest		Latest		Float		
				Start	Finish	Start	Finish	Total	Free	Indept.
1	2	Demolition	8	0	8	0	8	0	0	0
2	3	Const. new fdns.	14	8	22	8	22	0	0	0
2	5	Install undergrd.	6	8	14	27	33	19	13	13
3	4	Erect str. steel	5	22	27	22	27	0	0	0
4	5	Dummy	0	27	27	33	33	6	0	0
4	6	Const. 2d fl. slab	6	27	33	27	33	0	0	0
4	7	Install rf. & rfg.	6	27	33	39	45	12	12	12
5	7	Const. 1st fl. slab	4	27	31	41	45	14	14	8
5	8	Start M&E services	12	27	39	33	45	6	6	0
6	7	Const. ext. walls	12	33	45	33	45	0	0	0
7	8	Dummy	0	45	45	45	45	0	0	0
7	9	Const. int. partitions	10	45	55	47	57	2	2	2
8	9	Fin. M&E services	12	45	57	45	57	0	0	0
9	10	Painting & finishing	8	57	65	57	65	0	0	0

Figure 3

Although every job in a project is important, in practice a few jobs control the completion date of the project. These are called the *critical* jobs, because they must follow in sequence and on schedule if the completion date of the project is to be met. There is no float—the term used for spare time—associated with the critical jobs. The time required for each critical job exactly equals the time available for it. In the diagram, shown in Figure 2, the critical jobs are indicated by slanted parallel lines. All other jobs are noncritical because they have some spare time or float. However, once the float associated with a noncritical job has been used, that job also becomes critical.

Float on noncritical jobs can be used to stabilize the level of manpower demands, to obtain better material or equipment price quotations on the basis of relaxed delivery schedules, or to regulate equipment or material deliveries to a site with limited storage.

The *total float* for a job is the total time available to do the job minus the duration of the job. Consider Job 5–7, construction of first floor slab. This job can start as early as day 27 and be completed as late as day 45. There are 45 minus 27 or 18 days available for performing this job. The job itself requires 4 days. Thus the total float for Job 5–7 is 14 days.

The total float for one particular job often interferes with the total float available for a succeeding job. Consider Job 2–5, installation of underground services, which can be finished as late as day 33. Job 5–7, construction of first floor slab, can start as early as day 27. But Job 5–7 cannot start until Job 2–5 has been completed. If Job 2–5 is not complete until day 33, it has interfered with the total float of Job 5–7 by 33 minus 27, or 6 days. That portion of the total that remains after subtracting the interfering float is called the *free float.* Stated in another way, the free float is that portion of the total float that is available when all the jobs are started at the earliest event times. The free float is equal to the difference between the earliest event times at the head and tail of the arrow, minus the job duration.

Certain jobs have float that is independent of, or unaffected by, the float of preceding or following jobs. This is called *independent float.* A job having independent float can be shifted backwards or forwards by that amount of time without disturbing the preceding or following jobs. The independent float is equal to the difference between the earliest event time at the head of the job arrow and the latest event time at the tail of the job arrow. Independent float can never be less than zero.

Each phase of the critical path method offers definite benefits to the user. If the system were carried no further than the planning phase, the user would have

| Job | Normal | | Crash | | Cost Slope |
Code	Days	Dollars	Days	Dollars	Dollars/Days
1-2	8	7,200	6	10,000	1,400
2-3	14	25,000	11	31,000	2,000
2-5	6	4,000	4	6,000	1,000
3-4	5	5,000	4	6,500	1,500
4-5	0	0	0	0	—
4-6	6	30,000	3	39,000	3,000
4-7	6	18,000	4	23,000	2,500
5-7	4	18,000	3	22,000	4,000
5-8	12	32,000	8	37,000	1,250
6-7	12	24,000	9	28,500	1,500
7-8	0	0	0	0	—
7-9	10	16,000	6	20,000	1,000
8-9	12	36,000	8	40,000	1,000
9-10	8	9,000	6	14,000	2,500
		224,200			

Figure 4

a clearer picture of the project, the jobs to be performed, and the sequence in which they are to be performed, than would be possible otherwise. Completion of the scheduling phase will enable the user to determine the project completion date and the jobs which must be completed on schedule if that date is to be met. The greatest benefit of all will be obtained when the third phase—costs —is employed.

The critical path method is based on the premise that time and cost are interrelated. Most projects can be performed in a number of different ways from minimum cost-maximum time to minimum time-maximum cost. The method permits an educated choice between the two extremes, a choice that will be best for the particular construction operation under consideration.

For the office building in this example, if the 65 day time duration is unacceptable, time can be saved by expediting one or more of the jobs along the critical path. This is more efficient than placing all jobs along the critical path on a crash basis. In the example, each activity was assigned a normal time duration. For each activity, there is also a crash time duration—a minimum time in which the activity can be performed. For each of the time durations, there are also associated normal and crash costs. Once the normal and crash times and costs are known, the cost slope for each activity can be determined.

$$\text{Cost Slope} = \frac{\text{Crash Cost—Normal Cost}}{\text{Normal Time—Crash Time}}$$

The cost slope gives the rate of increase in cost for decrease in time. The cost data for the present example is shown in Figure 4 on the following page. Now, if a schedule of time less than 65 days is desired for the completion of the project, an intelligent choice of which job to expedite can be made by compressing the time schedule of the critical job with the least cost slope. Starting with Job 8-9, a two day reduction can be effected at an additional cost of $1,000 per day. At this point Job 7-9 also becomes critical and any further reduction in Job 8-9 would also require a reduction in Job 7-9, which would increase the cost by $2,000 per day. However, Job 1-2 can be reduced in duration by two days at a cost of $1,400 per day. This process is repeated until the project duration has been reduced to its minimum time of 47 days as shown in Figure 5.

In making the time reduction, a direct cost for each day interval between 47 and 65 days has been obtained. Since a decrease in project time requires additional capital expenditure, the direct costs obviously rise as the project time is decreased from 65 days. However, the total project cost is comprised of both

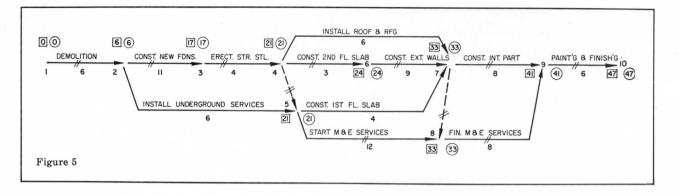

Figure 5

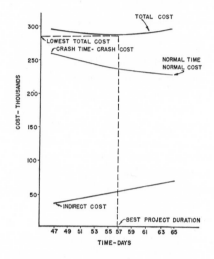

Figure 6

indirect costs and direct costs. Indirect costs consist of such items as overhead, insurance, interest on capitalization, production loss and liquidated damage clauses. Costs of this type have a tendency to increase in cost with an increase in project duration. The optimum project duration usually falls somewhere between the normal time and the crash time when the total project cost (the sum of indirect and direct costs) is considered. The relationships between these variables are represented, graphically, in Figure 6, for the building of the present example.

Regardless of how thoroughly the scheduling of a project has been studied, some changes will inevitably be required in the construction stage. As such changes appear, their effect on the project as a whole is made immediately apparent by the arrow diagram. If a delayed job is noncritical, and the delay does not exceed the float time for the job, the project completion will not be delayed. If a delay occurs on a critical job, the extension of the project completion and the effect on other related jobs will be apparent.

One of the very real advantages of the critical path method is its simplicity. None of the operations discussed in the example require anything other than paper, pencil and simple arithmetic. If only the first two phases of the method—planning and scheduling—are utilized for small or medium-sized projects, no more than manual computations will probably be required. For large, complex projects or projects for which the cost phase of the system is to be employed, electronic computers are almost a necessity. The almost infinite number of variations and combinations that will be encountered in critical path scheduling for projects of this sort makes manual computation impractical and inaccurate; accordingly, computers are the only practical answer. However, consulting firms as well as computer manufacturers regularly provide programing and computer service.

The following extract from the book, "Professional Construction Management and Project Administration" by William B. Foxhall, owes much to a presentation by Paul Spindel of McKee-Berger-Mansueto at a Spring 1971 conference on Advanced Management Research. The book is published jointly by The American Institute of Architects and Architectural Record, 1972.

Computers: Tools for construction management

Computers play a dual role as tools for time, cost and quality control in construction management. First, they serve as highspeed mathematical aids—especially in the areas of engineering, estimating and scheduling. Second, computers are a sorting, collating and reporting tool for the management process. They can relate the emplacement schedule to, for example, purchasing, cash flow, inspection, meetings and approvals. The special conditions of client procedures, the myriad variations in emphasis and detail for communicating the same body of information to, say, the contractor, the purchasing agent and the project administrator—all can be sorted out by the computer with idiot speed.

The computer can make infinite lists. It can list all the systems and activities in a project in several ways: by date of early or late start in a CPM network, by longest-lead time for purchasing, by cost, by supplier, by contractor or (for the project administrator) by overall summary of cost and schedule.

The listing and sorting process is perhaps the least demanding on the potential skills of the computer and its programers. It has been called a trivial use of great capacity. But it can be, on complex projects, the computer's most rewarding use in terms of savings in time and money; in terms of coordinated communications; and in terms of evaluating the cost/quality options.

The myth of the computer as supermachine that takes over all tasks and has its accomplishments measured in stacked feet of print-out paper is long past. Now the machine is more maturely regarded as a high-level investment in the *profitable* (i.e. rapid) manipulation of *massive* and relevant data. It has a mindless talent for repetitive scanning, with key (and keyed) variations in either the core-memory of applied parameters or the daily input of job data.

But building design and construction are exceptionally non-repetitive—in comparison with manufacturing or accounting procedures. Although both manufacturing and accounting are within the purview of construction management, the idiosyncracies of each job and each client call for rigorous assessment of the computer's applicability job by job. The key words emphasized in the preceding paragraph are: *profitable, massive,* and *relevant.*

There are two major considerations that bear on the construction manager's assessment of computer applicability.

1. No management program can be turned over to a computer to the total exclusion of manual calculation and verbal communication. Someone has to read the printout, make decisions, write reports and orders, negotiate, see that things get done. Even cost estimating, a chore of massive detail that would seem readily amenable to computerization, becomes progressively more refined and immediate, to the point where the real price is the bid price. Computerized costing is a well-developed service, but there comes a

time on every project where the computer must give way to the pencil sharpener.

2. The smaller the project, the larger is the proportion of manual and verbal (i.e., non-computerized) components in the management task. Considering the difference between, say, the World Trade Center and a $500,000 factory, that seems a simplistic statement. But somewhere on the scale of size and complexity between those two extremes is a point below which no job-developed software is warranted—no matter how much in-house hardware is standing by to handle it. The location of that point is itself a management decision based on the answer to a simple question. Does it pay?

The answer to that question is not always revealed by simple arithmetic. It can be distorted by two opposing attitudes. One that has cost untold amounts in overkill is the compulsion to "keep the hardware busy." The other, equally costly, has been a reluctance to use expensive and exotic machines in the trivial role of giant tickler file. A judgment must be made based on the particulars of

1 available hardware in-house

2 its cost to own or rent

3 its current loading

4 software programing cost for the project

5 available core programs

6 management demands of the project

7 management fees available

At risk of offering figures that are dated and otherwise limited by special conditions, we report the following yardsticks of computer cost mentioned at a 1971 seminar of the Advanced Management Research International.

1. Engineering firms with repetitive usage of well developed programs and good load factor spend about $40 per month per graduate engineer on staff.

2. The cost of in-house hardware is about one-third to one-half of the cost of computing; the rest goes into people, programing, supplies and space.

3. A minimum cost for in-house hardware alone is between $1500 and $2000 per month.

4. Initial cost for time-sharing at a service center is much less, but the added cost of communication and travel brings the total to almost $1500—not counting personnel.

The two major considerations previously stated having to do with the limits of computer application (i.e.: no program can be 100 per cent computerized; and small projects may not warrant any computerization at all) set the stage for developing management systems for cost, quality and time control using the computer at key points. Those points are determined by the criteria of project characteristics in size and complexity and by the resources of the managing firm itself.

The ideal management system would be totally flexible so that it could be applied logically and economically over a full scale of job and firm criteria. It turns out, however, that the development of a computer-oriented system capable of serving the management of large projects calls for a certain commitment of the management firm to full-time staffing for computer programing, cost estimating and field operating personnel. That commitment sets a high break-even point that almost automatically precludes the handling of small projects except on a fragmentary basis.

A well-designed management system for the control of construction projects will combine capabilities in cost estimating, critical path analysis, financial status and progress reports, and administrative procedures in a well-organized format. Individual reports should be designed for each level of project administration and construction management. In each case, the system should be able to use either a manual or a computerized mode of reporting in order to approach as closely as practicable the kind of ideal flexibility previously described.

Because of the mass of data available and the immense capability of the machine to absorb and report, an essentially editorial judgment should be made as to content and format of these reports. That judgment should be based on the function and preoccupation of individual recipients. For example, the project administrator might receive a summary schedule and financial status report while the on-site construction manager would require a more detailed list of all work items for each phase of the job.

Individual reports and input documents should not only be tailored to each user but should also have consistent format one with another, so that translation of data into decision and action is handled readily.

The information presented by the system should be coordinated on the basis of a scheduled flow of input related to stipulated intervals and classifications of output. That is, the data sources, such as estimators, field inspectors, job captains, clerks of the works, etc., should be encouraged to report back to the system at stipulated intervals and in patterned format readily convertible to input data.

A workable system might be designed to present four basic areas of information (schedule, cost, financial and administrative) to three key decision-making groups: project administration, construction management and a third level comparable to job captain or field superintendent which might be labeled "technical management." Definition of the four areas of information might be amplified as follows:

A. Scheduling, planning, and control of project duration usually employs the CPM technique or one of its variations. The system should develop a detailed model of each project's design-delivery-occupancy process as a single identity made up of many parts. The network technique both views the process as a whole and separates its parts into manageable modules.

B. Cost control systems should present timely cost data in useful format. These data are exceptionally sensitive to the chance conditions of the market and the phase of design development. For that reason, its reporting method usually has a high manual component.

C. Financial summaries integrate data generated in the estimating and scheduling areas in order to show how much of the project's total cost has been spent and how much will be committed in designated future periods. These summaries also indicate the extent to which funding and cash flow have been approved and appropriated for the job.

D. The administrative applications of the system tend to be less rigidly structured than other areas and are tailored to the in-house capabilities and methods of the owner and/or project administrator. In order to provide full services to a variety of clients, public and private, over a substantial spread of project size, the construction management firm should be prepared to fit its own capabilities to those of the client. The danger lies in overstaffing for a level of administrative participation that may not be required to a consistent degree from one client to another.

Some of the administrative backup services to be considered might include manuals of procedure, either general to the construction management process or specific for the project at hand, outlines of useful administrative reports, step-by-step procedures and background literature on construction markets and practices that may be helpful to the less sophisticated client.

Develop sets of useful management reports

In order to discipline the unlimited computer output at a manageable level, the professional construction manager should establish specific sets of reports. These reports will draw upon the complete reservoir of project data, but will be assembled in format relating the four categories of information previously described to the needs of recipients. The reports will also be tailored to the management level to which they are directed.

TOP-LEVEL REPORTS. Most major projects have a senior decision-making group made up of client representatives, and principals of the architectural, engineering and construction management firms. Ordinarily, these people have more than one center of interest in addition to the project itself. Their objective as a group is to maintain adequate surveillance of the project development in order to respond intelligently when top level decisions are required. Useful reports for this group should give clear and concise information about a project's general progress, its cost status related to the schedule and its financial status related to the budget. This information might be usefully divided into:

1. A narrative report from the principal in charge of construction management, summarizing overall development and pointing up significant problems that might call for action of the top management group.
2. A financial-status report summarizing critical aspects of the budget-schedule relationship, noting any significant change between the current and prior period, alerting management to any need for additional or progress funding;
3. A master schedule chart in some readily comprehensible form (usually a bar chart) which serves as a summary of current status of the CPM schedule condensing all significant aspects of the project delivery process through a display of key activities.

ACTION-LEVEL REPORTS. At the second level of management, directly related full-time to the project, is a second category of reports also tailored to the problems of the individuals concerned. The objective is to avoid inundating all members of this management echelon with the massive data typical of large projects. The "need to know" principle should be applied to the editing of these reports, which might include:

1. A narrative report based on cost and progress information from the field or from "technical management" summarizing current developments;
2. A summary of the master schedule detailing activities of the network for the entire project and serving as a central scheduling checklist for the project;
3. A critical list of items within the network with minimal float time that must be watched most carefully;
4. A list of important dates on individual schedules of the project;
5. An alerting list of key activities scheduled to take place within the immediate future; a period of, say, 60 to 90 days, in a printout arranged in sequence by early start date;
6. A master tickler for central management summarizing the upcoming

activities of staff and compiled from the individual tickler files of staff members in a uniform format;

7. Current working estimates bringing out significant detail from the data used as background for the top management cost and financial status reports;

8. Detailed current cost estimates identifying building system costs and noting changes from the preceding period to readily spot any system in danger of a cost overrun;

9. A cash flow summary providing a monthly check against schedule activity and not only projecting cash flow requirements but implementing the payment process for upcoming schedules.

The sorting and format of these reports, the intervals of their issuance, and the lists of individuals to whom they are directed are all subject to the characteristics of the project and the organization of the management firm itself. Computer printouts are not the most readable of documents, although as users become familiar with them and programers edit their physical volumes to manageable dimensions, they become increasingly useful as both management tools and field documents.

Index

Quality control, 6